The Story of God Bible Commentary Series Endorsements

"Getting a story is about more than merely enjoying it. It means hearing it, understanding it, and above all, being impacted by it. This commentary series hopes that its readers not only hear and understand the story but are impacted by it to live in as Christian a way as possible. The editors and contributors set that table very well and open up the biblical story in ways that move us to act with sensitivity and understanding. That makes hearing the story as these authors tell it well worth the time. Well done."

Darrell L. Bock
Dallas Theological Seminary

"The Story of God Bible Commentary series invites readers to probe how the message of the text relates to our situations today. Engagingly readable, it not only explores the biblical text but offers a range of applications and interesting illustrations."

Craig S. Keener
Asbury Theological Seminary

"I love The Story of God Bible Commentary series. It makes the text sing and helps us hear the story afresh."

John Ortberg
Senior Pastor of Menlo Park Presbyterian Church

"In this promising new series of commentaries, believing biblical scholars bring not only their expertise but their own commitment to Jesus and insights into today's culture to the Scriptures. The result is a commentary series that is anchored in the text but lives and breathes in the world of today's church with its variegated pattern of socioeconomic, ethnic, and national diversity. Pastors, Bible study leaders, and Christians of all types who are looking for a substantive and practical guide through the Scriptures will find these volumes helpful."

Frank Thielman
Beeson Divinity School

"I'm a storyteller. Through writing and speaking I talk and teach about understanding the Story of God throughout Scripture and about letting God reveal more of his story as I live it out. Thus I am thrilled to have a commentary series based on the story of God—a commentary that helps me to Listen to the Story, that Explains the Story, and then encourages me to probe how to Live the Story. A perfect tool for helping every follower of Jesus to walk in the story that God is writing for them."

Judy Douglass
Director of Women's Resources, Cru

"The Bible is the story of God and his dealings with humanity from creation to new creation. The Bible is made up more of stories than of any other literary genre. Even the psalms, proverbs, prophecies, letters, and the Apocalypse make complete sense only when set in the context of the grand narrative of the entire Bible. This commentary series breaks new ground by taking all these observations seriously. It asks commentators to listen to the text, to explain the text, and to live the text. Some of the material in these sections overlaps with introduction, detailed textual analysis and application, respectively, but only some. The most riveting and valuable part of the commentaries are the stories that can appear in any of these sections, from any part of the globe and any part of church history, illustrating the text in any of these areas. Ideal for preaching and teaching."

Craig L. Blomberg
Denver Seminary

"Pastors and lay people will welcome this new series, which seeks to make the message of the Scriptures clear and to guide readers in appropriating biblical texts for life today."

Daniel I. Block
Wheaton College and Graduate School

"An extremely valuable and long overdue series that includes comment on the cultural context of the text, careful exegesis, and guidance on reading the whole Bible as a unity that testifies to Christ as our Savior and Lord."

Graeme Goldsworthy
author of *According to Plan*

RUTH, ESTHER

The Story of God Bible Commentary

RUTH, ESTHER

Marion Ann Taylor

Tremper Longman III & Scot McKnight

General Editors

ZONDERVAN ACADEMIC

ZONDERVAN ACADEMIC

Ruth, Esther

Published in Grand Rapids, Michigan, by Zondervan. Zondervan is a registered trademark of The Zondervan Corporation, L.L.C., a wholly owned subsidiary of HarperCollins Christian Publishing, Inc.

Requests for information should be addressed to customercare@harpercollins.com.

Zondervan titles may be purchased in bulk for educational, business, fundraising, or sales promotional use. For information, please email SpecialMarkets@Zondervan.com.

ISBN 978-0-310-49089-0 (hardcover)
ISBN 978-0-310-49090-6 (ebook)

Cover design: Ron Huizinga
Cover image: iStockphoto ®
Interior composition: Kait Lamphere

Printed in the United States of America

26 27 28 29 30 31 32 34 35 /TRM/ 14 13 12 11 10 9 8 7 6 5 4 3

In loving memory of my sister and soulmate
Mary Catherine Campbell

Old Testament series

1 ▪ Genesis—*Tremper Longman III*
2 ▪ Exodus—*Christopher J. H. Wright*
3 ▪ Leviticus—*Jerry E. Shepherd*
4 ▪ Numbers—*Jay A. Sklar*
5 ▪ Deuteronomy—*Myrto Theocharous*
6 ▪ Joshua—*Lissa M. Wray Beal*
7 ▪ Judges—*Athena E. Gorospe*
8 ▪ Ruth/Esther—*Marion Ann Taylor*
9 ▪ 1–2 Samuel—*Paul S. Evans*
10 ▪ 1–2 Kings—*David T. Lamb*
11 ▪ 1–2 Chronicles—*Carol M. Kaminski*
12 ▪ Ezra/Nehemiah—*Douglas J. Green*
13 ▪ Job—*Martin A. Shields*
14 ▪ Psalms—*Elizabeth R. Hayes*
15 ▪ Proverbs—*Ryan P. O'Dowd*
16 ▪ Ecclesiastes/Song of Songs—*George Athas*
17 ▪ Isaiah—*Mark J. Boda*
18 ▪ Jeremiah/Lamentations—*Andrew G. Shead*
19 ▪ Ezekiel—*D. Nathan Phinney*
20 ▪ Daniel—*Wendy L. Widder*
21 ▪ Minor Prophets I—*Beth M. Stovell*
22 ▪ Minor Prophets II—*Beth M. Stovell*

New Testament series

1 ▪ Matthew—*Rodney Reeves*
2 ▪ Mark—*Timothy G. Gombis*
3 ▪ Luke—*Kindalee Pfremmer DeLong*
4 ▪ John—*Nicholas Perrin*
5 ▪ Acts—*Dean Pinter*
6 ▪ Romans—*Michael F. Bird*
7 ▪ 1 Corinthians—*Justin K. Hardin*
8 ▪ 2 Corinthians—*Judith A. Diehl*
9 ▪ Galatians—*Nijay K. Gupta*
10 ▪ Ephesians—*Mark D. Roberts*
11 ▪ Philippians—*Lynn H. Cohick*
12 ▪ Colossians/Philemon—*Todd Wilson*
13 ▪ 1, 2 Thessalonians—*John Byron*
14 ▪ 1, 2 Timothy, Titus—*Marius Nel*
15 ▪ Hebrews—*Radu Gheorghita*
16 ▪ James—*Mariam J. Kamell*
17 ▪ 1 Peter—*Dennis R. Edwards*
18 ▪ 2 Peter, Jude—*C. Rosalee Velloso Ewell*
19 ▪ 1, 2, & 3 John—*Constantine R. Campbell*
20 ▪ Revelation—*Jonathan A. Moo*
21 ▪ Sermon on the Mount—*Scot McKnight*

Contents

Acknowledgments

My thanks go to the staff and board of Wycliffe College at the University of Toronto for their encouragement and support of this project. Thanks also to the staff at Graham Library who helped me track down hard to find books and articles on Ruth and Esther.

I am especially thankful to my students at Wycliffe College and my friends at the Church of the Resurrection who read and studied the books of Ruth and Esther with me. I am also grateful to fellow parishioners at the summer parish of St. John's Anglican Church, Eagle Lake, who provided helpful feedback on sermons preached on Ruth and Esther over the course of several summers. I am particularly indebted to my friend Maud Sandbo for her careful reading, corrections, and helpful suggestions.

I am also grateful for the support and feedback provided by Tremper Longman III and George Athas who were the editors assigned to this volume. Thanks also to Katya Covrett for her encouragement throughout the writing and editing process. Special thanks to Nancy Erickson whose careful reading, editing, and impressive knowledge of Scripture made the final task of editing the manuscript of Ruth and Esther much more enjoyable.

I also want to express my deepest thanks for my family's encouragement and patience as I researched and wrote this commentary. My special thanks to my sister Catherine who, like Ruth, modelled a life of faith and *hesed* and sadly died before the book was published.

The Story of God Bible Commentary Series

Why another commentary series?

In the first place, no single commentary can exhaust the meaning of a biblical book. The Bible is unfathomably rich and no single commentator can explore every aspect of its message.

In addition, good commentary not only explores what the text meant in the past but also its continuing significance. In other words, the Word of God may not change, but culture does. Think of what we have seen in the last twenty years: we now communicate predominantly through the internet and email; we read our news on iPads and computers. We carry smartphones in our pockets through which we can call our friends, check the weather forecast, make dinner reservations, and get an answer to virtually any question we might have.

Today we have more readable and accurate Bible versions in English than any generation in the past. Bible distribution in the present generation has been very successful; more people own more Bibles than previous generations. However, studies have shown that while people have better access to the Bible than ever before, people aren't reading the Bibles they own, and they struggle to understand what they do read.

The Story of God Bible Commentary hopes to help people, particularly clergy but also laypeople, read the Bible with understanding not only of its ancient meaning but also of its continuing significance for us today in the twenty-first century. After all, readers of the Bible change too. These cultural shifts, our own personal developments, and the progress in intellectual questions, as well as growth in biblical studies and theology and discoveries of new texts and new paradigms for understanding the contexts of the Bible—each of these elements work on an interpreter so that the person who reads the Bible today asks different questions from different angles.

Culture shifts, but the Word of God remains. That is why we as editors of The Story of God Bible Commentary, a commentary based on the New International Version 2011 (NIV 2011), are excited to participate in this new series of commentaries on the Bible. This series is designed to speak to this generation with the same Word of God. We are asking the authors to explain what the Bible says to the sorts of readers who pick up commentaries so they can understand not only what Scripture says but what it means for today.

The Bible does not change, but relating it to our culture changes constantly and in differing ways in different contexts.

As editors of the Old Testament series, we recognize that Christians have a hard time knowing exactly how to relate to the Scriptures that were written before the coming of Christ. The world of the Old Testament is a strange one to those of us who live in the West in the twenty-first century. We read about strange customs, warfare in the name of God, sacrifices, laws of ritual purity, and more and wonder whether it is worth our while or even spiritually healthy to spend time reading this portion of Scripture that is chronologically, culturally, and—seemingly—theologically distant from us.

But it is precisely here that The Story of God Commentary Series Old Testament makes its most important contribution. The New Testament does not replace the Old Testament; the New Testament fulfills the Old Testament. We hear God's voice today in the Old Testament. In its pages he reveals himself to us and also his will for how we should live in a way that is pleasing to him.

Jesus himself often reminds us that the Old Testament maintains its importance to the lives of his disciples. Luke 24 describes Jesus' actions and teaching in the period between his resurrection and ascension. Strikingly, the focus of his teaching is on how his followers should read the Old Testament (here called "Moses and all the Prophets," "Scriptures," and "the law of Moses, the Prophets and Psalms"). To the two disciples on the road to Emmaus, he says:

> "How foolish you are, and how slow to believe all that the prophets have spoken! Did not the Messiah have to suffer these things and then enter his glory?" And beginning with Moses and all the Prophets, he explained to them what was said in all the Scriptures concerning himself. (Luke 24:25–27)

Then to a larger group of disciples he announces:

> "This is what I told you while I was still with you: Everything must be fulfilled that is written about me in the law of Moses, the Prophets and the Psalms." Then he opened their minds so they could understand the Scriptures. (Luke 24:44–45)

The Story of God Commentary Series takes Jesus' words on this matter seriously. Indeed, it is the first series that has as one of its deliberate goals the identification of the trajectories (historical, typological, and theological) that land in Christ in the New Testament. Every commentary in the series will, in the first place, exposit the text in the context of its original reception. We will interpret it as we believe the original author intended his contemporary audience to read it. But then we will also read the text in the light of the death and resurrection of Jesus. No other commentary series does this important work consistently in every volume.

To achieve our purpose of expositing the Old Testament in its original setting and also from a New Testament perspective, each passage is examined from three angles.

Listen to the Story. We begin by listening to the text in order to hear the voice of God. We first read the passage under study. We then go on to consider the background to the passage by looking at any earlier Scripture passage that informs our understanding of the text. At this point too we will cite and discuss possible ancient Near Eastern literary connections. After all, the Bible was not written in a cultural vacuum, and an understanding of its broader ancient Near Eastern context will often enrich our reading.

Explain the Story. The authors are asked to explain each passage in light of the Bible's grand story. It is here that we will exposit the text in its original Old Testament context. This is not an academic series, so the footnotes will be limited to the kinds of books and articles to which typical Bible readers and preachers will have access. Authors are given the freedom to explain the text as they read it, though you will not be surprised to find occasional listings of other options for reading the text. The emphasis will be on providing an accessible explanation of the passage, particularly on those aspects of the text that are difficult for a modern reader to understand, with an emphasis on theological interpretation.

Live the Story. Reading the Bible is not just about discovering what it meant back then; the intent of The Story of God Bible Commentary is to probe how this text might be lived out today as that story continues to march on in the life of the church.

Here, in the spirit of Christ's words in Luke 24, we will suggest ways in which the Old Testament text anticipates the gospel. After all, as Augustine famously put it, "the New Testament is in the Old Testament concealed, the Old Testament is in the New Testament revealed." We believe that this section will be particularly important for our readers who are clergy who want to present Christ even when they are preaching from the Old Testament.

The Old Testament also provides teaching concerning how we should live today. However, the authors of this series are sensitive to the tremendous impact that Christ's coming has on how Christians appropriate the Old Testament into their lives today.

It is the hope and prayer of the editors and all the contributors that our work will encourage clergy to preach from the Old Testament and laypeople to study this wonderful, yet often strange, portion of God's Word to us today.

Tremper Longman III, general editor Old Testament
George Athas, Mark Boda, and Myrto Theocharous, editors

Abbreviations

AB	Anchor Bible
ABD	*Anchor Bible Dictionary*. Edited by David Noel Freedman. 6 vols. New York: Doubleday, 1995
ACCS	Ancient Christian Commentary on Scripture
AKJV	American King James Version
Anab.	Xenophon, *Anabasis*
ANET	*Ancient Near Eastern Texts Relating to the Old Testament*. Edited by James B. Pritchard. 3rd ed. Princeton: Princeton University Press, 1969
Ant.	Josephus, *Jewish Antiquities*
AOTC	Abingdon Old Testament Commentaries
ApOTC	Apollos Old Testament Commentary
Art.	Plutarch, *Artaxerxes*
b. Meg.	Babylonian Megillah
BBR	*Bulletin for Biblical Research*
BibInt	*Biblical Interpretation*
BT	*The Bible Translator*
CAT	*The Cuneiform Alphabetic Texts from Ugarit, Ras Ibn Hani, and Other Places*. Edited by Manfried Dietrich, Oswald Loretz, and Joaquín Sanmartín. 2nd edition. Münster: Ugarit-Verlag, 1995 (first English edition of KTU)
CEB	Common English Bible
ConcC	Concordia Commentary
COS	*The Context of Scripture*. Edited by William W. Hallo. 3 vols. Leiden: Brill, 1997–2002
Cyr.	Xenophon, *Cyropaedia*
Doctr. chr.	Augustine, *De doctrina christiana*
DOTW	*Dictionary of the Old Testament: Wisdom, Poetry & Writings*. Edited by Tremper Longman III and Peter Enns. Downers Grove, IL: InterVarsity Press, 2008
DSf	Darius 1 Susa foundation inscription
DTIB	*Dictionary for Theological Interpretation of the Bible*. Edited by Kevin J. Vanhoozer, Craig G. Bartholomew, Daniel J. Treier, and N. T. Wright. Grand Rapids: Baker Academic, 2005

Ep. fest.	Athanasius, *Epistulae festales*
EvQ	*Evangelical Quarterly*
fl.	flourished
Geogr.	Strabo, *Geographica*
Hist.	Herodotus, *Histories*
HTR	*Harvard Theological Review*
IB	*Interpreter's Bible.* Edited by George A. Buttrick et al. 12 vols. New York, 1951–1957
IBC	Interpretation: A Bible Commentary for Teaching and Preaching
IDBSup	*The Interpreter's Dictionary of the Bible, Supplementary Volume.* Edited by Keith Crim. Nashville: Abingdon, 1976
IEJ	*Israel Exploration Journal*
JB	Jerusalem Bible
JBL	*Journal of Biblical Literature*
JPSBC	Jewish Publication Society Bible Commentary
JQR	*Jewish Quarterly Review*
JSOT	*Journal for the Study of the Old Testament*
JTS	*Journal of Theological Studies*
KAI	*Kanaanäische und aramäische Inschriften.* Edited by Herbert Donner and Wolfgang Röllig. 2nd ed. Wiesbaden: Harrassowitz, 1966–1969
KJV	King James Version
KTU	*Die keilalphabetischen Texte aus Ugarit.* Edited by Manfried Dietrich, Oswald Loretz, and Joaquín Sanmartín. First edition. Kevelaer: Butzon & Bercker, 1976.
LW	*Luther's Works.* Edited by Jaroslav Pelikan. St. Louis: Concordia, 1955
LXX	Septuagint
Mor.	Plutarch, *Moralia*
MT	Masoretic Text
NAB	New American Bible
NAC	New American Commentary
NASB	New American Standard Bible
NCB	New Century Bible
NET	New English Translation
NIBCOT	New International Biblical Commentary, Old Testament Series
NIDOTTE	*New International Dictionary of Old Testament Theology and Exegesis.* Edited by Willem A. VanGemeren. 5 vols. Grand Rapids: Zondervan, 1997
NIV	New International Version

NIVAC	New International Version Application Commentary
NJB	New Jerusalem Bible
NKJV	New King James Version
NLT	New Living Translation
NPNF[1]	*Nicene and Post-Nicene Fathers*, Series 1
NRSV	New Revised Standard Version
NSTB	New Studies in Biblical Theology
OEBI	*The Oxford Encyclopedia of Biblical Interpretation*. Edited by Steven L. McKenzie. 2 vols. Oxford: Oxford University Press, 2013
OTL	Old Testament Library
Phillips	*The New Testament in Modern English*, J. B. Phillips
Rab.	Rabbah
REC	Reformed Expository Commentary
RSV	Revised Standard Version
R&T	*Religion and Theology*
RW	*Reformed Worship*
SBLWAW	Society of Biblical Literature Writings from the Ancient World
SMN	Cuneiform Texts in the Semitic Museum at Harvard (catalogue numbers)
SPCK	Society for Promoting Christian Knowledge
TEV	Today's English Version
Tg.	Targum
Them.	Plutarch, *Themistocles*
TOTC	Tyndale Old Testament Commentary
UBOT	Understanding the Bible Commentary Series, Old Testament
Vulg.	Vulgate
VT	*Vetus Testamentum*
WBC	Word Biblical Commentary
YLT	Young's Literal Translation
ZAW	*Zeitschrift für die alttestamentliche Wissenschaft*

Introduction to Ruth

Composition, Transmission, and Canonicity

Authorship, Date, and Occasion for Writing

Suggestions abound as to who wrote the book of Ruth, and when and why it was written. The Talmud suggested that Samuel wrote Ruth (Baba Batra 14b), but the book's language, style, and purpose point to a later date. Some recent scholars suggest that a woman (perhaps David's daughter Tamar) or a group of women wrote Ruth or at least first told the story, as it uniquely features the words, perspectives, and traditions of women.[1] The identity of the author of this carefully crafted book, however, remains elusive.

Scholars' opinions about the book's date vary, ranging from the time of David to the postexilic period, and are tied to observations about its language, style, customs, socio-political setting, and literary dependence on Pentateuchal texts, as well as suggestions about the book's purpose and themes.[2] Scholars favoring a postexilic date argue that Ruth was written as a polemic against the exclusionary policies of Ezra and Nehemiah regarding outsiders (see Ezra 9–10; Neh 10:28–30; 13:3, 23–30). Evidence used to support a postexilic date includes the use of late biblical Hebrew (including the presence of Aramaic and Aramaic-like features), the narrator's explanation of an "ancient" custom regarding the symbolic use of a sandal during the legal transactions at the gate (Ruth 4:7), and differences in marriage and redemption customs between Ruth and earlier texts.[3] L. Daniel Hawk, one of a number of contemporary scholars who continue to argue for a mid-fifth to early fourth-century BC date, argues that "against Ezra's and Nehemiah's attempts to redefine Israel along the lines of genetic purity, Ruth presents a vision of Israel as a

---

1. K. Lawson Younger, Jr., *Judges/Ruth*, NIVAC (Grand Rapids: Zondervan, 2002), 389. See Richard Bauckham, "The Book of Ruth and the Possibility of a Feminist Canonical Hermeneutic," *Bib Int* 5 (1997): 29–45; A. J. Bledstein argues for Tamar as author in "Female Companionships: If the Book of Ruth Were Written by a Woman. . .," in *A Feminist Companion to Ruth*, ed. A. Brenner (Sheffield: Sheffield Academic, 1993), 116–35.

2. For helpful recent discussions of the date of Ruth's composition, see Jeremy Schipper, *Ruth: A New Translation with Introduction and Commentary*, AB 7D (New Haven: Yale University Press, 2015), 20–22, and L. Daniel Hawk, *Ruth*, ApOTC 7B (Downers Grove, IL: InterVarsity Press, 2015), 31–36.

3. Tamara Cohn Eskenazi and Tikva Frymer-Kensky, *Ruth*, JPSBC (Philadelphia: Jewish Publication Society of America, 2011), xvi-xvii.

nation that welcomes outsiders and presents the conditions on which they may be incorporated."[4]

Scholars who support a variety of earlier dates in the tenth to ninth centuries BC tie the question of the date of composition to such figures as David.[5] They suggest that Ruth was written to legitimate the Davidic dynasty, exonerate David's Moabite origins, and support inclusive policies regarding foreigners advocated by various members of the Davidic dynasty. The book's connections to David and the Davidic dynasty support this view: David is referenced twice, and the concluding genealogies end with David (4:17, 22), by implication placing David's imprimatur on the book and giving weight to its teachings and theology. Also supportive are such themes as the obligation to provide care for those outside the covenant community and God's providential work that brought about the birth of the one who was promised an enduring kingdom (2 Sam 7:11–16).[6] Arguments supporting a monarchic date based on language include "the decidedly pre-exilic use of classical Hebrew idioms, syntax, and style . . . comparable to that in the books of Samuel and [which] differ markedly from the post-exilic conventions in Esther, Ezra, Nehemiah, and Chronicles."[7]

Suggestions about the book's purpose can be disentangled from questions of dating by speaking more abstractly about the book's purpose as entertainment, edification, or teaching. Those who stress the book's didactic purpose usually cite Naomi, Ruth, and Boaz as models of such virtues as covenant faithfulness (*hesed*), trust, initiative, boldness, generosity, commitment, and female friendship. An example of the didactic approach is Rabbi Ze'ira's proposal that Ruth was written to "teach how great is the reward of those who do deeds of *hesed*" (*Ruth Rabbah* 2.14). Ruth's message of hope and inclusion for the destitute and the outsider and its teachings about divine-human cooperation and God's providence are not ultimately determined by the question of the book's date.

Title, Canonicity, and Textual Witnesses

The book of Ruth is one of two Old Testament books named after a woman, the other being Esther. Some have asked why the book is named after Ruth,

---

4. Hawk, *Ruth*, 36.

5. For a comprehensive discussion of date, see Daniel I. Block, *Judges, Ruth*, NAC 6 (Nashville: Broadman & Holman, 1999), 590–98.

6. Kirsten Nielsen, *Ruth*, OTL (Louisville: Westminster John Knox, 1997), 29; J. Fentress-Williams, *Ruth*, AOTC (Nashville: Abingdon, 2012), 21–22.

7. John R. Wilch, *Ruth*, ConcC (St. Louis: Concordia, 2006), 15. For an alternative perspective that sees Standard Biblical Hebrew and Late Biblical Hebrew as concurrent dialects, see Ian Young, Robert Rezetko, and Martin Ehrenvärd, *Linguistic Dating of Biblical Texts* (London: Routledge, 2008).

the widowed Moabite daughter-in-law of the main character Naomi, and not Naomi, whose story drives the plot, or even Boaz, who speaks more than either woman, models inclusion of outsiders, marries Ruth, and fathers David's ancestor, Obed. In support of the title Ruth, we can argue that it appropriately draws our attention to the faithful, caring, loyal, and hardworking Moabite ancestor of David who models *hesed* for the people of God of every generation.

While the canonicity of the book of Ruth was never questioned, its placement within various collections of texts fluctuated, dividing along two main lines. Most English translations of the Bible follow the ordering of the Greek Septuagint (LXX) and the Latin Vulgate (Vulg.) that place Ruth after Judges, with its dark portrayal of life without a king, and before Samuel, which marks the transition to monarchy. This chronologically determined placement of Ruth in the second division of the Hebrew canon (The Former and Latter Prophets) invites us to read Ruth as a bridge that joins the stories of the conquest and settlement with the rise of kingship.

In other editions of the Hebrew Bible, Ruth is placed in the third division of the Hebrew canon (The Writings) for literary and liturgical reasons. In the oldest extant copy of the Hebrew Bible, Ruth stands as the first of the Five Scrolls (*Megilloth*) read at major festivals—the others being Lamentations, Esther, Song of Songs, and Ecclesiastes. In another edition, Ruth is placed after Proverbs, where it answers the book's final question, "Who can find a woman of worth (*'eshet hayil*)?" (Prov 31:10). (See Ruth 3:1–18: Explain the Story.) In more recent arrangements of the Hebrew Bible, however, Ruth stands second in the Five Scrolls, following Song of Songs, and is associated with the festival Pentecost (Shavuot).

Comparisons of extant Hebrew versions of Ruth, including fragments of four Hebrew manuscripts of Ruth found at Qumran, with other ancient versions (LXX, Vulg., Syriac, and the Targums) show that the Hebrew text of Ruth is very well preserved.[8] The NIV translation is based on the standard Hebrew text, the Masoretic Text (MT), as represented in the complete early eleventh-century manuscript *Codex Leningradensis*.

Changes made to the MT of Ruth based on other Hebrew manuscripts and versions are generally noted in the footnotes of NIV study Bibles. In the sections Explain the Story in the commentary that follows, significant textual and translation issues are noted. For example, the Hebrew of Ruth 4:5 allows the text to be read as either, "on the day you buy land . . . *you will acquire* the man's widow" or "on the day you buy land . . . *I will acquire* the man's widow."

8. Block, *Judges, Ruth*, 590.

The reading we choose affects our understanding of the deal that Boaz was negotiating, but in the end, it is Naomi's closer relative's refusal that moves the plot of the story forward (see comments on Ruth 4:1–12 in Ruth 4:1–22: Explain the Story).

Literary Analysis

Genre

The book of Ruth is a prose narrative that has been classified variously as a tale, folktale, novella, migration narrative, comedy, and edifying historical short story. The latter designation accurately describes the "intricately woven, magnificently crafted tale that "communicate[s] to his audiences things very close to the heart of the Old Testament."[9] In this commentary, I shall read the story as an edifying historical short story but also draw on the insights of those who classify it differently.

Style and Structure

The book of Ruth is a literary masterpiece. It features poignant thematic reversals as it moves from famine to fullness, barrenness to fruitfulness, isolation to community, death to life.[10] The story is laden with various types of rhetorical devices, including wordplay and repetition. The most obvious wordplay is Naomi's renaming of herself as Mara (Bitter) since the Almighty had made her life very bitter (1:13, 20). Key Hebrew words are often playfully clustered together for an effect that is regularly lost in dynamic equivalent English translations such as the NIV. Examples of word clusters include "return" in chapter 1; "glean" in chapter 2; "threshing floor," "lie down," and "redeem" in chapter 3; and "redeem" and "buy/acquire" in chapter 4. Other words that are repeated in Hebrew but found somewhat separated from each other include "sons"/ "child"(1:5; 4:16); "wings"/ "corner" (2:12; 3:9); "rest"/ "home" (1:9; 3:1); "kindness" (*hesed*) (1:8; 2:20; 3:10); "cling"/ "stay here"/ "stay close" (1:14; 2:8, 21, 23); "stay" (1:16; 3:13); "brought back" / "renew" (1:21; 4:15); and "standing"/ "noble" (*hayil*) (Ruth 2:1; 3:11). Such doubles, as Campbell suggests, are not merely repetitions: "they constitute brackets, as plot problems are transferred from one set of circumstances to another, from difficulty to be overcome to resolution of that difficulty. The first use of the

---

9. Edward F. Campbell Jr., *Ruth*, AB 7 (Garden City, NY: Doubleday, 1975), 3.

10. I am indebted to Jack M. Sasson's discussion of style in *Ruth: A New Translation with a Philological Commentary and a Formalist-Folklorist Interpretation*, 2nd ed. (Sheffield: Sheffield Academic, 1995), 222–25.

word constitutes a foreshadowing of what is to come, perhaps not recognized as such until the term reappears."[11]

A related kind of rhetorical bracketing or chiasm occurs when the order of a word pair is reversed the second time it occurs: "go"/"return" in 1:8 ("go back" NIV) becomes "return"/"go" in 1:12 ("return home" NIV); "kiss"/ "weep" in 1:9 becomes "weep"/ "kiss" in 1:14; "Almighty"/ "LORD" in 1:20–21a becomes "LORD"/ "Almighty" in 1:21b.[12] In addition, the book of Ruth features dramatic dialogue. Fifty-five of its eighty-five verses involve conversations that reveal much of the book's theology.

The artistry is seen in the author's use of rhetorical devices is also apparent in the book's structure. Its four chapters are similar in structure: each has three sections in which the middle section involves dialogue. The book begins and ends in Bethlehem. The emptiness, uncertainty, and death in chapter one are replaced by fullness, security, and new birth in chapter four. Between these bookends, the middle chapters center on the harvest: chapter 2 takes place during the day in a very public agrarian setting and chapter 3, by contrast, features a private night scene on the threshing floor. The narrative moves quickly as unresolved complications push the story relentlessly forward to its happy end.

Furthermore, Ruth's skillful author engages other stories, traditions, motifs, and patterns in the story of God that open up new conversations about its meaning. The book's relationship with the book of Genesis, for example, goes far beyond the mention of Rachel, Leah, Judah, Tamar, and Perez in Ruth 4 to encompass an intricate web of biblical parallels, including the journeys of Abram and Ruth (Gen 12; Ruth 1) and the unusual encounters that Lot's daughters, Tamar, and Ruth had with older men (Gen 19; 38; Ruth 3). Harold Fisch speaks of "the Ruth-corpus (Gen 19; 38; Ruth 1–4)" as giving us "in miniature the very essence of all *Heilsgeschichte* [a history of salvation] . . . beginning with Sodom and its overthrow and ending with the birth of David, the father of a messianic dynasty . . . a drama unfolding in time and involving at each point momentous and irreversible decisions, which will weigh down upon the succeeding generations."[13]

Ruth's author adds depth to the story by engaging with Israel's legal traditions (e.g., laws about the treatment of the marginalized, levirate marriage, and redemption). Stories from the books of Judges and Samuel also inform our reading of Ruth as they provide poignant contrasts and comparisons (Judg 17:7; 19:1–21:25; 1 Sam 1:8). In addition, the concluding genealogy links the past, present, and future, as it reaches back to Tamar's son, Perez (Gen 38:29),

11. Campbell, *Ruth*, 14.

12. Ibid.

13. Harold Fisch, "Ruth and the Structure of Covenant History," *VT* 32 (1982): 433.

features Boaz as the important seventh male in the list of ten, and looks forward to the messianic figure, King David (Ruth 4:22). (See Ruth 4:1–22: Listen to the Story and Explain the Story.)

Although there are many ways to outline the structure of the book of Ruth, what follows is the structural breakdown followed in this commentary:

1:1–5	The Road to Unbearable Emptiness
1:6–18	The Return Home
1:19–22	Hope Dawns: The Beginning of the Barley Harvest
2:1–3	"As It Turned Out": Ruth Gleans in Boaz's Field
2:4–17	Ruth Meets the Exceedingly Generous Boaz
2:17–23	Ruth Arrives Home with "Seed" and the Guardian-Redeemer Is Identified
3:1–5	The Plan Proposed
3:6–15	The Plan Enacted
3:16–18	The Report on the Plan, More "Seed," and the Waiting Game
4:1–12	Boaz Redeems Ruth
4:13–17	A Son Is Born
4:18–22	Connecting the Dots

Historical and Ancient Near Eastern Background

The book of Ruth assumes a basic knowledge of ancient Israelite society. Scholars typically describe Israelite society as patriarchal (the head of the household is the father), patrilineal (kinship is traced through the male line), and patrilocal (a woman leaves her family to join her husband's family). These terms describe much of what we see in the book of Ruth. In the final chapter especially, we witness men negotiating their "ownership" of land and of Ruth the Moabite, and the closing genealogy traces descent through the male line. However, since the power differentials in ancient Israel were a function not simply of gender but also of age, class, and ethnicity, Carol Meyers challenges the designation of Israelite society as patriarchal. She argues convincingly that "heterarchy," a term derived from the Greek *heteros* ("differ" or "other") and *archein* ("to rule"), more accurately describes the multiple horizontal, vertical, and sometimes intersecting relationships at work among individuals, households, professional associations, village communities, and kinship groups in ancient Israel.[14] The complex relationships found in the book of Ruth demonstrate how age, race, class or position, as well as gender, affect power relations between mothers and daughters, masters and servants, women

14. Carol Meyers, *Rediscovering Eve: Ancient Israelite Women in Context* (Oxford: Oxford University Press, 2013), 195–98.

and men, men related by blood, and even between diverse members living together in community.

The book of Ruth provides a unique window into women's culture and concerns. It reveals that women functioned as autonomous actors in multiple aspects of household and community life and, in addition, participated in multilayered heterarchical relationships.[15] The deaths of the head of the household and of his married sons provoke a catastrophe that leaves three widows without traditional kinship structures to support them (Ruth 1). Naomi and Ruth become dependent for survival on the generosity and faithfulness of relatives, the community, and their own ingenuity (Ruth 2–4). As head of the family, Naomi orders her daughters-in-law to return to their mothers' houses to find husbands. She later concocts the risky plan that involves Ruth proposing to Boaz, the family's guardian-redeemer, at night on the threshing floor (1:11; 3:2–4). While Ruth most often is respectful and deferential toward Naomi, asking her permission, for example, to glean (2:2), she refuses to follow the directive of the senior head of the household and return to Moab (1:16–18).

The book of Ruth also raises concerns about women's safety. Unattached women working the land were at risk of sexual exploitation and harassment. This reality explains Boaz and Naomi's concerns for Ruth's personal safety (2:8–9, 15–16, 22). The processing of grain took place on threshing floors and the nightly parties that followed were often associated with immorality and perhaps even fertility rites. Such traditional associations add to the mystery and suspense created by the night scene linking a man who had been partying with a Moabite woman (3:6–15; see discussion of Moabites in Ruth 1:1–22: Listen to the Story).

The complex interactions that take place in Boaz's field in chapter 2 and at the city gate in chapter 4 also attest to a variety of gender, age, class, and ethnic hierarchies, including those that reveal traditional male power and privilege related to ownership of land and female sexuality (2:9, 13, 20, 22; 4:5). The threshing floor scene in chapter 3 is itself a study of cross-cutting power dynamics as Ruth reports back to Naomi only to have her insist that she wait to find out what happens, as the power to decide their future resides in the male members of their family and community (3:16–18). Another set of hierarchies is present among the women who witness Naomi's declaration of emptiness when she arrives in Bethlehem, and later speak words of truth into Naomi's life as they remind her that Ruth is of more value to her than seven sons (1:19–21; 4:14–15). The book's concluding genealogies also give witness to another set of hierarchies: the first involving Naomi (4:17) and the second

15. Ibid., 27.

a more traditional male-membered genealogy (4:18–22; see fuller discussion in Ruth 4:1–22: Listen to the Story).

Families like those of Elimelek and Naomi were part of larger clan structures. Relatives were expected to protect and provide for their kin, including widowed, orphaned, or poor relatives, as well as foreigners or sojourners who fell outside ancient societies' safety nets. Provisions for marginalized at-risk individuals were encoded in a number of ancient law codes. Israel's levirate marriage, for example, mandated that a childless widow's brother-in-law marry her to draw her back into protective care of family and produce a male heir to carry on the name of the dead brother (Deut 25:5–10; Gen 38; see Ruth 2:1–23: Listen to the Story for examples of similar but more flexible provisions for widows in surrounding cultures).

Similarly, laws were in place to redeem the land when needy relatives had either sold it or given the rights to work the land to another (Lev 25:25–34). Other laws allowed the redemption of relatives sold into slavery, objects dedicated to the sanctuary, and, by the principle of a life for a life, the blood of a murdered relative (Lev 25:47–50; Num 35:9–21). Boaz's levirate-like marriage to Ruth may be viewed as an unattested example of "redemption" or as a generous extension of the principles behind both "redemption" and levirate marriage as outlined in Israel's legal codes (see discussion in Ruth chs. 3 and 4).

Land was valued highly in Israel, as the variety of laws related to land use, land redemption, and inheritance suggest. Israel and her neighbors associated land with deity. Naomi, for example, speaks of Orpah returning to her gods in Moab (1:15), although Naomi also embraces the belief that Israel's God would be with the women in Moab (1:8). The question, "Should Elimelek and his family have left the land given by the Lord?" lingers behind the text, as Elimelek's family faces one disaster after another in the land associated with Chemosh and the other gods venerated by the Moabites. The question of what happened to Elimelek's land does not surface until Boaz parcels together the sale of Naomi's land and marriage to Ruth (4:3).

Also presupposed in the book of Ruth is a basic understanding of ancient farming practices and laws related to the provision of food for those in need. Naomi and Ruth arrive back in Bethlehem at the beginning of the barley harvest (1:22); Ruth takes advantage of one of the few sanctioned means that widows had to provide for themselves and gleans for food in accordance with Israel's laws that mandated leaving behind produce in the fields and vineyards for those in need (2:2–3); Ruth's proposal on the threshing floor takes place approximately seven weeks later at the end of the wheat harvest (3:2, 5).

Knowledge about Moab is important in this book that features an Israelite family's move to Moab and a Moabite woman's move to Bethlehem. Israel's account of Moab's origins in an incestuous relation between Lot and his eldest daughter and other stories about sexual and religious improprieties involving Moabite women, undoubtedly raised questions about the suitability of David—the descendant of a Moabite—and his successors for kingship (Gen 19:30–38; Num 25:1–5; 1 Kgs 11:1–8).

Antagonism toward the Moabites was ensconced in Israel's law, which forbade Ammonite and Moabite males and their descendants from entering "the assembly of the LORD, not even in the tenth generation" (Deut 23:3). It also commanded the Israelites "not to seek peace" or good relations with the Moabites (Deut 23:6). The exemplary qualities of Ruth, David's Moabite ancestor, did much to ameliorate the reputation of the Moabites. It helped to answer such questions as "How could David, the descendant of Ruth the Moabite, become king and 'enter the assembly of the Lord'?"

The section Listen to the Text in the Story features texts that add to our understanding of the customs, laws, and traditions that Israel shared with her neighbors. It also enables us to see the connections between the world of the story of Ruth and the wider world of the ancient Near East. These texts illuminate the needs, rights, and vulnerabilities of widows; agricultural practices; comparative examples of personal greetings; blessings; laments; laws; preparation for love-making; genealogies; metaphorical uses of footwear; and connections between land and divinity.

Theological Message

The book of Ruth is theologically rich. It presents a compelling account of how most of us experience God in our everyday lives. Israel's God acts *directly* on behalf of his people only twice in Ruth: first, when God comes to the aid of his people suffering famine by providing food; and second, when God enables the previously barren Ruth to conceive (1:6; 4:13). More often we see God working *indirectly* behind the scenes, answering prayers and rewarding faithfulness, bringing life where there is death, hope where there is despair, fullness where there is famine, and inclusion where there is exclusion (1:8–9, 20–22; 2:11–12, 19–23; 3:10–11; 4:11–12, 14–15). The story enacts a theology of divine and human cooperation, as those who pray for God's blessings participate in answering their own petitions as well as the prayers of others. Boaz prays that Yahweh will reward Ruth richly (2:12) and then offers Ruth food, protection, and the sort of security marriage brought for ancient widows (chs. 2–4). This theology reminds us that God works through people to bring healing to our very broken and needy world. Renowned hymn writer Frances Ridley Havergal expressed this idea well when she penned:

Take my hands, and let them move
At the impulse of Thy love,
Take my feet and let them be
Swift and beautiful for Thee.[16]

We also see God's providence embedded in such "aha" moments as Ruth's "finding herself" gleaning in Boaz's fields (2:3), Boaz's perfectly "timed" arrival at his fields (2:4), and the nearer guardian-redeemer's appearance at the town gate (4:1). Psalm 113's description of the Lord raising up the poor from the dust and the needy from the ash heap and settling a barren woman in her home as a happy mother of children reminds us of God's superintendence over Ruth's journey from destitute Moabite widow to faithful follower of Israel's God, to wife, and to blessed mother (Ps 113:7–9). The book of Ruth calls us to be more mindful of God's providential workings in our lives.

Reading the book of Ruth as a story deeply embedded in the larger story of God in Scripture opens up its theological significance in ever expanding ways. The story portrays the ways of God's working in the lives of faithful people during a time not unlike the present, when "everyone did as they saw fit" (Judg 21:25). Reading Ruth alongside stories such as the dismembering of the Levite's concubine and its violent repercussions (Judg 19–21) makes many of Ruth's theological lessons more poignant. These include *hesed*, redemption, returning/turning or conversion, friendship, migration/immigration, the inclusion of the marginalized, including women, widows, and foreigners, and the victimization of the vulnerable. As Lawson Younger notes, in Judges, we see "covenant, custom, and institutions gone awry," while in Ruth, we see "things go as they should, people make the right decisions, and Yahweh is anything but lost."[17]

Further, links with stories such as Abram's leaving his homeland and the plots by Lot's daughters and Tamar to produce progeny provide further points of comparison that illuminate Ruth's faith on the one hand, and Ruth and Boaz's integrity on the other (see Style and Structure, above). Boaz's generous interpretation of his kinship responsibilities to Ruth and Naomi illustrates the principles of redemption encoded in Israel's laws and fleshed out by Jesus' redeeming sacrifice on the cross.

The book of Ruth also arches into the future story of God. With the links to the messianic figure of David that Matthew's genealogy of Jesus makes

16. Havergal's hymn, "Take My Life and Let it Be," was first published in 1876. Some suggest it was inspired by Mephibosheth's response to King David's order that Mephibosheth divide the land with Ziba: "Let him take everything, now that my lord the king has returned home safely" (2 Sam 19:30).

17. Younger, *Judges/Ruth*, 392.

explicit (Matt 1:5–6, 17), the story of Ruth looks forward to David's greater son Jesus and the blessings his incarnation, crucifixion, and resurrection bring to the world.

For most of the history of the church, Christians have located Ruth's primary theological message in the "fuller" or spiritual senses of the text. Specifically, they looked for what the book teaches about Christ and about how to live in this life and in preparation for the next. Typological readings of the book build on the connections the closing genealogy makes between Ruth, Boaz, and Obed on the one hand, and David's greater son, Jesus, on the other. Boaz, Ruth's redeemer and husband, is understood as a type of Christ; Naomi and Ruth the Moabite foreshadow the unity of Jew and gentile in the church; Ruth is seen as a type of the gentile church, delivered out of her afflictions and blessed with fruitfulness.

Interpreters also identify implicit thematic correspondences between actions or actors in Ruth and actions and actors in the New Testament. Notably they find New Testament parallels to the inclusion of the outsider, the feeding of the hungry, and models of *hesed*, self-sacrifice, redemption, and marriage. Some traditional interpreters such as nineteenth-century writers Charles Spurgeon and the anonymous Anglican M. G. also developed allegorical readings of the book of Ruth (see Ruth 2:1–23: Live the Story).

Many scholars, teachers, and preachers in the modern period set figural readings of the book of Ruth aside. Peter Hawkins speaks for many when he describes the downside of "traditional Christian interpretations of Ruth [which] tend to drain the biblical text of particularity—despite their relevance 'as examples for us.' With a kind of plodding predictability, characters become ideas and individual stories are subsumed into a theological master plan that offers few surprises."[18]

Still, reading Scripture together with the great cloud of witnesses that have come before us with critical discernment can have great value; like a beautiful glass prism, our forebears can open our eyes to theological truths we have not seen in the text, or might not even be able to see. Hugh of St. Victor's reading of Ruth (ca. 1096–1140) as "a model of the obedient soul and as such an inspiration for individuals and for the church," has merit, as does his counsel to "take the book of Ruth to heart so that [we ourselves] might be transformed as Ruth herself was, from Moabite to Israelite, from widow to bride."[19] He exhorts his audience to imitate Ruth:

18. Peter S. Hawkins, "Ruth Amid the Gentiles," in *Scrolls of Love; Ruth and the Song of Songs*, ed. Peter S. Hawkins and Lesleigh Cushing Stahlberg (New York: Fordham University Press, 2006), 80.

19. Ibid., 81.

> Let us [like Ruth] cling to him truly by loving him; . . . let us bring [the ears of wheat] into our house by reading the words of the Savior, by reflection on them, by storing them in memory. . . . Let us remove the cloak from part of his feet . . . by seeking in humble contemplation the mystery of our redemption. And let us cast ourselves down there until the end of his passion by asking humbly, again and again, to be united to him . . . at last to be joined to him in marriage and to taste the inward sweetness of the untouched bridal chamber and the glory of bliss in heaven."[20]

Hugh of St. Victor sees Ruth as much more than a type of the gentile church or convert. While it is true that he sees in her [unspoken] love for Boaz a model for loving Christ, he also sees in her willingness to make sacrifices for Naomi a reminder of Christ's ultimate sacrifice. For others, Ruth models female friendship, bold risk-taking for the greater good, and resilience following catastrophic loss or change.

Reading Boaz both as a type of both Christ and of an individual Christian also has merit. Boaz's protection of Ruth and his inclusion of Ruth in the community and later, more fully, as his wife anticipates Jesus' inclusion of the poor, the outsider, and the unclean. Boaz's care for the widows, Naomi and Ruth, also points to the New Testament's teaching about the Christian community's continued responsibility for the care of widows, and by extension all in need (1 Tim 5:3–16).

Naomi can also be read as a picture or type of the life of faith and discipleship. She models a female Job who acknowledges that God's hand is heavy upon her, and she gives us permission to voice our own laments. Her story also shows us how living in community can support individuals experiencing grief and depression. She gives us hope in the darkness as we witness her journey from emptiness to fullness, from death to life. As the women of Bethlehem recognized, God provided Naomi with Ruth, whom they suggested was worth more than seven sons, and with the child Obed, who, like Ruth, is seen by many as a type of Jesus, our redeemer who brings us also from death to life.

Reading from the Perspective of the Twenty-First Century

The twenty-first century brings new reading lenses to the book of Ruth that shift its primary signification away from personal piety to a more holistic approach that includes social justice. Our global awareness of problems related to famine, migration, sexual harassment, human trafficking, and the plight of the poor, widows, orphans, and outsiders suggests new ways of understanding

---

20. Hugh of Saint Victor, sermon 56, "De anima obediente," PL, vol. 177, cols. 1064C–1067A. English based on Latin translation by Nancy Sullas, quoted in Hawkins, "Ruth Amid the Gentiles," 82.

the plight of the members of Elimelek's family and especially, the perils Ruth faced as a "migrant worker." It pushes us to explore the book's significance for us as individuals and as the church. We need to become the Boazes for today's Ruths. We need to care for the hungry, the displaced, the disenfranchised, and the sexually violated, inside and outside our communities of faith.

A related theological insight comes with new awareness of the importance of place, community, and what Christians traditionally referred to as a parish. The book of Ruth tells the story of how a broken family was healed after moving back into a community that offered both practical and spiritual support. It models how *hesed*-like commitment to people living in community transforms lives, bringing God's healing, care, and compassion into their midst. It models a vision of life together that is at the heart of the Christian gospel. This vision has been lost in many Christian communities, but can be found in Christian groups that are forming intentional communities who live in co-housing or close enough to their neighbors to share meals, resources, and, most importantly, to support one another and those in surrounding communities for the sake of the gospel.

Insights gleaned from recent studies of grief and trauma also open up new avenues for theological reflection. Naomi's anger toward God, her silences, and her self-centered focus as she fails to introduce Ruth to the community should not be seen as evidence of character flaws, but rather as normal human responses to human tragedy.[21] Further, Ruth's journeying with Naomi from darkness into light can be evaluated in terms of what we now know to be best practices of care for those suffering grief and trauma (see Ruth 1:1–22: Listen to the Story).

The book of Ruth also informs our theological understanding of male and female. With its focus on women and their role in the story of God, the book of Ruth reminds readers of Scripture of women's importance and presence even when they are explicitly excluded, as in the closing ten-member genealogy of David.

Finally, as we read the book of Ruth with global conversation partners, we are blessed with new insights into the text, as well as an awareness of our own culturally-framed reading biases. While Western readers may be critical of Asian preachers who hold up Ruth as the model Christian daughter-in-law—submissive, selfless, and willing to sacrifice everything for her mother-in-law—we too can also fall into the sin of reading the text through the lens of the present with no consideration of the original context. Popular bloggers

---

21. Danna Nolan Fewell and David M. Gunn, "'A Son is Born to Naomi!': Literary Allusions and Interpretation in the Book of Ruth," *JSOT* 40 (1988): 99–108; David G. Garber, Jr., "Trauma Theory," *OEBI* 2 (New York: Oxford University Press, 2013): 421–28.

giving "biblical" advice on Christian dating based on the book of Ruth, for example, generally pass over details related to the night on the threshing floor (Ruth 3) and ignore Ruth's status as property (4:5).[22] As Katharine Sakenfeld suggests, "the underlying societal vision of this story, not its particular form of enfleshment in Israel's particular ancient economic and family system, offers a proper and valuable basis for theological appropriation of its story."[23]

22. Linda Martin, "The Book of Ruth Lends Dating Advice," *Cache' Connections Christian Matchmaking*, 27 February 2011, https://cacheconnections.blogspot.com/2011/02/book-of-ruth-lends-dating-advice.html.

23. Katharine Doob Sakenfeld, *Ruth*, IBC (Louisville: Westminster John Knox, 1999), 56.

Resources for Teaching and Preaching

Many excellent commentaries on the book of Ruth are cited in this commentary. Most helpful for teaching and preaching Ruth are the commentaries of Sakenfeld, Younger, Hawk, Hamlin, Block, and Campbell. Ellen F. Davis's *Who Are You, My Daughter?: Reading Ruth Through Image and Text* provides a great translation, as well as notes on the text of Ruth and Margaret Adams Parker's provocative woodcuts of key scenes and figures in the book of Ruth. Helpful for studying the history of the interpretation of the book of Ruth from the end of the New Testament era to AD 750 is John R. Franke, ed., *Joshua, Judges, Ruth, 1–2 Samuel* (ACCS).

Additional resources include Yairah Amit's wonderful introduction to reading biblical narratives, *Reading Biblical Narratives: Literary Criticism and the Hebrew Bible* (Philadelphia: Fortress, 2001).

For those who know Hebrew, a very helpful resource is Robert Holmstedt's *Ruth: A Handbook on the Hebrew Text* (Waco, TX: Baylor University Press, 2010).

For further background material, see Bill T. Arnold and Bryan E. Beyer, eds., *Readings from the Ancient Near East: Primary Sources for Old Testament Study* and the three volumes of *Context of Scripture* (*COS*), edited by William W. Hallo and K. Lawson Younger, Jr.

Helpful popular works on Ruth include:

Charles, Elizabeth Rundle. *An Old Story of Bethlehem: One Link in the Great Pedigree*. London: SPCK, 1884.

Chittister, Joan D. *The Story of Ruth: Twelve Moments in Every Woman's Life*. Grand Rapids: Eerdmans, 2000.

James, Carolyn Custis. *The Gospel of Ruth: Loving God Enough to Break the Rules*. Grand Rapids: Zondervan, 2008.

CHAPTER 1

Ruth 1:1–22

LISTEN to the Story

1In the days when the judges ruled, there was a famine in the land. So a man from Bethlehem in Judah, together with his wife and two sons, went to live for a while in the country of Moab. 2The man's name was Elimelek, his wife's name was Naomi, and the names of his two sons were Mahlon and Kilion. They were Ephrathites from Bethlehem, Judah. And they went to Moab and lived there.

3Now Elimelek, Naomi's husband, died, and she was left with her two sons. 4They married Moabite women, one named Orpah and the other Ruth. After they had lived there about ten years, 5both Mahlon and Kilion also died, and Naomi was left without her two sons and her husband.

6When Naomi heard in Moab that the LORD had come to the aid of his people by providing food for them, she and her daughters-in-law prepared to return home from there. 7With her two daughters-in-law she left the place where she had been living and set out on the road that would take them back to the land of Judah.

8Then Naomi said to her two daughters-in-law, "Go back, each of you, to your mother's home. May the LORD show you kindness, as you have shown kindness to your dead husbands and to me. 9May the LORD grant that each of you will find rest in the home of another husband."

Then she kissed them goodbye and they wept aloud 10and said to her, "We will go back with you to your people."

11But Naomi said, "Return home, my daughters. Why would you come with me? Am I going to have any more sons, who could become your husbands? 12Return home, my daughters; I am too old to have another husband. Even if I thought there was still hope for me—even if I had a husband tonight and then gave birth to sons—13would you wait until they grew up? Would you remain unmarried for them? No, my daughters. It is more bitter for me than for you, because the LORD's hand has turned against me!"

[14]At this they wept aloud again. Then Orpah kissed her mother-in-law goodbye, but Ruth clung to her.

[15]"Look," said Naomi, "your sister-in-law is going back to her people and her gods. Go back with her."

[16]But Ruth replied, "Don't urge me to leave you or to turn back from
you. Where you go I will go, and where you stay I will stay. Your people
will be my people and your God my God. [17]Where you die I will die, and
there I will be buried. May the LORD deal with me, be it ever so severely,
if even death separates you and me." [18]When Naomi realized that Ruth
was determined to go with her, she stopped urging her.

[19]So the two women went on until they came to Bethlehem. When they arrived in Bethlehem, the whole town was stirred because of them, and the women exclaimed, "Can this be Naomi?"

[20]"Don't call me Naomi," she told them. "Call me Mara, because the
Almighty has made my life very bitter. [21]I went away full, but the LORD
has brought me back empty. Why call me Naomi? The LORD has afflicted
me; the Almighty has brought misfortune upon me."

[22]So Naomi returned from Moab accompanied by Ruth the Moabite, her daughter-in-law, arriving in Bethlehem as the barley harvest was beginning.

Listen to the Text in the Story: Biblical Texts: Genesis 19:30–38; 31:14–16; 38:13–19; Exodus 15:22–27; 34:12–16; Numbers 25:1–9; Deuteronomy 23:3–6; 25:5–10; 27:19; 28:15–68; Joshua 2; Judges 2:6–23; 3:15–30; 11:23–28; 1 Samuel 22:3–4; 2 Samuel 8:12; 1 Kings 17:8–24; 2 Kings 3:1–27; Ezra 10:2–4; Nehemiah 13:23–27; Job 12:9–10; 27:2–4; Psalms 146:9; Isaiah 1:17; Ancient Near Eastern Texts: The Mesha Stela (known also as the Moabite Stone); Hittite and Middle Assyrian laws concerning the provision of husbands for widows; "The Widow's Plea"; the Sumerian Job-like wisdom poem, "Man and His God"; The Hittite "Treaty Between Mursilis and Duppi-Teshub"; The Sumerian "Lamentation of the Destruction of Ur."

Background Texts

A number of Old Testament and ancient Near Eastern texts provide helpful background information and commentary on the opening chapter of Ruth. Judges 2:6–23 summarizes the period leading up to the time of the judges. It speaks of Israel's recurrent unfaithfulness to the covenant, God's use of Israel's enemies as vehicles of punishment, and God's raising up of judges to deliver his penitent people. The covenant curses in Deuteronomy 28:15–68 include famine, sickness, infertility, and death. Given what we know about the period of the judges, it is possible that the famine in Bethlehem and perhaps even the deaths of Elimelek and his sons and their childless marriages were linked to covenant unfaithfulness. Naomi certainly saw the hand of God behind her afflictions (Ruth 1:21).

Moab and the Moabites

Other Old Testament narratives mentioning Moab and the Moabites provide a helpful backdrop to the story of Elimelek's move to Moab and his sons' marriages to Moabite women. Genesis 19:30–38 traces the origins of Moab to the incestuous relation between Lot and his eldest daughter. Other stories involving the Moabites feature seduction, idolatry, and duplicity (for example, the seduction of Israelite men by Moabite women that led to idolatry in Num 25:1–9). Moab is most often portrayed as an enemy in the Old Testament, and stories of military incursions dominate the history of Moab and Israel. Eglon, king of Moab, for example, oppressed Israel for eighteen years, only to be duped and his country subdued by a repentant Israel in Judges 3:15–30. David, on the other hand, whose ancestry is traced to Ruth the Moabite, entrusted his family to the king of Moab early in his career (1 Sam 22:3–4); later David regarded them as enemies (2 Sam 8:12).

Old Testament laws prohibiting covenants with foreigners, including marriage (Exod 34:12–16), provide an important commentary on Elimelek's move to Moab, the subsequent marriages of his sons to Moabite women, and the repeated identification of Ruth as "the Moabite" now living in Bethlehem. Mosaic Law barred Moabite men and their sons from entering "the assembly of the LORD, not even in the tenth generation" (Deut 23:2–3). However, not all exogamous marriages were censured in Scripture: Tamar (Gen 38:13–19), Rahab (Josh 2:1), Ruth (Ruth 3:1–9; 4:12), and Bathsheba (2 Sam 11:2–5) were integrated into the community and named in the lineage of Jesus (Matt 1:3, 5–6). By contrast, foreign women such as Jezebel and Solomon's wives were linked with apostasy and licentiousness; Solomon's wives in particular were used as negative examples to support the extreme measures taken against foreigners in the postexilic period (Neh 13:23–27; Ezra 10:2–4).

As the following excerpt from the ninth-century BC Mesha Stela attests, hostilities between Moab and Israel were very real (see 2 Kgs 3:1–27):

> I am Mesha son of Chemosh-yat, king of Moab. . . . I built this high place for Chemosh in Qarhoh, a high place of salvation, because he

> delivered me from all assaults, and because he let me see my desire upon all my adversaries. King Omri of Israel had oppressed Moab many days, for Chemosh was angry with his land. His son succeeded him, and he too said, I will oppress Moab. In my days he said it; but I saw my desire upon him and his house, and Israel perished utterly forever. Omri had taken possession of the land of Medeba, and dwelled there his days and much of his son's days, forty years; but Chemosh dwelled in it in my days.[1]

This passage also introduces the assumption shared by Jephthah, Naomi, and many others in the Old Testament that deity, people, and land are intimately connected (Judg 11:23–28). This being the case, Elimelek's decision to leave the "promised" land to sojourn in Moab, where Chemosh ruled, suggests desperation and perhaps even lack of faith (Judg 2:18). Not surprisingly, Naomi felt that God's hand had turned against her family (Ruth 1:13).

Widows

Israelite law identifies widows as a group who, like orphans and sojourners, need to be provided for and protected by God and God's people (Exod 22:21–24; Deut 27:19; see also Ps 146:9; Isa 1:17). Deuteronomy 25:5–10 prescribes the marriage of a childless widow to her brother-in-law, who would provide security and an heir, thus keeping the name of the deceased alive. Old Testament stories featuring widows help us to empathize with Naomi. The story of the widow of Zarephath who planned to make the last supper that she and her son would share with just "a handful of flour in a jar and a little olive oil in a jug" helps us to appreciate an ancient widow's dire straits (1 Kgs 17:8–24).

Legal texts from other ancient Near Eastern civilizations demonstrate concern for the welfare of widows. The following Hittite law (ca. 1650–1500 BC) makes provision for the care of a childless widow through marriage to another male in her husband's family:

> If a man has a wife, and the man dies, his brother shall take his widow as wife. (If the brother dies,) his father shall take her. When afterwards his father dies, his (i.e., the father's) brother shall take the woman whom he had.[2]

1. Bill T. Arnold and Bryan E. Beyer, eds. *Readings from the Ancient Near East: Primary Sources for Old Testament Study* (Grand Rapids: Baker Academic, 2002), 161–62. See also Rusty Russell, "The Moabite Stone," *Bible History Online*, www.bible-history.com.

2. Harry A. Hoffner, Jr., "Hittite Laws," *COS* 2.19:118 §193.

Middle Assyrian Laws from the eleventh century BC expand the list of potential husbands to include male children as young as ten and address the issue of what happens to the widow's dowry. These laws imply the same sense of urgency for finding a husband that Naomi expresses. Ruth's choice to align herself with an old woman who cannot provide what the culture says she needs seems all the more remarkable:

> If a man either pours oil on her head or brings (dishes for) the banquet, (after which) the son to whom he assigned the wife either dies or flees, he shall give her in marriage to whichever of his remaining sons he wishes, from the oldest to the youngest of at least ten years of age. If the father is dead and the son to whom he assigned the wife is also dead, a son of the deceased who is at least ten years old shall marry her. If the sons of the (dead) son are less than ten years old, if the father of the daughter wishes, he shall give his daughter (to one of them), but if he wishes he shall make a full and equal return (of gifts given). If there is no son, he shall return as much as he received, precious stones, or anything not edible, in its full amount; but he shall not return anything edible.[3]

Suffering

Like Naomi, Job believed that his life was in God's hand (Job 12:9–10) and that the Almighty had made his life bitter (Job 27:2–4). Naomi's situation, as well as the words she uses to describe it, finds parallels not only in Job but also in the Sumerian lament, "Man and His God," from about 2000 BC:

> My god . . . *How long* will you leave me unguided? . . .
>
> The man—his bitter weeping was heard
> by his god,
> when the lamentation and wailing that
> filled him had soothed the heart of
> his god for the young man
> . . . *and* his god withdrew his hand from
> the evil word,
> . . . he turned the [young man's] suffering
> into joy . . .
> [The man uttered] constantly the
> exaltedness of his god.[4]

---

3. See also Laws 30, 33, and 43, *COS* 2.132: 356–58.

4. Arnold and Beyer, Readings, 176; see also "A man and his god: translation," Black, J.A., Cunningham, G., Fluckiger-Hawker, E, Robson, E., and Zólyomi, G., *The Electronic Text Corpus of Sumerian Literature*, Oxford 1998–, http://www-etcsl.orient.ox.ac.uk/section5/tr524.htm.

Curses

The curse section of the second millennium Hittite "Treaty Between Mursilis and Duppi-Teshub" makes explicit what is implicit in Ruth's oath, "May the Lord deal with me, be it ever so severely" (Ruth 1:17):

> Should Duppi-Teshub not honor these words of the treaty and the oath, may these gods of the oath destroy Duppi-Teshub together with his person, his wife, his son, his grandson, his house, his land and together with everything that he owns.
>
> But if Duppi-Teshub honors these words of the treaty and the oath that are inscribed on this tablet, may these gods of the oath protect him together with his person, his wife, his son, his grandson, his house *and* his country.[5]

Responses to Trauma and Disaster

Survivors of trauma and disaster in the ancient world and today often experience anger and feelings of bitterness. Those who are able to speak of their losses often find it helpful to blame God/gods for what has happened. The Sumerian "Lamentation of the Destruction of Ur" from circa 2000 BC contains a cluster of responses to trauma also present in Naomi's response to her losses and pain.

> The lord of all the lands has abandoned
> *his stable*, his sheepfold *has been*
> *delivered* [to] the wind. . . .
> His righteous city that has been
> destroyed—bitter is its lament. . . .
> Your lament, which is bitter—how long
> will it grieve your weeping lord?
> Your lament, which is bitter—how long
> will grieve the weeping Nanna? . . .
> The utter destruction of my city truly
> they [the gods] directed. . . .
> To Kingaluda, the tender of the storm,
> he entrusted it.
> The storm that annihilates the land he
> called; the people groan. . . .
> The storm ordered by Enlil in hate, the
> storm that wears away the land.[6]

---

5. Arnold and Beyer, *Readings*, 100.
6. "Lamentation of the Destruction of Ur," in Arnold and Beyer, *Readings*, 223.

EXPLAIN the Story

The Road to Unbearable Emptiness (Ruth 1:1–5)

The introduction to the book of Ruth tersely reports a series of family tragedies in a compressed fashion. The deaths of Naomi's husband and sons left her, together with her Moabite daughters-in-law Orpah and Ruth, far from home in the country (lit., "the field[s]") of Moab. The narrator does not provide reasons for the series of disasters that the family experiences, but as nineteenth-century commentator Elizabeth Baxter observes, the family's trials are presented "as though to show us there was ample ground for this severe discipline."[7] Baxter, like many other interpreters, uses clues embedded in the book of Ruth and in other parts of the story of God to fill in the gaps in the story (see Listen to the Story, above).

The reasons for famine in Bethlehem (lit., "House of Bread") are not given, though famine is often linked in Scripture to God's judgment for covenant breaking (Deut 28:15–68). The same phrase, "there was a famine in the land" (Ruth 1:1), introduces the story of Abraham and Sarah's move to Egypt (Gen 12:10–20) and Isaac and Rebecca's sojourn in Gerar among the Philistines (Gen 26:1–16), and invites us to compare these stories. During their sojourns, Abraham and Isaac put their wives and the future promised line at risk, but each time their families ended up benefitting financially from the experience. Elimelek certainly put himself and his family at risk with his move. The allusions to the stories of Abraham and Isaac hint that blessings may be in store for the survivors of Elimelek's family. The family's identification as "Ephrathites from Bethlehem, Judah" at the beginning of the story forms the opening bracket or inclusio with the genealogy of David, "the son of an Ephrathite named Jesse, who was from Bethlehem in Judah," that closes the book (1 Sam 17:12; Ruth 4:17, 22).

The death of Elimelek (whose name means "My-God-is-King") in 1:3 changes everything for Naomi (whose name means "My-Pleasantness").[8] Unlike most of the other names in the book, which say something about the character's nature or role in the story, My-God-is-King suggests one of the book's themes: it points to the divine reality who acts providentially to provide for Elimelek's family who is experiencing the grim impact of death.

---

7. Mrs. M. (Elizabeth) Baxter, *The Women in the Word,* 2nd ed. (London: Christian Herald, 1897), 88.

8. For a discussion of meaning of the names see Block, *Judges, Ruth,* 624–28; Ellen F. Davis, *Who Are You, My Daughter? Reading Ruth through Image and Text* (Louisville: Westminster John Knox, 2003), 4–10; and Bruce W. Waltke, *An Old Testament Theology: An Exegetical, Canonical, and Thematic Approach* (Grand Rapids: Zondervan, 2004), 853.

After her husband's death, Naomi, an Israelite widow living outside the land of Israel and likely beyond child-bearing years, must find security and hope in her sons, both of whom marry Moabite women—marriages she may or may not have supported initially. Orpah's name is associated with "neck" and bespeaks her future, as she later turns her neck or back on Naomi to return to Moab (Ruth 1:14). The meaning of Ruth's name is less clear: it might mean "refreshment or satiation" or perhaps "female companion."

The marriages of Naomi's sons, Mahlon (whose name means "Critically-ill") and Kilion (whose name means "Terminally-ill") did not produce the children who would have assured a future for the family (1:2–5). Naomi was, as nineteenth-century English commentator Clara Balfour suggests, "a stranger in a strange land," who had first lost her husband, "the prop of her declining years—the head of the house—the guide of the young manhood of her sons," and then her adult sons, and had truly experienced "the desolation of grief."[9] We can imagine Naomi using the words of eighteenth-century poet Edward Young to describe the series of fatal blows she experienced:

> Insatiate archer! Could not one suffice?
> Thy shaft flew thrice, and thrice my peace slain.[10]

Naomi had lost everything—including her name; the Hebrew says "the woman" was left without her two sons (lit., "her two boys") and her husband (1:5). Without an extended family to provide legal, social, and economic support, Naomi and her daughters-in-law would have to resort to extraordinary measures to provide for themselves. Naomi's empty arms would not be filled again until she embraced her grandson in the closing scene of the book (Ruth 4:16; the word for "sons" in 1:5 is repeated in 4:16; see Introduction to Ruth).

The Return Home (Ruth 1:6–18)

Naomi's journey home with her daughters-in-law to the "House of Bread" begins when she hears that Yahweh has "visited" (KJV) his people with bread. Although God's visitations sometimes brought judgment, as in Leviticus 18:25 where God "visits" or "punishes" the defiled land, the psalmist reminds us that God's visitations sometimes bring blessing (Ps 65:9–10), as it does here with the provision of food (Ruth 1:6). This direct action of God at the beginning of the story, together with the only other direct action of God that is revealed in Ruth—God's enabling Ruth's conception to conceive (4:13)—frames the story and reminds us of God's providence.

---

9. Clara Lucas Balfour, *The Women of Scripture* (London: Houlston and Stoneman, 1847), 109.

10. Edward Young, *Young's Night Thoughts: With Life, Critical Dissertation, and Explanatory Notes,* ed. George Gilfillan (Edinburgh: James Nichol, 1853), 11, lines 212–13.

In an undesignated place on the road between Moab and Bethlehem, Naomi begins the first of fifty-five verses of dialogue—in a book that contains only eighty-five verses. This liminal space is the perfect place for the farewell scene. The geographic uncertainly is also a locus of reckoning; it contains Naomi's three impassioned speeches, the responses of Orpah and Ruth to the first two speeches, and Ruth's response to the third, at which point the arguments cease (1:8–10, 11–14, 15–18).

The theme of returning is central to the entire chapter. The Hebrew verb "return" (*shub*) is repeated twelve times, although the force of the repetition is lost in the NIV, which renders the verb variously as "return" (1:6, 8, 11, 22), "take back" (7, 15), "go back" (8, 10, 15), "turn back" (16), and "brought back" (21), and omits translating the second occurrence of the verb in verse 22. In addition to denoting physical actions of turning and returning, the Hebrew verb "return" frequently describes spiritual transformation or conversion. This theme is evident in Ruth's vow to make "your God my God" (1:16), and is also linked to other reversals such as Naomi's transformation from empty to full by the end of the story (4:14–17).

Naomi's speech begins with the double directive in Hebrew that her daughters-in-law "go, return" literally, each to her "mother's house" (1:8). This latter expression is unusual. The standard phrase, "the house of the father," indicated the place where other women at risk such as Tamar and the Levite's concubine returned (Gen 38:11; Judg 19:2, 3). "Mother's house" or "household" is found elsewhere in Scripture only three times, and only in contexts of love and marriage (Gen 24:28; Song 3:4; 8:2). This idea is more commonly expressed through combinations of "mothers" and "marriage" (Gen 24:67; 27:46; 28:2; Song 3:11) and of "woman," "house" or "household," "marriage," and the concept "wisdom" (Prov 9:1; 14:1; 24:3; 31:10–31). As Ellen Davis suggests, "in the context of this book, the unusual term [mother's house] quietly marks the fact that the book portrays the sphere of women and the power they wielded. This power would prove to be world shaping, even though in a traditional society such as Israel, the exercise of women's power was less publicly visible than that of men."[11]

As the excerpts from the ancient Near Eastern texts cited above and from Scripture (i.e., Deut 10:17–18; 14:28–29; Ps 68:5) show, the widow's plight in the ancient world was desperate. Without the support of a husband or son(s), a widow could become a slave or prostitute, or die (Amos 7:17). Independent women like Rahab, who worked both as a prostitute and in the production of

11. Davis, *Who Are You*, 17. Alternatively, it could show that Orpah and Ruth had come from contexts that lacked a leading male to care for them, because their mothers were also vulnerable widows.

flax were exceptional (Josh 2). Not surprisingly, Naomi, who likely assumes that the community in Bethlehem would not welcome her Moabite daughters-in-law, believes that remarriage in Moab holds the greatest promise for a full and secure life for her daughters-in-law. Leah and Rachel's comments regarding their freedom to leave their father's house since he no longer provided financial security for them in Genesis 31:14–16 may shed light on Naomi's decision to liberate Orpah and Ruth of any sense of familial obligation to her, as she could not provide for them (Ruth 1:11–13).

Naomi's seemingly harsh directive to Orpah and Ruth to return is followed by two prayers (1:8–9). Naomi asks that the Lord show the women the same "kindness" or "commitment" (*hesed*) that they have shown to their dead husbands and to Naomi. The full sense of the term *hesed* is difficult to capture simply in English. *Hesed* embraces the kind of covenant love, loyalty, and commitment that the psalmist associates with God's character: "The LORD is compassionate and gracious, slow to anger, abounding in love [*hesed*]" (Ps 103:8). This term is also a quality that God's covenant people are to demonstrate (1 Sam 20:8). Naomi expects that Israel's covenant God will continue to be involved in the lives of her daughters-in-law even as they return to Moab, an expectation that challenges the traditional association of god-land-deity discussed above.

In her second prayer for "rest in the home of another husband" (1:9), Naomi asks that Ruth and Orpah find the kind of security and sense of belonging that a family and community provide for women in a society in which living alone is untenable. What Naomi desires for her forsaken daughters-in-law is beautifully described by Isaiah in his use of three parallel expressions to describe God's future kingdom: "My people will live in peaceful dwelling places, in secure homes, in undisturbed places of rest" (Isa 32:18).

After Ruth and Orpah refuse to return to Moab, Naomi begins her second emotive appeal, asking rhetorical questions that introduce the problem of Naomi's inability to provide them new husbands (Ruth 1:11–13). Naomi is most likely alluding to the ancient custom of levirate marriage that mandated that the brother of a man who died without children should marry the widow so as to produce a son who would "carry on the name of the dead brother so that his name will not be blotted out from Israel" (Deut 25:5–6; see Introduction to Ruth and Listen to the Story in chs. 3 and 4). The story of Tamar, who disguised herself as a prostitute to force her father-in-law to perpetuate the name of her dead husband, looms large in the background. Ruth, like Tamar, was a gentile who needed to find a husband (Gen 38). Tamar's story is referenced both in the blessing that Boaz's "family be like that of Perez, whom Tamar bore to Judah," and in the closing genealogy that traces the line of David back through to the descendants of Perez (Ruth 4:12, 18; see Introduction to Ruth).

Naomi's argument becomes more personal as she turns her gaze inward (1:13). The NIV translation, "It is more bitter for me than for you," suggests that Naomi considers her losses to be greater than those of her daughters-in-law. The text can also be translated: "It is very bitter for me because of you" (RSV, JB). This translation suggests that the Moabite women are in some way responsible for making Naomi bitter, for causing her sons' deaths, or perhaps for contributing to her distress. In any case, in her bitterness Naomi places the ultimate blame for her troubles on the Lord.

Naomi's passionate speech convinces Orpah to return to Moab (1:14). Her logical decision provides a foil for Ruth's: Orpah kisses Naomi and departs, whereas Ruth "clings" to Naomi, a term that is used for the bond between husband and wife (Gen 2:24) and the bond God requires of his covenant people (Deut 10:20). The same verb appears again in Ruth 2:8, 21, and 23, when Ruth is mandated to stay close or "cling to" the other workers for protection (see Introduction to Ruth).

Naomi's third speech is much shorter (1:15). Perhaps she already knows she has met her match in the resolute and strong-willed Ruth. Ruth's poetic declaration speaks of her commitment, loyalty, and devotion to Naomi and Naomi's God. Ruth's decision was not impulsive (1:16–17). She would have been familiar with Israelite customs and beliefs from her years of living with Naomi's family. The God she was embracing, after all, was the God Naomi believed could show covenant kindness to her daughters-in-law even in Moab, just as he was the God who had made her life so difficult.

Ruth's declaration includes a vow to be buried where Naomi was buried, and an oath to Yahweh (1:17). This decision marks a clear sign that she is leaving aside her Moabite identity—her family, Moab, and Moab's gods—and committing herself to Naomi, Israel's land, and Israel's God. The practice of being buried with one's family was common and was usually associated with claims to the land, as Abraham's purchase of property in the "promised land" for Sarah's burial demonstrates (Gen 23:3–20). Ruth's oath to the Lord does not spell out the consequences of oath breaking, as Mursillis did in his treaty with Duppi-Teshub (see Listen to the Story, above). However, Ruth may have made some sort of hand gesture calling for punishment to prove the seriousness of her oath.

Seeing Naomi's "whitened locks" and "the lines of sorrow in [her] grief worn countenance [and her] feeble limbs," Ruth senses Naomi's great need for someone to walk with her into what she regards as a bleak and hopeless future.[12] When Naomi sees that Ruth is resolute in her decision, she says no

---

12. Harriet Livermore, *Scriptural Evidence in Favour of Female Testimony in Meetings for Christian Worship* (Portsmouth, NH: R. Foster, 1824), 40. Livermore assumes Naomi is elderly, but she may

more. Naomi's silence may indicate anger; it may also be one more sign of trauma—her pain is unspeakable, her depression is overwhelming. Recent studies of trauma survivors help us understand Naomi's behavior, state of mind, and sense of identity. As Erikson suggests, those who have experienced trauma reckon life's chances differently and see the world through a different lens. Indeed, they "experience not only a *changed sense of self* and a *changed way of relating to others* but a changed *worldview*."[13]

Hope Dawns: The Beginning of the Barley Harvest (Ruth 1:19–22)

Chapter 1 ends where it began—in Bethlehem, a small village of a few hundred people. The famine is over; barley harvest is just beginning (mid-to late April). But Naomi's personal famine is not over. She returns to Bethlehem empty; the fullness and identity she had found in her husband and sons are no more. She does not even acknowledge the presence or value of Ruth, her Moabite daughter-in-law.

The arrival of a journey-weary and timeworn woman causes great excitement and commotion. The women of Bethlehem ask, "Can this be Naomi?" (1:19). Naomi breaks the silence of her journey with the news of a name change. No longer "Pleasant One," she is now to be called Mara, "Bitter," a name that takes us back to Marah in the wilderness where God's people complained about bitter waters that later became sweet (Exod 15:22–25). By the end of the story, Naomi would experience the kind of rest and nourishment that the Israelites enjoyed at Elim following their sojourn in Marah (Exod 15:27), and the women of Bethlehem would gather around Naomi with the baby and identify her not as "bitter" but as truly blessed and loved by both Yahweh and Ruth (Ruth 4:15–17).

Like Naomi, the author of the lament over the destruction of Ur associates tragedy with punishment by the gods and responds in "bitter" lamentation. Job's protestations against God provide an even closer parallel with Naomi's words of complaint. Just as Job complains "in the bitterness of [his] soul" (Job 7:11) to Shaddai—an ancient title for God traditionally rendered as the Almighty—who has made his life bitter (27:2), so Naomi identifies herself, her experiences (Ruth 1:13), and the Lord's actions against her as bitter, and also

---

have been in her 40s or 50s since women married young in the ancient world. Still, as Carol Meyers has argued, ancient Israelite women did not normally live long lives: "the "estimated average life span for women. . .based on the analysis of skeletal remains found in tombs or graves, was about thirty years old. Men, spared the dangers of the reproductive process, lived an average of ten years longer." Meyers, "Everyday Life: Women in the Period of the Hebrew Bible," in *Women's Bible Commentary*, exp. ed., ed. Carol A. Newsom and Sharon G. Ringe (Louisville: Westminster John Knox, 1998), 255.

13. Kai Erikson, "Notes on Trauma and Community," in *Trauma: Explorations in Memory*, ed. C. Caruth (Baltimore: Johns Hopkins University Press, 1995), 194, italics original.

complains against Shaddai (1:20–21). Since Shaddai is possibly derived from an ancient Semitic word meaning mountains and is associated in Hebrew with breasts, some scholars wonder if the use of Shaddai in a book that so prominently features women and their reproductive value goes beyond coincidence. Their argument is not based on etymology but rather on "a wordplay between the epithet *shadday* ("mountains") and the noun *shadayim* ("breasts") [in Genesis 49:25]."[14] Ellen Davis develops this appealing idea, noting that "Naomi presents herself as a woman whose body has been emptied of all possibility of nurturance." She asks: "Could this bitter naming of God be a reminder of her own breasts, which once nurtured sons who are no more?"[15]

Naomi has been called the female Job, but unlike Job, who cries out for intellectual answers to the question of his undeserved suffering, Naomi simply sets out her case against the Lord before her old community (1:20–21). So, too, the Lord's solution to Naomi's plight will be found in community, as Ruth and Boaz reach out through their acts of *hesed* to bring fullness, security, rest, and a future hope to Naomi.

Naomi uses the metaphors "full" and "empty" to describe her life's journey (1:21). The famine-induced journey to Moab is ironically described as "full"—fullness linked not to food, land, or community, but rather to her immediate family, as she was both wife and mother. In contrast, Naomi disdainfully identifies her return to the land where signs of God's abundance are evident as "empty"—an emptiness initiated by the Lord who is known throughout Scripture for sustaining and defending widows and paying special attention to their cries (Pss 68:5–6; 146:9; Exod 22:21–24). The play of contrasts between the seedless woman returning to the well-seeded land is powerful; the fullness of the land will become key to the restoration of seed for Naomi in the child, Obed (Ruth 4:17).

Naomi draws a straight line from her afflictions to her Lord, the Almighty (1:21). The verb that the NIV renders as "afflicted" can also mean "testified." Perhaps, as Michael Moore suggests, both meanings are possible here: they convey Naomi's "sense of legal impotence (testimony) and her sense of theological abandonment (affliction)."[16] If Naomi had the Psalms, she could have prayed with David: "Turn to me and be gracious to me, for I am lonely and afflicted. Relieve the troubles of my heart and free me from my anguish. Look on my affliction and my distress. . . . Guard my life and rescue me; do not let me be put to shame, for I take refuge in you" (Ps 25:16–20).

14. Phyllis Trible, "God, Nature of, in the OT," 368–69.

15. Davis, *Who Are You,* 35.

16. Moore argues for the polysemantic nature of the Hebrew verb *'anah,* which can mean "to afflict" or "to testify" or perhaps both in v. 21. Michael Moore, "Ruth," in *Joshua, Judges, Ruth,* NIBCOT 5 (Peabody, MA: Hendrickson, 2000), 324.

LIVE the Story

> "*Troubles, troubles. That's all you ever hear from me right? But who else can we simple people take our troubles to?* . . . I know, I know. We are the chosen people. But, once in a while, can't you choose someone else?"
>
> —Tevye in *Fiddler on the Roof*[17]

Trauma, Grief, and Lament

Judah's bereft daughter, Naomi, takes center stage at the beginning of Ruth. Naomi experienced what the woman of Tekoa had claimed would happen to her if the authorities "put out the only burning coal [she had] left, leaving [her] husband neither name nor descendant on the face of the earth" (2 Sam 14:7). As the only "burning coal" or remnant of Elimelek's family, Naomi has been interpreted as a figure of Mother Zion in exile, "bereaved and barren, exiled and rejected . . . left all alone (Isa 49:21)."[18] She has also been seen as a figure of "the *remnant* that is *left*" of God's people, whom God will gather from many nations (Isa 11:11; Jer 23:3), and of Jesus, weak . . . low and despised in the world (1 Cor 1:27–28).[19] Naomi's significance goes beyond that of figure though. Her story resonates with all readers who have experienced trauma or disaster. In fact, her expression of anger and bitterness points to the importance of the place of lamenting, protesting, and questioning God in the Christian life.

There is a place for lament in the Christian life. Gregory the Great (AD 590–604) recognized this in his allegorical reading of Naomi's complaint as the complaint of the Christian soul lamenting "the groans of [her] fallen state . . . [and] exile . . . from the face of the Lord."[20] Many of Scripture's great saints raised their fists to God: Moses, Jeremiah, the psalmists, Job, Habakkuk, and, of course, Naomi. The voice of lament continues in the New Testament alongside the more prominent themes of the hope of the resurrection and patience in suffering. Jesus, as both man and God, simultaneously "prays (Mark 15:34) and embodies lament. . . . [Jesus is] the beginning of the fulfillment of lament's cries, and . . . points forward to the consummation of God's kingdom as guaranteed in [his] resurrection."[21] God's spirit also groans

17. The words of the Jobian character Tevye in the 1971 musical *Fiddler on the Roof* by Joseph Stein. See "Fiddler on the Roof Script—Dialogue Transcript," *Drew's Script-O-Rama*, http://www.script-o-rama.com/movie_scripts/f/fiddler-on-the-roof-script.html.

18. E. John Hamlin, *Ruth: Surely There is a Future* (Grand Rapids: Eerdmans, 1996), 10.

19. Ibid., 11.

20. Gregory the Great, "Letter 1.6" quoted in John R. Franke, ed., *Joshua, Judges, Ruth, 1–2 Samuel*, ACCS 4 (Downers Grove, IL: InterVarsity, 2005), 184.

21. Rebekah Ann Eklund, *Lord, Teach Us How to Grieve: Jesus' Laments and Christian Hope* (ThD diss., Duke University, 2012), https://dukespace.lib.duke.edu/dspace/handle/10161/5730.

our pain for us (Rom 8:26–27). Laments are not failures of faith; they embody faith. We can cry out to God from the depths of our sorrow and pain believing that God will hear us, that Jesus is with us in our suffering, and that God's spirit groans on our behalf when the pain is unbearable.

The classic five-stage model of grief proposed by Elizabeth Kübler-Ross (denial, anger, bargaining, depression, and acceptance) and the more recent six "R" processes of mourning put forward by Therese Rando (recognize the loss, react to the separation, recollect and re-experience, relinquish old attachments, readjust, and reinvest), and William Worden's four tasks of mourning (work through the pain of grief, accept the reality of the loss, adjust to an environment in which the deceased is missing, and find an enduring connection with the deceased while embarking on a new life) are all valuable tools for helping us deal with personal and community losses.[22] They also help us understand Naomi's journey from fullness to emptiness, and finally to fullness again.

A number of Christian communities, including spiritual and medical caregivers who recognize the value of lament, have developed services, liturgies, and rituals to help individuals and communities to express loss, acknowledge feelings, and raise questions.[23] When we grieve, lament, and mourn in community, we are able to support the most vulnerable with our presence and love. Biblical laments help us bring our feelings of anger, fear, and perplexity before God. Giving voice to our personal pain using the words of the psalmist or Jeremiah, or even the words of Naomi, allows us to speak the unspeakable and admit our feelings of fear, anger, and perplexity before God. Knowing that God hears our cries somehow begins to relieve the burden of our agony. Various forms of social media that allow "friends" to respond can be used for individual and communal lament. Kate Hall's blog, written after her husband died tragically in a construction accident, helped her to voice pain and suffering, thankfulness, and faith:

> It has been just over three months since Rob has gone and I have lived through the gamut of unbelief, shock, sleepless nights, tears, numbness and the reality that I still need to function, parent and love my kids. I have had the unmatched support of a family who will fly to Africa to get me, let me live with them, and bend over to push my son on a tricycle for the

22. David Kessler, "The Five Stages of Grief," www.grief.com; Therese A. Rando, *How to Go On Living When Someone You Love Dies* (New York: Bantam Books), 1991; Litsa Williams, "Worden's Four Tasks of Mourning," *What's Your Grief?*, 24 June 2013, http://whatsyourgrief.com/wordens-four-tasks-of-mourning/; Litsa Williams, "Rando's Six R Processes of Mourning," *What's Your Grief?*, 19 July 2013, https://whatsyourgrief.com/randos-six-r-processes-of-mourning/.

23. For a very helpful article on liturgical lament see John D. Witvliet, "A Time to Weep: Liturgical Lament in Times of Crisis," *RW* 44 (June 1997), https://www.reformedworship.org/article/june-1997/time-weep-liturgical-lament-times-crisis.

> thousandth time. . . . Then there has been the financial love given to me by friends, family and those who I have never met. . . . I also know that I can't answer the question "why." I doubt I will ever be able to understand such mystery, but I can say that I have never identified with Christ in his sufferings more than at this time. God has shown himself as a God of compassion to me even in this darkest of nights in ways that I am yet unable to express clearly so I won't. All I will say is that comfort has been tangible and not of my own making.[24]

Transformation and Redemption

Meeting the needs of hurting people like Naomi who in their despair cannot see the way forward is a challenge. Naomi was not in a place where she was ready to accept help, as her refusal to even acknowledge Ruth shows. Naomi had a number of basic needs that had to be met before she could begin to hope and to care again. As the rest of the book of Ruth unfolds, we will witness Naomi's transformation as her needs begin to be met through the *hesed* of Ruth and Boaz. Change came, in this case, from within the patriarchal system. Today however, many Christians are challenging oppressive heterarchical structures, including patriarchy, directly and to develop the kind of alternative structures and relationships envisioned in the early Christian baptismal formula cited by Paul in Galatians 3:28: "There is neither Jew nor Gentile, neither slave nor free, nor is there male and female, for you are all one in Christ Jesus." The work of abolitionists William Wilberforce and Sarah and Angelina Grimké, anti-apartheid advocate Nelson Mandela, and peace activist and advocate for victims of sexual violence Mariliana Morales provide inspiring models for how change can happen. The Ladder of Hope designed by Minas Hiray of Hope Enterprises in Ethiopia is a great example of a project for sustainable development that not only helps individuals like Ruth and Naomi, but also addresses the systemic issues that bring people into crises like those faced by ancient widows.[25] It first meets the basic needs of the destitute and marginalized, and then offers educational and training programs oriented toward longer sustainability.

Life-Changing Decisions: Orpah and Ruth

Somewhere on the road between Moab and Judah, Naomi begins a conversation that leads to life-changing decisions. Orpah returns to Moab, but Ruth commits herself to Naomi and her God. Interpreters throughout history have explored the significance of their decisions. Naomi's desire to return to

24. Kate Hall, personal blog. Used with permission.
25. You can find more about Hope Enterprises at www.hopeenterprises.org.

the land, to the place of God's visitation and thus his blessing and presence, reflects her continuing faith in the God of Israel whose hand she feels has gone out against her (Ruth 1:13). The move toward the land of promise is a key impulse within redemptive history and is linked to the patriarchal promises of progeny and the blessings of the nations that would come from a descendant of the tribe of Judah. The role of the land and of the nation of Israel change however, with the introduction of the new covenant that embraces all nations in Christ (Gen 49:10; Mic 5:2–5). Naomi's return to the land brings the redemption of her land, a new son, and rest for Naomi. But rest in the promised land was never fully realized; the author of Hebrews suggests that the opportunity for entry into God's rest remains for the people of God (Heb 4:6–11).

Paulinus of Nola (AD 354–431) contrasts Ruth and Orpah while placing "eternal" signification on their decisions: "Ruth follows after her holy mother-in-law, whereas Orpah abandons her; one daughter-in-law demonstrates faithlessness, the other fidelity. The one puts God before country, the other puts country before life. Does not such disharmony continue through the universe, one part following God and the other falling headlong through the world? If only the two groups seeking death and salvation were equal! But the broad road seduces many, and those who glide on the easy downward course are snatched off headlong by sin which cannot be revoked."[26]

Isidore of Seville (ca. AD 560–636) explores parallels between Ruth and the gentile church, suggesting that Ruth "is a type because she is a stranger from the Gentile people who renounced her native land [idolatry] and all things belonging to it. She made her way to the land of Israel; . . . she confessed that he in whom the saints believed is the Lord God; and that she herself will go where the flesh of Christ ascended after his passion; and that on account of his name she would suffer in this world unto death; and that she will unite with the community of the saints, that is, the patriarchs and the prophets." Isidore also sees Ruth as a fulfillment of Old Testament prophecies about the gentile nations rejoicing together with God's chosen ones (Rom 15:7–12).[27] Early American preacher Harriet Livermore extends this typology further by comparing Ruth and the gentile princess who will marry the King/David/Christ in Psalm 45: "Hear, O daughter, consider and incline your ear; forget your people and your father's house"[28] (Ps 45:10).

Other interpreters draw spiritual lessons from Orpah. Etty Woosnam (1849–ca.1883), for example, compares Orpah to the rich young ruler who, like

26. Paulinus of Nola, "Poems 27.511," quoted in Franke, *Joshua, Judges, Ruth, 1–2 Samuel*, 183.
27. Isidore of Seville, "On Ruth," quoted in Franke, *Joshua, Judges, Ruth, 1–2 Samuel*, 184.
28. Livermore, *Scriptural Evidence*, 41.

Orpah, weighed his options and "went away sad" (Mark 10:17–22). She then develops an evangelistic message about "the valley of decision" from the moving scene in which "Orpah stood regretfully clasping the hand of the kind and motherly Naomi while looking back to her native vales, like the 'Multitudes, multitudes in the valley of decision.' (Joel 3:14)." Woosnam then reminds us that we, too, have to pass through "such a moment" of decision.[29]

By reading the story within the fuller context of the story of God, Paulinus, Isidore, Livermore, and Woosnam understand the decisions of these women as types or symbols of the spiritual decisions we are all called to make. Just as Moses set before God's people a choice between "life and prosperity, death and destruction," calling Israel to "choose life" so that they might live (Deut 30:15–20), so Jesus called those who heard him to make the decision to follow him. Isidore viewed Ruth as a model disciple: "Whoever wants to be my disciple must deny themselves and take up their cross and follow me. For whoever wants to save their life will lose it, but whoever loses their life for me will find it" (Matt 16:24–25). Isidore did not differentiate between "turning" or conversion in ancient Israel and Christian conversion. However, unlike Ruth, who turned her back on her gentile identity to follow Yahweh into the land of promise, gentiles who decide to follow Jesus do not have to become Jews or be in the land to be in Christ, as Paul so clearly argues: "in Christ Jesus you are all children of God through faith, for all of you who were baptized into Christ have clothed yourselves with Christ. There is neither Jew nor Gentile, neither slave nor free. . . . If you belong to Christ, then you are Abraham's seed, and heirs according to the promise" (Gal 3:26–29). In other words, for the Israelite, repentance or conversion necessitated active cultural changes, but Christian conversion or repentance is about receiving God's Spirit into our hearts (Gal 4:6).

Many readers also contrast assumed or implied character traits of Ruth and Orpah. For nineteenth-century devotional writer Margaret Black, Orpah models selfishness: "Kiss Naomi and go. What matter though in her old age she goes forth alone to meet and struggle with poverty. Let her go. Selfishness must return to her people and her gods."[30] The noble Ruth, by contrast, models unselfishness, love, and hard work.[31]

Using a similar exemplary hermeneutic, some contemporary pastors exhort women to make personal and professional sacrifices for their mothers-in-law.[32] But surely the application of this passage should not be restricted to women!

---

29. Etty Woosnam, *The Women of the Bible: Old Testament* (London: Partridge and Co, 1881), 110–11.

30. Margaret Black, *The Woman's Daily Text Book: Homely Lessons from Women's Lives: Old and New Testament* (Paisley: J. and R. Parlane, n.d.), Fourteenth Day, n.p.

31. Ibid., Fifteenth Day, n.p.

32. Sakenfeld, *Ruth*, 34.

Rather we are all called to live lives that model *hesed*, the kind of covenant loyalty, commitment, and love that Ruth showed to Naomi, that Jesus demonstrated, and that he expects us to display (Luke 10:27).

History presents us with countless examples of the kind of love and commitment that Ruth showed Naomi. The love, devotion, and care that Margaret Roper (1505–1544) showed for her father, Sir Thomas More (1478–1535), who courageously faced execution for criticizing King Henry VIII's divorce of Catherine of Aragon, is one example;[33] another is Father Damien's (1840–1889) commitment to the leprous "living dead" in Kalaupapa that led to his own death from leprosy;[34] and still another is Mother Teresa of Calcutta's (1910–1997) devotion to Calcutta's poorest of the poor, which inspired countless others to live lives of covenant love and loyalty.

The choice Naomi set before her daughters-in-law was countercultural. According to Israelite law and custom, a widow was expected to remain a part of her husband's family after his death, and his family was expected to provide for her needs. In parts of the world, this expectation is still in place. In the Northern Sotho culture of South Africa even today, death does not release a woman from her husband's family. According to Madipoane Masenya, Naomi's advice that her two daughters-in-law return to their own families and Orpah's subsequent action of returning would be viewed with distaste.[35] Thus Naomi's offer must be seen as unexpected; she gives her daughters-in-law the opportunity to determine their own futures, an opportunity few women are given in patriarchal societies.

In her own way, Ruth also counters traditional ideas of deference by refusing to obey Naomi. Ruth shapes her own future and, paradoxically, also shapes Naomi's future. Together Ruth and Naomi exemplify strong women who counter the assumptions still held by some that women/girls should not shape their own futures but that such decisions are to be made by the male authorities in their lives. Ruth and Naomi also show women that life is not over when one becomes a widow. It is true that life is forever changed, but life is not over. Important decisions need to be made and women need to be given leave to make the kind of choices Naomi blesses her daughters-in law with—choices that change the future.

---

33. For a review of a recent book on Margaret Roper see Claire Tomalin, "A Woman for All Seasons," review of *A Daughter's Love: Thomas More and His Dearest Meg*, John Guy, *The New York Times Sunday Book Review*, 2 April 2009, https://www.nytimes.com/2009/04/05/books/review/Tomalin-t.html.

34. See Jack Voelkel, "Saint Damien: The Leper Priest," *Urbana Articles*, 1 April 2007, https://urbana.org/blog/saint-damien.

35. Madipoane Masenya, "A Commentary on the Book of Ruth," in *Global Bible Commentary*, ed. Daniel Patte (Nashville: Abingdon, 2004), 88.

Human Suffering, Sin, the Ways of God, and God's Call

When we think about the ways God works in Ruth and the larger story of God, we are reminded that God's ways are often hidden, as are the reasons behind much human suffering. Naomi believed that God was the author of her personal suffering. She shared this belief with many living under the old covenant, who drew a straight line between natural and personal disasters and covenant breaking. And given what occurred at the time, as recorded in the book of Judges, it was quite understandable to think that the famine in Bethlehem was God's judgment on God's people, that Elimelek was judged for leaving the land, and his sons judged for marrying Moabite women. As Job, Ecclesiastes, and Jesus teach however, the line between suffering and sin should not be neatly drawn. Jesus clearly taught that neither the man born blind nor his parents were responsible for his suffering (John 9:1–12). At the same time, sin and suffering continue to be inextricably linked in some ways. Many Haitians died during the 2010 earthquake, for example, because building materials were substandard and/or they had been forced by poverty to build with poor foundations high on dangerously steep hillsides.

To acknowledge the role of human sin in suffering is different than pointing the finger of God's judgment toward individuals and nations who suffer unimaginable loss and pain—an approach to the problem of suffering that most theologians today agree is troubling if not actually abhorrent. God is the Lord of nature and history, but that does not mean that God is the direct, unmediated cause of the suffering caused by natural disasters. We simply do not know enough to be in a position to definitively answer the question of why suffering occurs. The Christian response to suffering should be practical rather than theoretical, a bearing of each other's sorrows, as Christ bore and continues to bear ours (Isa 53:4).[36]

Opportunities to help the staggering numbers of suffering Naomis in our world are limitless. The World Food Program reports that 815 million people go to bed hungry in the world today, and one in nine are malnourished.[37] The Office of the United Nations High Commissioner for Refugees (UNHCR) reports the highest levels of displacement of people on record—65.6 million people—many of them under eighteen.[38] Statistics like these can numb us to the personal pain of so many in our world. Listening to the stories of people who have experienced personal disaster and trauma helps to put a human face

---

36. For helpful theological reflections on the problem of suffering see David Bentley Hart, *The Doors of the Sea* (Grand Rapids: Eerdmans, 2005) [written in light of the 2004 tsunami] and Stanley Hauerwas, *God, Medicine, and Suffering* (Grand Rapids: Eerdmans, 1990).

37. See "Zero Hunger," World Food Programme: www1.wfp.org/zero-hunger.

38. See "Figures at a Glance," *UNHCR: The UN Refugee Agency*, www.unhcr.org/figures-at-a-glance.html.

on the kind of suffering experienced by Naomi and her family. The stories of refugees living in Kenya's Dadaab refugee camp help us to become more aware of problems God may be calling us to do something about.[39]

The call to God's people to care for the most vulnerable in society—the widow, the orphan, and the sojourner—runs like a scarlet thread throughout Scripture. God's people were among the oppressed and marginalized foreigners in Egypt, and God calls them to remember their own experiences and to treat the marginalized and disenfranchised with justice, loving-kindness, and mercy (Exod 22:21–24). The often-repeated message to God's people who ignored the cries of the oppressed was one of judgment:

> Woe to those who make unjust laws,
> to those who issue oppressive decrees,
> to deprive the poor of their rights
> and withhold justice from the oppressed of my people,
> making widows their prey
> and robbing the fatherless. (Isa 10:1–2)

The media remind us daily of the urgent needs of victims of famine, displacement, death, and other forms of trauma. How can we as individuals and as a church bring God's hope into situations of darkness? The rest of the book of Ruth will help us answer these and other questions about how to live out God's call "to act justly and to love mercy and to walk humbly with [our] God" (Mic 6:8).

39. For more information, see www.dadaabstories.org.

CHAPTER 2

Ruth 2:1-23

LISTEN to the Story

[1]Now Naomi had a relative on her husband's side, a man of standing
from the clan of Elimelek, whose name was Boaz.

[2]And Ruth the Moabite said to Naomi, "Let me go to the fields and
pick up the leftover grain behind anyone in whose eyes I find favor."

Naomi said to her, "Go ahead, my daughter." [3]So she went out, entered
a field and began to glean behind the harvesters. As it turned out, she was
working in a field belonging to Boaz, who was from the clan of Elimelek.

[4]Just then Boaz arrived from Bethlehem and greeted the harvesters,
"The LORD be with you!"

"The LORD bless you!" they answered.

[5]Boaz asked the overseer of his harvesters, "Who does that young
woman belong to?"

[6]The overseer replied, "She is the Moabite who came back from Moab
with Naomi. [7]She said, 'Please let me glean and gather among the sheaves
behind the harvesters.' She came into the field and has remained here from
morning till now, except for a short rest in the shelter."

[8]So Boaz said to Ruth, "My daughter, listen to me. Don't go and glean in
another field and don't go away from here. Stay here with the women who
work for me. [9]Watch the field where the men are harvesting, and follow along
after the women. I have told the men not to lay a hand on you. And whenever
you are thirsty, go and get a drink from the water jars the men have filled."

[10]At this, she bowed down with her face to the ground. She asked him,
"Why have I found such favor in your eyes that you notice me—a foreigner?"

[11]Boaz replied, "I've been told all about what you have done for your
mother-in-law since the death of your husband—how you left your father
and mother and your homeland and came to live with a people you did
not know before. [12]May the LORD repay you for what you have done. May
you be richly rewarded by the LORD, the God of Israel, under whose wings
you have come to take refuge."

13“May I continue to find favor in your eyes, my lord,” she said. “You
have put me at ease by speaking kindly to your servant—though I do not
have the standing of one of your servants.”

14At mealtime Boaz said to her, “Come over here. Have some bread
and dip it in the wine vinegar.”

When she sat down with the harvesters, he offered her some roasted
grain. She ate all she wanted and had some left over. 15As she got up to
glean, Boaz gave orders to his men, “Let her gather among the sheaves and
don’t reprimand her. 16Even pull out some stalks for her from the bundles
and leave them for her to pick up, and don’t rebuke her.”

17So Ruth gleaned in the field until evening. Then she threshed the
barley she had gathered, and it amounted to about an ephah.

18She carried it back to town, and her mother-in-law saw how much
she had gathered. Ruth also brought out and gave her what she had left
over after she had eaten enough.

19Her mother-in-law asked her, “Where did you glean today? Where
did you work? Blessed be the man who took notice of you!”

Then Ruth told her mother-in-law about the one at whose place she had
been working. “The name of the man I worked with today is Boaz,” she said.

20“The Lord bless him!” Naomi said to her daughter-in-law. “He has
not stopped showing his kindness to the living and the dead.” She added,
“That man is our close relative; he is one of our guardian-redeemers.”

21Then Ruth the Moabite said, “He even said to me, ‘Stay with my
workers until they finish harvesting all my grain.’ ”

22Naomi said to Ruth her daughter-in-law, “It will be good for you, my
daughter, to go with the women who work for him, because in someone
else’s field you might be harmed.”

23So Ruth stayed close to the women of Boaz to glean until the barley
and wheat harvests were finished. And she lived with her mother-in-law.

Listen to the Text in the Story: Biblical Texts: Exodus 15:13; 16:4–22; Leviticus 19:1, 9–10; 23:22; 25:9–34, 47–50; 27:9–28; 35:12; Deuteronomy 24:19–22; 28:1–68; 2 Samuel 3:39; Psalms 17:8; 28:4; 36:7; 57:1; 61:4; 63:7; 91:4; 126:5; 129:8; Proverbs 19:16–17; 23:10–11; Isaiah 9:3; 16:9–10; 41:13–14; Matthew 23:37–39; Luke 13:34–35; Ancient Near Eastern Texts/Images: the Gezer Calendar; Egyptian tomb paintings; The Egyptian Instruction of Amenemope; Hebrew inscription from Kuntillet ‘Ajrud.

Gleaning, Farming Practices, and Vulnerable Widows

In imitation of God's holiness, landowners in Israel were to leave produce in the fields and on the vines for gleaners (Lev 19:1, 9–10; Deut 24:19–22). God's people were to remember their own experiences as outsiders in Egypt and as wandering gleaners dependent on God's provision of manna (Deut 24:22; note the Hebrew verb meaning "glean" or "gather" occurs nine times in Exod 16:4, 5, 16, 17, 18, 21, 22, 26, 27).

Information on farming practices found in Ruth chapters 2 and 3 is consistent with data found in other ancient texts as well as the findings of archaeologists. They include a number of Egyptian tomb paintings that contain images of landowners, laborers, reapers, and gatherers with baskets, and the poor gleaning produce left behind.[1] Those working the fields hand-pulled or cut grain with sickles, bound it into sheaves, and separated the grain from the chaff by throwing the mixture of straw, chaff, and grain up into wind with a winnowing fork on the threshing floor. The heavier grain fell to the floor while the rest blew away. The grain was then collected and stored in jars or pits. The end of the harvest was marked by celebration (Isa 9:3; 16:9–10; Ruth 3:7). The late tenth-century Hebrew inscription unearthed in 1908, known as the Gezer Calendar, is an ancient farmer's almanac:

> His double-month is ingathering
> His double-month is sowing
> His double-month is late-planting
> His month is chopping flax
> His month is barley harvest
> His month is harvest and measuring
> His double-month is pruning
> His month is summer fruit.[2]

The Egyptian Instruction of Amenemope from the Ramesside period (1292–1069 BC) mentions the vulnerability of widows like Ruth who work in the fields (Ruth 2:8–9, 15–16, 22). It also speaks of God's love for those who care for the poor.

> Do not expose a widow if you have caught her in the fields,
> Nor fail to give way if she is accused.

---

1. André Dollinger, "Ancient Egypt: The Grain Harvest," *Ancient Egypt*, www.reshafim.org.il/ad/egypt/timelines/topics/harvesting_grain.htm; Oded Borowski, "Harvests, Harvesting," *ABD* 3:63–64; Borowski, "Agriculture," *ABD* 1:95–98.

2. P. Kyle McCarter, "The Gezer Calendar," *COS* 2.85:222; W. F. Albright, "Palestinian Inscriptions," *ANET*, 320.

> Do not turn a stranger away [from] your oil jar
> That it may be made double for your family.
> God loves him who cares for the poor,
> More than him who respects the wealthy.[3]

Personal Greetings

Personal greetings that included a divine blessing were common in the ancient world. Similar to the personal greetings passed between Boaz and his workers (Ruth 2:4) are those found in Psalm 129:8, "The blessing of the LORD be on you; we bless you in the name of the LORD." A similar blessing is part of an eighth-century inscription found on a large storage jar at Kuntillet 'Ajrud in northeastern Sinai, which reads, "I bless you by Yahweh of Samaria and his asherah!"[4]

Theology of Curse and Blessing

When Boaz asks that the Lord compensate Ruth for her actions (Ruth 2:12), he is assuming a theology of retribution/curse and blessing associated with the Sinai covenant (Deut 28:1–68). The idea that God should punish evildoers for their wrongdoings was common in the ancient world. Following the murder of Abner, for example, David asks the Lord to "repay the evildoer according to his evil deeds!" (2 Sam 3:39). Similarly, the psalmist asks God to carry out retributive justice on the evildoers:

> Repay them for their deeds
>   and for their evil work;
> repay them for what their hands have done
>   and bring back on them what they deserve. (Ps 28:4)

Less common is the counter-idea found in Ruth 1:8 and 2:12, that God rewards and blesses those who do good and who keep the covenant/commandments. Proverbs 19:16–17 contrasts both ideas and articulates the notion present in Ruth that a person who is kind to the poor "lends to the LORD" who "will reward them for what they have done" (Prov 19:17; see also the Instruction of Amenemope 28:5, above).

---

3. From Instruction of Amenemope chapter 28:1–6. William Kelly Simpson, *Literature of Ancient Egypt; An Anthology of Stories, Instructions, and Poetry* (New Haven: Yale University Press, 1972), 264. For another translation of the Instruction of Amenemope see Miriam Lichteim, "Instruction of Amenemope," *COS* 1.47:115–22.

4. P. Kyle McCarter, "Kuntillet 'Ajrud: Inscribed Pithos 1," *COS* 2.47A:171. The reference to "asherah" here likely bears a connection to the same-named goddess, thus implicating the Samarian writer of this blessing as syncretistic.

Bird Imagery

The image of God's wings sheltering and protecting those in need is found in a number of Psalms (Pss 17:8; 36:7; 57:1; 61:4; 63:7; 91:4) and in the New Testament, where Jesus likens his own longing to provide refuge for Jerusalem's inhabitants to the actions of a mother bird who gathers her young under her wings to protect them (Matt 23:37–39; Luke 13:34–35). Boaz uses this common metaphor when he likens God's actions toward Ruth to that of a great bird whose wings protect the defenseless bird seeking refuge (Ruth 2:12). The Hebrew word for wing (*kanap*) is found again in Ruth 3:9, where it refers to the corner (lit., "wing") of the garment Ruth asks Boaz to spread over her. Boaz's spreading of the garment symbolizes God's bird-like protection of Ruth.

Guardian-Redeemers and Redemption

When Naomi identifies Boaz as "our close relative" and "one of our guardian-redeemers" (2:20), she introduces the subject of redemption, which pervades the book; the Hebrew root of the verb redeem (*ga'al*) is used of a person twenty-one times in Ruth (see Introduction to Ruth and relevant discussion in chs. 3 and 4). The basic function of redeemers, as Campbell suggests, is to take "responsibility for the unfortunate and stand as their supporters and advocates. They are to embody the basic principle of caring responsibility for those who may not have justice done for them by the unscrupulous, or even by the person who lives by the letter of the law."[5]

Redemption is an important theme in the larger story of God, which portrays God as redeemer of those in need—widows, the poor, and outsiders (Exod 15:13; Prov 23:10–11; Isa 41:13–14). Human redeemers such as Boaz embody and participate in God's redemptive care. The responsibilities of close relative guardian-redeemers include the redemption of such things as land forfeited by a family member—something Boaz does in chapter 4—(Lev 25:25–34); a relative sold into slavery (Lev 25:47–50); or objects dedicated to the sanctuary (Lev 27:9–28).[6] Although relatives were responsible to help more vulnerable family members in order to restore wholeness to the family or kinship group, they were not obligated to carry out the restoration (Ruth 4:6).[7]

---

5. Campbell, *Ruth,* 136.

6. Younger adds to this list the redemption of a widow in order to raise up his name on his property (Deut 25:5–10); the redemption of a clan widow facing old age alone (Ruth 4:14–15); assisting a clan relative in a lawsuit (Jer 50:34; Lam 3:58); acting as the recipient of restitution money when the wronged person is dead (Num 5:8). Younger, *Judges/Ruth,* 400–401.

7. Younger, *Judges/Ruth,* 401.

EXPLAIN the Story

"As It Turned Out": Ruth Gleaned in Boaz's Field (Ruth 2:1–3)

As it turns out, Ruth just happens to choose to glean in the field of Boaz, whose name may mean "strength is in him." Boaz is doubly introduced as "a relative" of Elimelek and a man "from the clan of Elimelek," because kinship with Elimelek makes Boaz a potential husband and redeemer of Ruth and, by extension, Naomi (Ruth 2:1, 3). Boaz is also "a man of standing" (Hebrew, *gibbor hayil*), an expression often used of valiant or powerful military leaders such as Jephthah (Judg 11:1) and Naaman, commander of the Aramean army (2 Kgs 5:1). It is sometimes used of competent, hardworking men such as Jeroboam (1 Kgs 11:28). Here, it likely denotes the favorable social and economic position of Boaz. Boaz would later use the word, *hayil* ("noble character"), to describe Ruth (3:11; Prov 31:10).

As a destitute and childless Moabite woman, Ruth had few honorable options open to her for employment. She chooses the hot, backbreaking dawn-to-dusk job of gathering up grain left behind by those working the fields. Ruth recognizes that she is at risk of abuse and exploitation and needs to find a person to glean behind "in whose eyes [she may] find favor" (Ruth 2:2). But "as it turned out," she gleans in the field of her wealthy distant relative Boaz. Is this chance or is it God's providence that brings Ruth to Boaz's field? The narrator does not say that God directs Ruth to Boaz's field, but such a conclusion is implied in the larger story. As John Hamlin suggests, "the narrator's statement that Ruth 'happened' to arrive at Boaz's field opens our understanding to the possibility that the hand of a loving God may be present in the events of our lives, providing opportunity to act according to God's will, even though we may feel, like Naomi, that God has turned against us."[8]

Ruth Meets the Exceedingly Generous Boaz (Ruth 2:4–17)

Boaz's greeting, "The Lord be with you!" and the reapers' response, "The Lord bless you!" are, as Psalm 129:8 suggests, conventional greetings. In a book filled with blessings and prayers (Ruth 1:8; 2:12, 19, 20; 3:10; 4:11), the interchange suggests that Boaz recognizes the Lord's presence in relationships and everyday life. The response of the reapers, however, whom Boaz thinks are capable of harming Ruth (2:9, 15), is more likely simply convention (See Listen to the Story: Personal Greetings, above).

Boaz's question, "Who does that young woman belong to?" (2:5) reminds us again this story was set in a time and place where women, male servants,

8. Hamlin, *Ruth: Surely There Is a Future*, 29.

and slaves were not autonomous. A woman's identity was inextricably linked to her father, husband, or in the case of a widow, her sons or distant male relatives (see Introduction to Ruth). Male servants and slaves were similarly identified by the person they served; Isaac, for example, expects Esau to ask the men who were bringing him gifts, "Who do you belong to?" (Gen 32:17); likewise, David's men ask an unidentified Egyptian slave in the open country, "Who do you belong to?" (1 Sam 30:13). But Ruth falls outside traditional patriarchal structures and belongs to no man. Boaz's servant doubly identifies her with Moab and notes her association with Naomi, as well as her polite request for permission to glean and her impressive work ethic (Ruth 2:6).

According to the NIV's rendering of the difficult Hebrew of the second part of verse 7, Ruth began her workday early, and, following the custom of resting when the sun was strongest, resumed work in the later afternoon. Another common reading of this verse has Ruth working without a break (NRSV). Both readings present Ruth as a tireless worker. A more recent interpretation of this unclear text suggests that Boaz's xenophobic overseer recasts Ruth's request to glean behind the harvesters (2:2) as a presumptuous request to glean and gather among the already bundled sheaves.[9] His prejudicial antagonism toward Ruth, together with that of Boaz's other young workers, contrasts with Boaz's kindness as he embraces the outsider.

Boaz's initial words to Ruth concern her personal welfare, as he feels she is at risk of physical and/or sexual abuse by his men, whom he suspects might take advantage of an unattached Moabite widow. Boaz clearly disapproves of such abuse and directs his men not "to lay a hand on" or "molest" her (Ruth 2:9 in the NJB; see Listen to the Story, above regarding the risks faced by unattached female gleaners). Boaz advises Ruth to "cling" (NIV: "stay") to the women, who were likely binding the stalks cut by the men. Boaz's directive to "cling," repeated in 2:21 and 22 recalls Ruth's "clinging" to Naomi (1:14). This repetition underscores the theme of the importance of choosing wisely both the people and deities one "clings" to (see Explain the Story in ch. 1). Boaz continues to anticipate Ruth's needs when he invites her to drink from the jars filled with water drawn for his regular workers (2:9). As Daniel Block suggests, Boaz's "extraordinary" invitation breaks with ancient convention, as foreigners would normally draw water for Israelites, and women for men.[10] We begin to wonder: why is Boaz taking such an interest in Ruth?

By falling on her face and bowing to the ground, the destitute Moabite widow, who would have expected contempt and indignity, shows her gratitude to Boaz and expresses surprise that he shows her favor and even takes notice

9. See the discussion of the proposals of Hurvitz and Grossman in Hawk, *Ruth*, 79–80.
10. Block, *Judges, Ruth*, 660.

of a foreigner (2:10). Abigail similarly prostrates herself before David, who praises God and blesses Abigail, whom he later marries (1 Sam 25:23–42). Reading these stories together heightens the sense building in the story that Boaz's protection and provision may eventually become permanent.

Boaz's testimony to Ruth's character is the high point in this scene; he calls attention to Ruth's exceptional care for Naomi and her courageous Abraham-like decision to leave family and country to accompany Naomi (Ruth 2:11). But unlike Abraham, who was promised land, children, and blessings (Gen 12:1–3), Ruth faces a future that promises risk, rejection, destitution, and possible death in the land of the God of Israel to whom she had committed herself (Ruth 1:17).

Boaz's prayers (2:12) that the Lord repay and reward Ruth reflect his view that God will justly and equitably reward the deserving and punish the undeserving (see Listen to the Story above). The psalmist, who has taken "refuge in the shadow of [God's] wings until the disaster has passed," similarly prays that God will reward him (Ps 57:1). Boaz believes that Ruth's actions and decisions, which he later calls "kindness" (*hesed*; 3:10), place her under Yahweh's protective wings. The concept of God's sheltering wings (the plural of *kanap*; the singular of "wing" is later used to describe the "corner" of Boaz's garment in 3:9) is paired with *hesed* in Psalm 36:7: "How priceless is your unfailing love (*hesed*), O God! People take refuge in the shadow of your wings." As Boaz's favor expands to include extravagant and generous acts of *hesed* that offer Ruth protection, provision, and inclusion, Boaz becomes part of the larger divine plan of rewarding Ruth for her decision to leave behind the gods of Moab to take refuge under God's wings. The eventual fulfillment of God's redemptive plan in Christ far exceeds what Boaz could have known or imagined.

Ruth responds to Boaz's prayer by asking for continuance of the favor that she recognizes she needs (2:1) but does not deserve as a "servant" (*shiphah*) lower in rank than the female servants who work for him (2:13; compare "servant" [*'amah*] in 3:9). But differences in nationality, social class, and economic position are not barriers for Boaz, who puts Ruth at ease by speaking "to the heart of your handmaid" (NIV: "kindly"). The expression "speak to the heart" is sometimes used in romantic settings; Shechem, for example, spoke to the heart of Dinah, whom he loved (Gen 34:3), and the Lord would speak to Israel's heart when he brought her into the wilderness (Hos 2:14). But "speak to the heart" can also mean "to speak kindly," something Joseph did to his brothers (Gen 50:21). The ambiguity in this expression teases us, providing fuel for those who read the chapter as the beginning of a romance. Ruth's claim to be *both* a servant and also not *even* or not *only* a servant presents a further ambiguity. Ellen Davis suggests "Ruth is also beginning to differentiate herself positively from the other servants and is hoping that Boaz will notice the difference. The next verse indicates that he does."[11]

Boaz then invites Ruth to leave her place of separateness as a foreign gleaner to join the community for a meal (2:14). He offers her bread for dipping in either wine vinegar (NIV) or some other kind of sour sauce used to moisten and flavor the bread. Boaz continues to break with custom when, as the male head of the community, he serves Ruth enough roasted grain to satisfy her hunger and have leftovers for Naomi. Boaz's remarkable hospitality to the Moabite gleaner, as Block suggests, is not just about "feeding the hungry." Rather, it "shows how Boaz took an ordinary occasion and transformed it into a glorious demonstration of compassion, generosity, and acceptance—in short the biblical understanding of *hesed*."[12] Boaz continues to demonstrate *hesed* by adding to his earlier directive that the men not lay a hand on Ruth (2:9), with a double order that they not humiliate her ("reprimand," "rebuke"),[13] but that they make Ruth's gleaning easier by pulling out some of the stalks from the bundles (2:15, 16).

When Ruth finishes gleaning, she beats the ears of barley to separate the grain from the hull on what is perhaps Boaz's threshing floor (2:17). She amasses about an ephah, a unit of measurement for dry goods estimated to be between thirty to fifty pounds or ten to thirty-six liters.[14] We gain a sense of Ruth's physical strength as well as the extent of Boaz's generosity by recalling that Jesse sent David with an ephah of roasted grain, ten loaves of bread, and ten cheeses to feed his three brothers who were fighting the Philistines in Saul's army (1 Sam 17:17–18).[15]

The twice-repeated description of Ruth's satiety (2:14, 17) and the narrator's stress on the abundance of grain both contrast with the earlier emptiness motif and sets up the book's empty/full theme: Naomi and Ruth had lost all in the fields of Moab and arrived empty in Bethlehem (1:1–5, 22); Ruth arrives empty at Boaz's field but returns home with abundance (2:3, 18). The association of the "seedless" Ruth with seed, garnered from the fields of Boaz anticipates the answer to Naomi's earlier prayer that the Lord would grant Ruth and Orpah rest in the home of another husband (1:9). Ruth's marriage to Boaz will produce seed that ties them to the promise of seed and the blessing of nations given to Abraham (Gen 12:1–3), to David's messianic line and, ultimately, to Jesus.

---

11. Davis, *Who Are You*, 51.

12. Block, *Judges, Ruth*, 667.

13. Hawk, *Ruth*, 83.

14. Lawson Younger suggests ten to twenty liters of barley, whereas Block cites evidence for twenty-two to thirty-six liters; Younger, *Judges/Ruth*, 448; Block, *Judges, Ruth*, 670.

15. Nielsen, *Ruth*, 61–62.

Ruth Arrives Home with "Seed" and the Guardian-Redeemer Is Identified (Ruth 2:18–23)

Naomi responds with an outpouring of questions and comments (2:18–22) upon seeing the abundance of grain Ruth had brought home after she "had eaten enough" (lit., "was satisfied"). This contrasts with the economy of her earlier words (1:18; 2:2) and is structurally parallel to Boaz's earlier blessing, questioning, and conversation with Ruth, including his concern for her safety (2:5, 8–9). The abundant seed not only solves the widows' immediate need for provisions, but also anticipates Ruth acquiring seed (i.e., progeny).

Naomi first blesses the unnamed benefactor (2:20) who has noticed Ruth who was a foreign woman who had "left" (lit., "abandoned") father, mother, and land and taken refuge under the wings of Israel's God (2:11–12). The identity of the benefactor who has "not stopped showing his kindness" (lit., "not abandoned his *hesed*") with the living and the dead (2:20)—words that evoke Naomi's in 1:8—is ambiguous in the Hebrew. The NIV translators understand the identity of the benefactor to be Boaz, but because the closest antecedent in Hebrew of the one who "has not stopped showing his kindness to the living and the dead" is the Lord, it is also possible that Naomi is referring to the Lord. The ambiguity in the Hebrew may be intentional, underscoring the book's clear theology of divine-human cooperation, as Boaz's *hesed* is an incarnation of the Lord's *hesed*.

Naomi then reveals the game-changing information that Boaz is "their" close relative and guardian-redeemer—a person obligated by law to care for vulnerable family members and buy back or repossess their family's land (see Listen to the Story, above and Introduction to Ruth for a further discussion of guardian-redeemers). Naomi now has reason to expect Boaz will "redeem" Ruth, an action that would provide both widows, the Moabite outsider and the Israelite insider, with the security they need.

Naomi's animated response to Ruth's news signals that she is moving on in the process of mourning, from depression to accommodation, to embrace hope.[16] Naomi no longer focuses on Yahweh's heavy hand of affliction; instead, she is able to acknowledge Boaz's/God's *hesed* to the living and the dead. As Judy Fentress-Williams suggests, "after the extended period of loss in chapter 1, the trajectory of the story is changed in one day by the faithfulness of one man in response to the faithfulness of one woman."[17] Naomi seems to view Ruth in a new light as she expresses the same concern for Ruth's safety in the field that Boaz expressed earlier (Ruth 2:8, 9, 15, 22). Naomi now directs Ruth to stay with Boaz's women, who would literally not "press themselves," a verb

16. See the discussion of the stages of grief in Live the Story, chapter 1.

17. Fentress-Williams, *Ruth*, 83.

used earlier by Ruth when she asked Naomi not to "urge" (lit., "press") her to leave (1:16). In the present context, the verb also suggests sexual pressure such as she might have received from the men whom Boaz had earlier instructed not to touch Ruth (2:9, 22).

Ruth continues to glean in the fields of her generous guardian-redeemer until the end of the barley and wheat harvests, which was a period of about three months. Gleaning, a sign of the movement from emptiness to fullness, from death to life, and from despair to hope, was only a temporary solution to the widows' problems, however. The note of the passing of time and the reminder that Ruth is still living with Naomi (2:23) call to mind that Naomi's prayer that Ruth would find "rest in the home of another husband" (1:9) has not yet been answered, preparing us for Naomi's bold plan for action that would move hope to realization in chapters three and four.

LIVE the Story

A Cute Little Love Story or Much More?

Many interpreters read Ruth as a happy-ending romance featuring Ruth, the beautiful young Moabite widow who captivated the heart of the older wealthy landowner Boaz. Nineteenth-century American historian Elizabeth Ellet imagines that Ruth's beauty and foreign appearance attracted Boaz's attention.[18] However, a contemporary of Ellet, Elmina Slenker, recognizes there are problems with overly romanticized retellings of "this neat and cute little love story" holding Ruth up as an example. Rather tongue-in-cheek Slenker asserts, "we hope the heroine will not be condemned as 'strong-minded' because she went out in the fields to glean, so that she might catch the eye of the rich farmer and captivate him by her charms. Perhaps it was leap year!"[19] Here Slenker is alluding to the Irish tradition going back to St. Patrick that women could propose to men on February 29th.

Although the story contains hints that support reading it as a romance, its explicit thrust pushes us to read it as much more. It contains a call to exercise *hesed* to those in need. Chapter two in particular brings us face to face with a vulnerable, destitute foreigner at risk of physical and psychological abuse as she seeks to provide food for her family. It similarly brings us face to face with an extraordinary Israelite man, who exceeds the requirements of the Mosaic Law regarding the inclusion of and provision and protection for an at-risk woman.

---

18. Elizabeth Ellet, *Family Pictures from the Bible* (New York: P. Putnam, 1849), 102–3.

19. Elmina Drake Slenker, *Studying the Bible: Or, Brief Criticisms on Some of the Principle Scriptural Texts* (Boston: Josiah P. Mendum, 1870), 27.

Boaz's care for Ruth reminds us of Jesus' care for such vulnerable women as the woman with the issue of blood (Mark 5:25–34), the desperate widow of Nain (Luke 7:11–17), and the crippled woman whom he healed (Luke 13:10–17). James reminds us that "look[ing] after orphans and widows in their distress" is indeed the "religion that God our Father accepts as pure and faultless" (Jas 1:27). In the book of Ruth, Boaz prefigures the sort of care modelled by Jesus and mentioned by James. God's people then and now are called to show *hesed* to the marginalized, the oppressed, the poor, the refugee, and the distressed.

Violence against Women

In her theological response to the problem of violence against women and girls, Elizabeth Gerhardt calls the church to embrace our responsibilities to care for those in need; specifically, she calls us to exercise *hesed* toward the vulnerable Ruths of our day:

> The time for ministering to abused women and girls is now. The time to work for structural change that will improve the lives of women and girls is now. The time to speak on behalf of those who cannot speak for themselves because of oppressive systems that deny their human dignity is now. Gendercide is a confessional issue. . . . [Jesus demands,] "Come, follow me."[20]

It is not difficult to recognize the Ruths in our world today who, because of their social, political, and economic situations, face uncertain futures that include violence and even death. Gender-based violence takes many forms, including the following: unwanted physical or sexual touching, rape, and physical and psychological harassment like that which threatened Ruth; child marriages that can result in pregnancies that threaten the lives of both mother and baby; female genital mutilation; trafficking of women and girls in modern-day slavery; and war-related rape. The issue of violence against women is highly complex. It entails ethical, moral, economic, cultural, political, and religious issues. It crosses borders, cultures, and classes; it affects all of us either directly or indirectly.

While there are many Boazes today who use their power and resources to show *hesed* to contemporary Ruths in need, many more of us must embrace our responsibilities to care for those who desperately need our help. We need to embrace the mission of the church ("religion that God our Father accepts as pure and faultless") and be modern Boazes (Jas 1:27). As members of Christ's church, we have

20. Elizabeth Gerhardt, *The Cross and Gendercide: A Theological Response to Global Violence against Women and Girls* (Downers Grove, IL: InterVarsity Press, 2014), 171.

> both the calling and the ability to help those who are vulnerable or oppressed, as well as to influence the world to prevent future exploitation from occurring. We *can* challenge the social, economic, political, and cultural conditions that force women to sell and endanger themselves for survival. We *can* help the Ruths and Naomis of today get safely across their deserts and find hope on the other side.[21]

As Gerhardt says, "The time . . . is now."[22]

Gleaning

The Israelite practice of leaving behind grain, olives, and grapes for the poor raises other contemporary justice issues. It assumes a worldview of theological social stewardship that challenges Western theories of economics, which are based on rational self-interest and the maximizing of profits without concern for the effects of particular enterprises on society and the environment. Moreover, the Old Testament practice of gleaning challenges our conventional ideas about land ownership, reminding us that what we call "our" land belongs to God and that we are stewards and keepers of God's creation.

The ancient practice of gleaning is experiencing a resurgence in many places today as individuals and communities experiment with a wide variety of gleaning practices, including sharing, conserving/preserving, and communal stewardship. Gleaning is certainly alive and well where I live in downtown Toronto. Every Wednesday on our quiet street, a few elderly women and men sort through our recycling and garbage bins looking for bottles and cans to redeem for cash. Many other people pick up furniture, dishes, clothes, books, and magazines that are routinely put out on the curb as part of my neighbors' commitment to reduce, reuse, and recycle.

Two other contemporary forms of gleaning are "dumpster diving" for food and products that have passed their expiration date or are damaged, and "freeganism" with its wider "anti-consumerist" ideology. In some communities, gleaners "freecycle," swap, or even lend a wide assortment of things—from coupons to clothes—using various social media networks. Although much gleaning today is not specifically faith-based, a number of Christians are initiating "gleaning" opportunities in their communities. Shane Claiborne's nonprofit, The Simple Way, in North Philadelphia is one such community. Their community works together to love God, to love people, and to follow

---

21. Donald Love and Emily Love Esworthy, "A Deeper Look at the Book of Ruth." *One In Three: Preventing Sexual Violence in Our Communities, A Health and Development Sermon Guide* (Maryland: IMA World Health and WeWillSpeakOut, US, 2012), 17–18, http://wewillspeakout.us/wp-content/uploads/2014/08/wwso_sermon_guide.pdf.

22. Gerhardt, *The Cross and Gendercide*, 171.

Jesus in and beyond their neighborhood. Their practices include a variety of "gleaning" enterprises. Gleaning nourishes the kingdom of God and models a biblical worldview.

God's Providence

This theologically rich chapter also invites reflections on God's providence. As we watch the events in the lives of Ruth, Boaz, and Naomi unfold providentially to bring about God's greater purposes, we are reminded that the God in whom we trust also works behind the scenes in our own lives to bring about his greater purposes. As Dean Ulrich reminds us,

> we trust in a God who provided redemption in Jesus Christ when circumstances looked as if no redemption was possible. The events of our lives are the scene of his providential and redemptive activity. Nothing occurs by chance, takes God by surprise, or exceeds his power to handle. This is the foundation of trust. . . . Both Ruth and Boaz illustrate the look of trust. To trust a God of providence is to go above and beyond conventional wisdom.[23]

Figural Readings of Chapter 2

As interpreters throughout the ages have recognized, this image-laden chapter lends itself to theological exegesis based on figural readings of the text. Traditionally, Ruth and Boaz were seen as examples to follow and as types of Christ and the gentile believer or church. The Greek theologian Theodoret of Cyr (ca. 393–ca. 457), for example, highlights Boaz as a model of servanthood and liberality:

> For he not only liberally shares his grain with Ruth but also consoles her with words. Not only does he share food with her but also was himself the minister of his kindness; so that whoever does not order another person to be his minister, but prepares the flour and bread himself, will have given very liberally indeed.[24]

Those who see in Boaz a type of Christ also see in Boaz's generous actions toward Ruth—of protection, provision, and inclusion—a picture of Christ's inclusion of the gentiles in the body of Christ. Ruth then is analogous to gentiles, "no longer foreigners and strangers, but fellow citizens with God's people and also members of his household" (Eph 2:19). More recently, Ruth has been

---

23. Dean R. Ulrich, *From Famine to Fullness: The Gospel of Ruth* (Phillipsburg, NJ: P&R Publishing, 2007), 63.

24. Theodoret of Cyr, "Questions on Ruth," quoted in Franke, *Joshua, Judges, Ruth, 1–2 Samuel*, 186.

seen as a model of courageous risk-taking for the higher good. According to Joan Chittister, "Ruth calls women to be everything they can be, whatever the odds, whatever the world thinks otherwise. Ruth goes out into strange fields alone—and takes all the women of the world with her, not simply for their sakes alone, but for the sake of the whole world."[25]

Finally, as interpreters throughout the ages have recognized, Ruth 2 also lends itself to allegory. Debates about the legitimacy of allegorical readings of Scripture are not new. The church fathers vigorously debated the issue as did the Reformers and Enlightenment scholars who called attention to the lack of controls on allegorical interpretation and thus dismissed allegorical readings. Recent interest in theological exegesis has reopened the debate over allegory. As the two examples of allegorical readings of Ruth 2 that follow suggest, theologically-sound allegorical readings can be spiritually edifying and very thought-provoking. Augustine's principle that a proper understanding of the biblical text promotes love for God and love for others is helpful to keep in mind when discerning the legitimacy of allegorical readings.[26]

In his three-point sermon, "Spiritual Gleaning," Charles Spurgeon (1834–1892) presents a mini-course on the Christian life using the metaphor of "the heavenly art of spiritual gleaning."[27] Boaz is a type of God, "the great husbandman," who encourages believers to glean in his various fields—God's doctrine field, with its sheaves of election and final perseverance; God's overflowing promise field; the field of the ordinances of baptism and the Lord's supper; and the most excellent field, hedged and sheltered field on a hill and called "Fellowship and Communion with Christ."[28] Spurgeon's Ruth, the humble gleaner, is the hard working and tired believer who has to glean the soul's food ear by ear and then thresh and winnow it. Finally, Boaz, Ruth's secret lover and redeemer, is our lover and redeemer, Jesus, the husband of the church. Spurgeon concludes his sermon with exhortation:

> Glean on with humble industry and hopeful confidence, and know that he who owns both fields and sheaves is looking upon you with eyes of love, and will one day espouse you to himself in glory everlasting. Happy gleaner who finds eternal love and eternal life in the fields in which he gleans![29]

---

25. Joan Chittister, *The Story of Ruth: Twelve Moments in Every Woman's Life* (Grand Rapids: Eerdmans, 2007), 43.

26. Augustine, *Doctr. chr.*, *NPNF*[1] 2:35–36.

27. Charles Haddon Spurgeon, "A Sermon for Gleaners," www.spurgeon.org/resource-library/sermons/a-sermon-for-gleaners#flipbook/.

28. Spurgeon, "A Sermon for Gleaners."

29. Ibid.

The anonymous Anglican writer M. G. (fl. 1893) also reads Ruth 2 allegorically. She follows many before her who see Boaz as a type of Christ, but she extends the figure. For M. G., Boaz is Christ, who offers Ruth inclusion in the mystical body of Christ, and the bread and wine vinegar are types of the body and blood of Christ:

> The whole history of Ruth's work in the field, her meeting with Boaz, her being numbered among his maidens, unworthy though she considered herself of the honour, and his blessing her, is a beautiful allegory of the Holy Communion, where we meet our Elder Brother, though at first we scarcely realize it, and where with His Blessing we are assured of our membership with "the blessed company of all faithful people,"[30] and where we receive heavenly Food from the hands of His servants as often as we will come for it. The morsel of bread, and the vinegar (a sort of common wine), which she might drink, is a plain type of the Bread and Wine given to us in the Holy Eucharist.[31]

---

30. Here M. G. is quoting the prayer used after communion in the Anglican service of Holy Communion. The Book of Common Prayer and the Administration of the Sacraments (Oxford: Oxford University Press, 1854), 134, https://archive.org/details/bookofcommonpray00unit/page/n37/mode/2up/search/blessed+company.

31. M. G., *Women like Ourselves: Short Addresses for Mothers' Meetings, Bible Classes, etc.* (London: SPCK, 1893), 77.

CHAPTER 3

Ruth 3:1–18

LISTEN to the Story

1One day Ruth's mother-in-law Naomi said to her, "My daughter, I must find a home for you, where you will be well provided for. 2Now Boaz, with whose women you have worked, is a relative of ours. Tonight he will be winnowing barley on the threshing floor. 3Wash, put on perfume, and get dressed in your best clothes. Then go down to the threshing floor, but don't let him know you are there until he has finished eating and drinking. 4When he lies down, note the place where he is lying. Then go and uncover his feet and lie down. He will tell you what to do."

5"I will do whatever you say," Ruth answered.

6So she went down to the threshing floor and did everything her mother-in-law told her to do.

7When Boaz had finished eating and drinking and was in good spirits, he went over to lie down at the far end of the grain pile. Ruth approached quietly, uncovered his feet and lay down. 8In the middle of the night something startled the man; he turned—and there was a woman lying at his feet!

9"Who are you?" he asked.

"I am your servant Ruth," she said. "Spread the corner of your garment over me, since you are a guardian-redeemer of our family."

10"The Lord bless you, my daughter," he replied. "This kindness is greater than that which you showed earlier: You have not run after the younger men, whether rich or poor. 11And now, my daughter, don't be afraid. I will do for you all you ask. All the people of my town know that you are a woman of noble character. 12Although it is true that I am a guardian-redeemer of our family, there is another who is more closely related than I. 13Stay here for the night, and in the morning if he wants to do his duty as your guardian-redeemer, good; let him redeem you. But if he is not willing, as surely as the Lord lives I will do it. Lie here until morning."

[14]So she lay at his feet until morning, but got up before anyone could
be recognized; and he said, "No one must know that a woman came to
the threshing floor."
[15]He also said, "Bring me the shawl you are wearing and hold it out."
When she did so, he poured into it six measures of barley and placed the
bundle on her. Then he went back to town.
[16]When Ruth came to her mother-in-law, Naomi asked, "How did it
go, my daughter?"
Then she told her everything Boaz had done for her [17]and added,
"He gave me these six measures of barley, saying, 'Don't go back to your
mother-in-law empty-handed.'"
[18]Then Naomi said, "Wait, my daughter, until you find out what
happens. For the man will not rest until the matter is settled today."

Listen to the Text in the Story: Biblical Texts: Genesis 19:37–38; 38:29, 30; Esther 2:12; Proverbs 7:17–18; Song of Songs 1:2–4; 7:2; Isaiah 41:13–14; 43:1, 14; 44:6, 22–24; Ezekiel 16:8; Hosea 9:1; Ancient Near Eastern Texts: Egyptian Love Song; the Story of Tammuz and Ishtar.

Marriage, Remarriage, and Set-ups

Most marriages in ancient Israel were monogamous and arranged by family members for economic, social, or religious reasons. Women had little say in terms of choosing a husband. Caleb's daughter, for example, was an item of property to be exchanged between men when her father offered her up as a prize of war (Josh 15:13–19; Judg 1:11–15). Some wealthy and privileged men and men whose marriages had produced no heirs married more than one woman; Solomon's marriage to 700 wives and 300 concubines was exceptional (1 Kgs 11:3). Marriage was normally endogamous, as marriage within the tribe and even between cousins was encouraged. Marriage outside the tribe or cultural and faith group was discouraged. Ahab's disastrous union with Jezebel, an ardent Phoenician follower of Baal and Asherah, provides an extreme example of what can go wrong in exogamous marriages (1 Kgs 16:29–33), whereas Ruth's marriage to Boaz and even Esther's marriage to Xerxes suggest that such unions have a place in the story of God. Although the Song of Songs testifies to the importance of passion, romantic love, and a woman's consent, romance rarely initiated ancient marital unions.

When death ended a marriage, remarriage was expected in the case of a childless young widow. Indeed, the levirate law mandated that a widow marry her brother-in-law as a way of protecting her from isolation and destitution. It also solved the problem of the transfer of the husband's land and legacy (Deut 25:5–10; see Introduction to Ruth). When family members shirked their responsibilities, widows such as Tamar (Gen 38) and Ruth, whose future security depended on being part of a family and community, had to take matters into their own hands. Older widows like Naomi faced a precarious future and needed to be cared for.

Naomi's unconventional scheme to have the outsider Ruth marry Boaz calls to mind the bold initiatives taken by the widowed daughters of Lot and the widow Tamar to acquire progeny (Gen 19:37–38; 38:27–30). Naomi's plan, like that of Lot's daughters, involved alcohol, but Boaz, unlike Lot, remained very self-aware on the threshing floor. Naomi's plan also involved solicitation, but Ruth did not dupe her intended mate as Tamar had done when she dressed as a prostitute to lure her father-in-law—who was not fulfilling his responsibilities toward her—into a sexual encounter. The links between these stories continue as the progeny born to these women play key roles in the story of salvation: Moab, the son of one of Lot's daughters, was Ruth's ancestor; Perez, Tamar's son, was Boaz's forefather; Ruth and Boaz's son, Obed, was David's forefather; Ruth is named in Jesus' genealogy (Ruth 4:18–22; Matt 1:1, 5, 16).[1] These links also remind us that Ruth and Naomi were not alone in taking bold initiatives to resolve the problems they faced as impoverished widows in a patriarchal culture. The female lover who goes to great lengths to find her lover in the Song of Songs provides example of a woman, who like Ruth, takes the initiative in the male/female relationship (Song 3:1–4).

Beautification, Change of Attire, and Love

Naomi's instructions to Ruth about how to prepare for her encounter with Boaz call to mind ancient stories and love songs that describe the use of beautifying preparations that were thought to awaken the senses for love making. In preparation for their one-night stand with the Persian King Xerxes, Esther and the other virgins were given twelve months of beauty treatments, "six months with oil of myrrh and six with perfumes and cosmetics" (Esth 2:12).

The Egyptian queen featured in the following love poem clearly associated perfumed oils and creams with lovemaking:

> My breasts are smothered with fruit,
> My hair glistens with balm,
> When I am with you . . .

---

1. Fisch, "Ruth and the Structure of Covenant History," 425–37.

I am a noble woman filled with pleasure,
I am the queen of Egypt.[2]

Occasionally, changing clothes was also associated with the preparation for an intimate encounter. For example, Tammuz, the Sumerian male vegetation god, was washed, anointed with oil, and changed his clothes before a sexual encounter:

Take Tammuz, her husband,
Wash him and anoint him with oil,
Clothe him in a purple garment
Allow him to play a flute of lapis lazuli,
Let him find contentment with prostitutes.[3]

This sequence of washing, anointing, and dressing found also in Ruth 3:3 may have been an ancient literary trope that readers would have recognized as the author's symbolic way of calling attention to a change in a character's situation.[4]

EXPLAIN the Story

The Plan Proposed (Ruth 3:1–5)

Like chapter two, chapter three begins and ends with conversations between Ruth and Naomi that enclose a longer scene involving Boaz and Ruth. In the first conversation, Naomi reveals her extraordinary plan to find a home for Ruth. This involves a risky nighttime encounter with Boaz on the threshing floor. No longer self-absorbed, Naomi takes up her responsibilities as head of this unsustainable family unit that needs the protective care of their kinship group. She introduces a scheme that sets in motion the answer to her earlier prayer, that Yahweh grant Orpah and Ruth "rest in the home of another husband" (1:9). Naomi expresses her desire for Ruth to find a place to settle "where you will be well provided for" (lit., "and that it go well with you"). This expression can mean much more than financial success. In Deuteronomy, the expression, "going well" with you and your children, together with long life, is associated with keeping Yahweh's decrees and commands (Deut 4:40; 5:29; 6:3).

Naomi's specific plan includes Ruth's marriage to Boaz, who has been attentive to the needs of both Naomi and Ruth throughout the harvest; he has

2. Victor Harold Matthews and Don C. Benjamin, *Old Testament Parallels: Laws and Stories from the Ancient Near East*, 3rd ed. (New York: Paulist Press, 2006), 301.

3. From the Sumerian story of Tammuz and Ishtar in Matthews and Benjamin, *Old Testament Parallels*, 311.

4. Eskenazi and Frymer-Kensky, *Ruth*, 51.

provided food for them to share, and included and protected Ruth in his fields. Naomi had earlier revealed that Boaz was a close relative of her husband (Ruth 2:1) and their guardian-redeemer (*go'el*) (2:20). But neither levirate marriage nor redemption as described in the legal texts in the Old Testament present an exact legal precedent for the marriage of Boaz and Ruth. Ruth's identity as a Moabite presents a major barrier to marriage to an Israelite. Did Naomi hope that Boaz's proven interest and commitment to Ruth was strong enough that he would figure out a way to make marriage to a Moabite woman who was a relative by marriage possible? (See Introduction to Ruth for discussion of the Moabites, levirate marriage, redemption, and guardian-redeemers; see also Explain the Story, below.)

Naomi's plan was to be enacted that very night at the threshing floor, where Naomi knew that Boaz would sleep following the traditional post-harvest winnowing celebration (3:2, 3, 6, 14; see Ruth 2:1–23: Listen to the Story). Why Boaz would be winnowing barley at the end of the harvest season is surprising, given that barley was one of the first crops harvested (2:23). However, traditional farmers in the Middle East today, like ancient farmers, sometimes delayed barley winnowing until the end of the season when it was winnowed together with the wheat.[5]

The signification of Naomi's initial instructions to wash, apply perfume, change clothes, and go down to the threshing floor (3:2) is debated.[6] The Hebrew preserves a double reading of Naomi's specific instruction for Ruth to change her clothes that allows either a singular or plural form of "clothes." Some scholars who prefer the singular (KJV: "put thy *raiment* upon thee") suggest that the change of clothing marked a change in Ruth's status from mourning widow to available spouse, as it did when David washed, anointed himself, and changed his clothes to signal that he was ready to move on from mourning his son's death (2 Sam 12:20). The sequence of washing, anointing, and dressing is also thought to be a way ancient authors called attention to change in a character's situation (see Listen to the Story, above). On the other hand, the NIV's "get dressed in your best clothes" reads the Hebrew as plural and follows ancient readings that put a "seductive" (or at least "romantic") spin on Naomi's plan. Both options signal a change that involves Ruth putting her best foot forward in presenting herself to Boaz for marriage, although one may wonder how Boaz would have been aware of the changes in Ruth's attire in the darkness of the night.

Naomi's idea for a night rendezvous following the celebrations that mark the end of harvest offers Ruth the opportunity of a private place to propose marriage in a setting pregnant with symbols of fecundity. Naomi's plan,

5. Sakenfeld, *Ruth*, 52.
6. See Wilch's discussion of the interpretive options, *Ruth*, 257.

however, places Ruth at risk of the kind of abuse and harassment vulnerable women especially experienced from men working in the fields (2:8–9, 15, 22). Naomi's risky plan also, as Hawk observes, "casts Ruth in the role of the Moabite seductress. A Moabite woman approaching an esteemed Israelite elder, secretly and in the middle of the night, epitomizes Israelite anxiety about Moabite women's aggressive and dangerous sexuality (see also Num 25:1–3)."[7]

Naomi's instructions to Ruth (Ruth 3:3–4) consist of a series of directions that invite readers into a scene filled with hints of sexual intrigue. These innuendoes include the use of "uncover" (Ruth 3:4, 7) (found in Lev 18:6 with reference to nakedness; ESV, KJV); "feet" (Ruth 3:4, 7 [sometimes used in Hebrew as a euphemism for male genitals, as in Ezek 16:25]); and "lie down" (repeated eight times in the chapter in Hebrew: 3x in Ruth 3:4; 2x in 7, 8, 13, 14, and used in Gen 26:10 as an expression of intercourse). Other sexually suggestive words and images in the account of the nighttime encounter at the threshing floor (3:6–15) are discussed below.

Ruth, who had earlier boldly defied Naomi's mandate to return to Moab, now defers to her mother-in-law and agrees to carry out Naomi's plan that Ruth propose to Boaz. If successful, this would make Ruth the Moabite a permanent insider (3:5). Although Ruth was undoubtedly aware of the risks involved in the plan, she trusted both Naomi and Boaz. She knew her gleaning provided a mere stopgap survival strategy, and that only marriage would provide a permanent solution for herself and for Naomi, with whom she had vowed to stay even unto death (1:16–17).

The Plan Enacted (Ruth 3:6–15)

As the plan unfolds, the sense of intrigue and danger increases. The adverb used to describe Ruth's approach toward the satiated Boaz in 3:7 is translated variously: "quietly" (NIV), "softly" (ESV), "secretly" (NASB), or "stealthfully" (NRSV). The latter implies clandestine action similar to that of David when he cut off a corner of Saul's robe (1 Sam 24:4) or Jael when she approached Sisera with tent peg and hammer in hand (Judg 4:21). Ruth finds Boaz at "the far end of the grain pile" where he guarded his grain as he slept (Ruth 3:7). This mound of grain evokes yet another sexual image, one made more explicit in the Song of Songs where the princess' belly is likened to a "mound of wheat" surrounded by lilies (Song 7:2).

The plethora of sexually evocative language, the sexually suggestive setting, and the act of uncovering part of Boaz's lower anatomy raise a number of questions: Did Naomi's desperate scheme to find Ruth a husband include sexual

7. Hawk, *Ruth*, 103.

intercourse? Did she hope that a pregnant Ruth, like Tamar (Gen 38), would force Boaz's hand into marriage? Or does a similar practice found among the Bowa in Mali that involves no physical contact suggest that the sexual innuendoes in this chapter are meant only to tease?[8] Perhaps the Victorian minister who simply sidestepped such questions by asserting that what happened on the threshing floor is "too beautiful, delicate, dangerous, and sublimely virtuous, to be recited here" was right, and questions about what happened are meant to be left open at this point in the story.[9]

Perhaps the chill of the night woke "the man," Boaz. Surprised that he was not alone, he asked "the woman" at his feet under the cover of darkness, "Who are you?" (3:8), a question that again raises the issue of Ruth's identity (Ruth 2:5). The Hebrew that identifies Boaz as "the man" (3:3, 8, 16, 18) and Ruth as "a woman" (vv. 8, 11, 14) recalls the "man" and "woman" in the Garden in Eden who were to become one flesh (Gen 2:23–24).[10] This repeated allusion to the garden scene is masked by the NIV translation of "him" in verse 3 and "Boaz" in verse 16. In 3:9, Ruth identifies herself as "Ruth, your servant" (*'amah*), a deferential term, similar in meaning to the term for servant she had earlier used to refer to herself (*shiphah*, 2:13), although possibly implying an increase in status. The eighth-century tomb inscription of Shebna, a royal steward in Hezekiah's court, contains a note to tomb robbers saying the tomb contains no silver or gold, but only the steward's bones together with those of his *'amah*, a term translated as wife or slave wife.[11] This translation supports Davis's argument that Ruth's new self-identification signifies "[Ruth] is now consciously representing herself as a prospect for marriage."[12]

Ruth's bold directive that Boaz spread the corner (lit., *kanap*, "wing") of his garment over her is a symbolic way of saying, "Marry me!" (3:9 TEV). A similar metaphor for the social and economic security marriage provided for women in this culture is found in Ezekiel 16:8, where God enters into a marriage covenant with Jerusalem by spreading "the corner of [his] garment" over the young woman who symbolized Jerusalem/Israel. Ruth's directive receives added significance when linked to Boaz's earlier prayer that the God of Israel, whose "wings" (plural of *kanap*) now provided Ruth with refuge, would richly reward her for what she has done (Ruth 2:12). As Katharine

8. Shadrac Keita and Janet W. Dyk, "The Scene at the Threshing Floor: Suggestive Readings and Intercultural Considerations on Ruth 3," *BT* 57 (2006): 31.

9. John P. Durbin, "Ruth: Or the Reward of the Daughter-in-law," in *The Opal: A Pure Gift for the Holy Days*, ed. Sarah J. Hale (New York: J. C. Riker, 1848), 98.

10. Hamlin, *Ruth: Surely There is a Future*, 43.

11. Philip J. King and Lawrence E. Stager, *Life in Biblical Israel* (Louisville: Westminster John Knox Press, 2001), 371.

12. Davis, *Who Are You*, 79.

Sakenfeld suggests, Ruth "in effect invites Boaz to make good on the prayer he made earlier on her behalf."[13]

Ruth justifies her marriage proposal by reminding Boaz that he was their guardian-redeemer (3:9). Boaz would have known that he was not obligated to marry Ruth on the basis of his kinship with her, as Old Testament legal texts only mandated marriage to the wife of one's deceased brother. He was also likely familiar with the generous ancient practices of levirate-like marriage and redemption that Naomi and Ruth knew about. At the same time, Boaz would have recognized that Ruth's identity as a Moabite would be a barrier to marriage with an Israelite.[14]

Boaz's positive response to Ruth's proposal, however, shows that he is open to marriage to a Moabite widow—an act that would enable him to extend his generosity not only toward Ruth but also toward Naomi, whom he would also care for as part of his extended family (3:10–11). His blessing (lit., "blessed are you by the Lord" echoes the blessing formula Naomi used earlier in regard to Boaz in 2:20) and suggests that Israel's God also approves of the proposal. The story of God shows that this was in fact the case, as the Lord blesses the widows' initiatives above and beyond their wildest dreams. David's greater son, Jesus Christ, "who is God over all, forever praised!" (Rom 9:5) is to come from the family line of Boaz and Ruth. Boaz's earlier praises of Ruth's actions and decisions were based on what she had done for Naomi (Ruth 2:11–12); now he highlights her even greater *hesed* in choosing him over the younger men. Boaz's comments about age (3:10) suggest that he is an older person who, given his age and stature in the community, was likely to have been already married. If this was the case, Ruth would become a second wife.

The expression, "all the people of my town" or more literally, "the whole gate of my people" (3:11), is a figure of speech (metonymy) that refers to all the people who met in the public square inside the city gate. Such meetings involved male heads of families who gathered to make decisions involving members of the community (4:1–12). Women's presence at the gate, as Davis suggests, was less obvious, "though their character and their work were no less essential to the well-being of the whole community than were those of men."[15] Indeed, the closing lines of praise for the noble woman in Proverbs 31:31 attest: "let her works bring her praise at the city gate."

Boaz also reports that all the people of Bethlehem call Ruth *'eshet hayil*, "a woman of noble character" or "a woman of standing or substance" (Ruth 3:11), the term used to describe the idealized woman praised for her hard work, initiative, and integrity in Proverbs 31:10–31. Earlier the narrator

13. Sakenfeld, *Ruth*, 58.
14. Hawk, *Ruth*, 107.
15. Davis, *Who Are You*, 83.

had similarly described Boaz as *gibbor hayil*, "a man of standing" or "a man of valor" (Ruth 2:1). The faith and character traits Boaz and Ruth shared outweigh their differences in age, status, and ethnicity.

After he reassures Ruth, Boaz introduces the problem of a more closely related relative who has first refusal rights to fulfill the responsibilities of guardian-redeemer (3:12). Using a strong oath, "as surely as the Lord lives," Boaz invokes the living God to help him fulfill his vow to redeem Ruth if the closer relative will not (3:13). The six-fold repetition of the idea of redemption in verses 12 and 13 is purposeful, as Boaz is committed to make redemption happen. Boaz is, as Hamlin observes, a "model of the covenant manner of life in Israel, which was to 'fear . . . worship . . . and swear by his name alone'" (Deut 10:20; see also 6:13).[16]

In the meantime, Ruth is instructed to lie with Boaz until morning, but leave before anyone notices that a woman had been with Boaz at the threshing floor (Ruth 3:13–14). As a sign of his commitment to Ruth, Boaz fills her shawl with a very generous gift of "six measures of barley" (lit., "six barleys"), which would have weighed between sixty and a hundred pounds.[17]

At this point we need to ask, what really happened during the "very strange and delicate proceeding" at the threshing floor? Or to put it more bluntly, did Ruth and Boaz have sex next to the pile of grain on the threshing floor? For Ephrem the Syrian (ca. 306–373) the answer was clear. He argued that Ruth slept with Boaz because she had a prophetic vision that the Messiah would come from his seed:

> Ruth: with a man on the threshing floor she lay down, for your sake.
> Her love was bold for your sake, you who teach boldness to all the repentant.
> Her ears despised all the voices because of your voice.
> The coal which crept into the bed of Boaz ascended and lay down.
> She saw the high priest who was hidden in his loins, (she) the fire for his censer.
> She hurried and she became the heifer (wife) of Boaz.
> For you she bore the fattened ox.
> She gleaned wheat out of love for you;—she gathered stalks of straw.
> You quickly gave her the reward for her humiliation.
> For the ears of wheat, a root of kings, and for the stalks of straw,
> the Sheaf of Life which issued from her.[18]

---

16. Hamlin, *Ruth: Surely There is a Future*, 49.

17. Davis, *Who Are You*, 87.

18. Phil J. Botha, "Tamar, Rahab, Ruth, and Mary—The Bold Women in Ephrem the Syrian's Hymn *De Nativatate* 9," *Acta Patristica et Byzantina* 17 (2006): 6. Botha's translation is very literal but conveys the sense of Ephrem's interpretation well.

Not all interpreters follow Ephrem on this matter. Even many who follow the narrator's clear lead and recognize the story's resplendent sexual innuendoes conclude that they did not have sex on the threshing floor. Their arguments are straightforward: the text says Ruth and Boaz consummated their marriage following the legal wrangling at the city gate and the blessing of the elders and witnesses in Bethlehem (4:13), and Ruth and Boaz are presented throughout the story as models of integrity and honor.[19] Betrothal and marriage in this setting, as in some cultures today, are not simply an agreement or commitment of individuals, but involve whole families and even the community.

The Report on the Plan, More "Seed," and the Waiting Game (Ruth 3:16–18)

The concluding dialogue that signals the end of the chapter also marks the last time we hear the voices of Naomi and Ruth. Naomi's query, "Who are you?" (NIV: "How did it go?") raises the question of Ruth's identity for a third time (2:5; 3:9). Again, Ruth returns with a generous gift from Boaz. Boaz's comment to Ruth that she not go back empty recalls Naomi's earlier self-narrative: "I went away full, but the LORD has brought me back empty" (1:21). Ruth's return with abundant grain encapsulates the story's larger journey: from emptiness to fullness, from destitution to abundance, from affliction to blessing, from despair to hope, from death to life—a journey that reaches its climax in chapter 4. Naomi's final word to Ruth, that she wait (3:18), is drawn out. It contrasts with the earlier rapid narration of Ruth's interaction with Boaz, Ruth's return, and the truncated dialogue between Ruth and Naomi. Both women now need to trust the traditional male decision-making process that "the man" Boaz would set in motion.

LIVE the Story

Working Together for Good

Although this chapter brings us into a world that is very different than ours, it has much to say to us as we try to live God's story faithfully today. It models how the human and divine "work together for good" (Rom 8:28 ESV) to fulfill God's great plans. As a faithful Israelite and a relative, Boaz enacts God's concern for the widow, the outsider, and the poor: "He raises the poor from the dust and lifts the needy from the ash heap" (Ps 113:7).

---

19. Ulrich, *From Famine to Fullness*, 90–93. This being said, Tamar, who had in desperation enticed her father-in-law Judah into sleeping with her by dressing as a prostitute, was judged by Judah as being more righteous than he was because he had not allowed her to marry his third son Shelah (Gen 38).

So too Naomi, who had earlier experienced God's hand as heavy upon her, acts to seal Ruth's relationship with Boaz, whose actions of *hesed* to the living and the dead incarnate God's *hesed* (Ruth 2:20). Naomi realizes that the timing is right to put in place her bold plan that will begin to answer her prayer that Ruth find rest/security in the home of another husband (1:9). Her plan becomes part of God's bigger plan of salvation, for in the fullness of time, God sent his son Jesus Christ, the son of David, son of Jesse, son of Obed, the son of Ruth and Boaz (Matt 1:1–17; Ruth 4:16–22).

The Question of Timing

While the timing of Naomi's initiative is spot on, other great saints have sometimes got it wrong. Sarah's plan to use Hagar as a surrogate mother, for example, made good sense and certainly fit with ancient practices, but it was neither God's plan nor God's timing: waiting was the better option for Sarah and Abram (Gen 16:1–16). The question arises: how do we know when to take the initiative to move a plan forward that seems to be God's plan, and when we should wait? Praying for wisdom and discernment, and following the lead of God's spirit and the counsel of other Christians, are important steps in what can often be a difficult process.

Boldness, Resilience, and Initiative

The widows' initiative sets them apart as exceptional examples of women who figure out ways to survive in a culture whose intersecting hierarchies leave little room for the marginalized to shape their future. South African scholar Madipoane Masenya praises Ruth and Naomi for refusing to be victims of their circumstances. Citing the northern Sotho proverb, *Kgomo go tsoswa yeo e itsosago*, literally, only a cow that tries to get up (from its fall) will be lifted up, Masenya exhorts us "as individuals and participants in structures of power [to] become willing agents and take upon ourselves the responsibility to transform our hopeless situations," trusting in God as Naomi and Ruth did "to make us rise above those circumstances."[20] What it will be like for us, as individuals and as the church, as we become willing and bold agents of transformation will look different for each of us. Standing aside and watching passively as outsiders of every kind try to negotiate our increasingly complex world is not a viable option.

Misreading the Threshing Floor Scene

The lines of continuity between the threshing floor and our varied postmodern contexts must be drawn carefully. Too often interpreters fail to

20. Masenya, "Ruth," 91.

recognize historical and cultural differences related to gender, ethnicity, age, class, and position between ancient Israelite and twenty-first-century society (see Introduction to Ruth). Instead, many focus on the common humanity we share with the characters in the text: we feel what they feel, we imagine what they are experiencing, and we use our own experiences to fill in any information the narrator has omitted in the story. Ruth, Naomi, and Boaz are, as nineteenth-century author M. G. declared, women and men like ourselves.[21]

By focusing on our sameness however, interpreters often apply the text in misleading ways. Western readers who mine the book for tips on dating and marriage without acknowledging our cultural differences are a case in point.[22] While it may be true that Ruth and Boaz exhibit many of the traits a person of faith would look for in a future mate (Ruth is faithful, committed to God and family, hardworking, mature, a self-starter, and respectful; Boaz is a man of integrity and faith, generous, respected, and respectful of his future mother-in-law), replicating the night rendezvous at the threshing floor is as highly problematic as the longstanding practice that women are acquired as chattel in marriage. Besides, what woman today would think it a good idea to propose marriage to a man awoken from sleep after partying in a place known for illicit sexual activity? Nineteenth-century author Clara Balfour was correct when she strongly advised against drawing lessons on male/female relationships from the book of Ruth. She warned young women, especially, against putting their trust in men for whom they have feelings, as they can easily be taken advantage of: "Woe to the unwary maiden who prematurely trusts her reputation in the keeping even of him to whom she has resigned her heart. In proportion to her affection must be her caution."[23]

Figural Readings

Given the highly suggestive nature of the threshing floor scene, it is not surprising that many interpreters have explored its various hidden senses. In most figural readings, Boaz is regarded as a type of Christ and Ruth a type of the individual believer or of the church. Some interpreters go further and find in specific details of the chapter spiritual truths about the Christian life. For example, Hugh of St. Cher (1200–1263) sees in the details of Ruth's washing, anointing, and dressing in preparation for meeting Boaz a picture of Christian

21. "The characters placed before us in Holy Writ are not impossible beings of a stained-glass window type, but real men and women of ordinary flesh and blood, with trials and temptations extremely like our own, who acted for the most part exactly as we ourselves would be likely to act under the same circumstances." M. G., *Women Like Ourselves*, iv.

22. Linda Martin, "The Book of Ruth Lends Dating Advice," *Cache' Connections Christian Matchmaking*, https://cacheconnections.blogspot.ca.

23. Balfour, *The Women of Scripture*, 122.

baptism, the anointing of the Holy Spirit, and virtue.[24] In his comments on Romans 4:7, Luther references Ruth 3:7 and 3:9, drawing an analogy between Ruth's lying down at Boaz's feet and how "the soul lays itself down at Christ's humanity and is covered with His righteousness."[25]

As noted above, Ephrem the Syrian (ca. 306–373) presents a most striking early theological reading of the threshing floor scene, as he reads it through the lens of Matthew's genealogy of Jesus.[26] Ephrem regards Tamar and Ruth as examples of Old Testament believers who had a prophetic vision that the Messiah would come from their seed. Their love for the Messiah impelled them to boldly pursue sexual relations with the carriers of the messianic seed, Judah and Boaz. According to Ephrem, "Ruth lay down with Boaz because she saw hidden in him the medicine of life; today her vow is fulfilled since from her seed arose the Giver of all life."[27] While we may not share Ephrem's conclusion that Boaz and Ruth actually had sex on the threshing floor—an act Ephrem suggests was excused by her "holy" motives as it led to a "holy" outcome—his theological insights bear careful consideration. He correctly notes the obvious connection between Ruth and "The Giver of all life," he picks up on important links between the stories of Ruth, Tamar, Bathsheba, and Mary, and he implies that Ruth's marriage proposal was motivated by much more than romantic attraction to Boaz.

---

24. B. P. Irwin, "Ruth 3: History of Interpretation," *DOTW* 697.

25. *LW*, 25:265.

26. Botha, "Tamar, Rahab, Ruth, and Mary," 1–21.

27. Ephrem, and Kathleen E. McVey, *Ephrem the Syrian: Hymns* (New York: Paulist Press, 1989), 65.

CHAPTER 4

Ruth 4:1–22

LISTEN to the Story

[1]Meanwhile Boaz went up to the town gate and sat down there just as the guardian-redeemer he had mentioned came along. Boaz said, "Come over here, my friend, and sit down." So he went over and sat down.

[2]Boaz took ten of the elders of the town and said, "Sit here," and they did so. [3]Then he said to the guardian-redeemer, "Naomi, who has come back from Moab, is selling the piece of land that belonged to our relative Elimelek. [4]I thought I should bring the matter to your attention and suggest that you buy it in the presence of these seated here and in the presence of the elders of my people. If you will redeem it, do so. But if you will not, tell me, so I will know. For no one has the right to do it except you, and I am next in line."

"I will redeem it," he said.

[5]Then Boaz said, "On the day you buy the land from Naomi, you also acquire Ruth the Moabite, the dead man's widow, in order to maintain the name of the dead with his property."

[6]At this, the guardian-redeemer said, "Then I cannot redeem it because I might endanger my own estate. You redeem it yourself. I cannot do it."

[7](Now in earlier times in Israel, for the redemption and transfer of property to become final, one party took off his sandal and gave it to the other. This was the method of legalizing transactions in Israel.)

[8]So the guardian-redeemer said to Boaz, "Buy it yourself." And he removed his sandal.

[9]Then Boaz announced to the elders and all the people, "Today you are witnesses that I have bought from Naomi all the property of Elimelek, Kilion and Mahlon. [10]I have also acquired Ruth the Moabite, Mahlon's widow, as my wife, in order to maintain the name of the dead with his property, so that his name will not disappear from among his family or from his hometown. Today you are witnesses!"

[11]Then the elders and all the people at the gate said, "We are witnesses.

May the LORD make the woman who is coming into your home like
Rachel and Leah, who together built up the family of Israel. May you
have standing in Ephrathah and be famous in Bethlehem. [12]Through the
offspring the LORD gives you by this young woman, may your family be
like that of Perez, whom Tamar bore to Judah."

[13]So Boaz took Ruth and she became his wife. When he made love to
her, the LORD enabled her to conceive, and she gave birth to a son. [14]The
women said to Naomi: "Praise be to the LORD, who this day has not left
you without a guardian-redeemer. May he become famous throughout
Israel! [15]He will renew your life and sustain you in your old age. For your
daughter-in-law, who loves you and who is better to you than seven sons,
has given him birth."

[16]Then Naomi took the child in her arms and cared for him. [17]The
women living there said, "Naomi has a son!" And they named him Obed.
He was the father of Jesse, the father of David.

[18]This, then, is the family line of Perez:

Perez was the father of Hezron,
[19]Hezron the father of Ram,
Ram the father of Amminadab,
[20]Amminadab the father of Nahshon,
Nahshon the father of Salmon,
[21]Salmon the father of Boaz,
Boaz the father of Obed,
[22]Obed the father of Jesse,
and Jesse the father of David.

Listen to the Text in the Story: Biblical Texts: Genesis 2:4; 5:1–32; 6:9; 10:1–32; 11:10–27; 25:12, 19; 36:1, 9; 37:2; 50:7; Exodus 3:5; Leviticus 25:14–16, 23; Numbers 22:4, 7; 27:9–11; Deuteronomy 25:5–10; Joshua 5:15; 9:11; 15:16–19; 1 Samuel 1:8; 24:21; 1 Kings 2:5; Job 1:2, 18; 42:13; Psalms 60:7–8; 113:7–9; Proverbs 15:25b; 31:16; Amos 2:6; Matthew 1:1–16; Ancient Near Eastern Texts: Nuzi Legal Text SMN 2338; "The Legend of Aqhat"; "The Widow's Plea"; *KAI* 214.16–22; "The Epic of Kirta"; the Assyrian King List.

Elders

Elders were senior male members of village households responsible in the ancient world for legal, social, and religious decision-making and administration. Egyptian, Midianite, Moabite, and Gibeonite elders are mentioned in the Old Testament (Gen 50:7; Num 22:4, 7; Josh 9:11). The elders in Bethlehem were called on to witness the deliberations about the redemption of Naomi's land and the marriage of Mahlon's widow, as these decisions impacted members of their community (Ruth 4:2, 9, 11–12).

Remembering and Venerating the Dead

Although the Israelites valued remembering the names of the dead, they did not normally venerate their dead. Part of Naomi's early despair was that she was not capable of having sons to perpetuate the ownership of the family's land and to carry on the names of the dead (Ruth 1:11; Deut 25:5–6). Saul speaks directly about the great misfortune of forgetting the names of the deceased when he asks David to swear that he would not kill off his descendants or wipe out his name from his father's family (1 Sam 24:21).

There is, however, evidence of various ancestor cult rites among Israel's neighbors. A late Bronze Age Ugaritic text outlining the responsibilities of a royal son, for example, suggests that a son's actions will affect the father's wellbeing after death:

> Let him have a son in his house.
> Offspring within his palace.
> To set up his Ancestor's stela,
> The sign of his Sib in the sanctuary:
> To rescue his smoke from the Underworld,
> To protect his steps from the Dust.[1]

Other ancient texts also point to various ancestor cult rites, including the veneration of the dead through ritual meals with the deceased. In an eighth-century BC inscription of the Aramean King Panammu, the king expresses his desire that his son remember to ask Hadad, the head of the Aramaic pantheon, to remember him by feasting with him:

> May the soul of Panammu eat with you,
> And may the soul of Panammu drink with you.[2]

Sandals

Leather sandals with straps or laces were commonly worn in the ancient world. Sandals had some "value" as implied by Amos's rebuke of Israelites who sold

1. *CAT* 1.17.26–28; repeated in 17.2.1–2; 17.2.14–17. As translated in Simon B. Parker, "Aqhat." In *Ugaritic Narrative Poetry*, ed. Simon B. Parker. SBLWAW 9 (Atlanta: Scholars Press, 1997), 53, 55, 56.

2. *KAI* 214.16–22 as cited in King and Stager, *Life in Biblical Israel*, 380.

the needy for a pair of sandals (Amos 2:6). Sandals also carried symbolic meaning. Staining blood on the sandals and belts of enemies signaled their defeat and shame (1 Kgs 2:5), as did the gesture of removing the sandal of a man who refused to marry his widowed sister-in-law (Deut 25:5–10). Gestures involving feet and sandals were also used in finalizing land claims and land transfers. God's gesture of throwing a sandal on Edom seems to symbolize God's possession of that land (Ps 60:7–8). God's command that Moses and Joshua remove their sandals because the land on which they stood was holy similarly indicates that the land belongs to God (Exod 3:5; Josh 5:15). A legal text from Nuzi, a second millennium BC Hurrian city, also depicts the landowner "lifting his foot" off his property and placing the new owner's foot on the land:

> My foot from my houses and fields I have lifted up,
> and the foot of Urhi-Sharri I have placed.[3]

The gesture involving a sandal in the negotiations at the gate in Ruth, like the practice of the lifting of the foot at Nuzi, likely symbolizes the transfer of Naomi's property from one guardian-redeemer to another.

Land Ownership

Land in Israel was Yahweh's land and "must not be sold permanently" (Lev 25:23; see Introduction to Ruth). Proprietary rights belonged to the clans, and individual clan members could "sell" the right to work the land and use its produce for a designated period of time (25:14–16). When a male clan member died, his land was normally passed down to his son; when there was no son, a daughter or the closest male family member inherited the land (Num 27:9–11). In exceptional cases, women owned land: the idealized wife in Proverbs 31:16 bought real estate, and Aksah, Caleb's daughter, received the upper and lower springs from her father (Josh 15:16–19). Proverbs 15:25b suggests that a widow could own land ("The Lord . . . sets the widow's boundary stones in place"). "The Widow's Plea," an ostracon from the period of the Israelite kings, raises the legal issue of whether a widow is eligible to an inheritance when land has already been given to the deceased's brother:

> May YHWH bless you in peace.
> And now, may my lord the official listen to your maidservant.
> My husband has died (leaving) no sons.
> (I request politely that the following) happen: (let) your hand (be) with me and entrust to your maidservant the inheritance about which you spoke to 'Amasyahu.

3. SMN 2338 in E. R. Lacheman, "Note on Ruth 4:7–8," *JBL* 56 (1937): 54.

As for the wheat field that is in Naamah, you have (already) given (it) to his brother.[4]

Naomi, by contrast, seems to have retained rights to Elimelek's fields (see Ruth 4:1–22: Explain the Story).[5]

Fertility and the Ideal Family

The blessings of fertility for the bride and honor for the groom were commonplace in the ancient world. The prayers for fertility in the mid-second millennium BC Ugaritic text, "The Epic of Kirta," are similar to those offered by the Bethlehemites (Ruth 4:11–15):

The woman you take, Kirta,
    the woman you take to enter your house,
    the girl who enters your courts,
She shall bear you seven sons,
    Even eight shall she produce for you.[6]

The ancients not only placed great value on male offspring, but also viewed seven or eight sons as ideal. God gave Job a new "ideal" family of seven sons and three beautiful daughters after his first "ideal" family of seven sons and three daughters were killed (Job 1:2, 18; 42:13). Voices like those of the women of Bethlehem, who valued Ruth as better than the ideal family of seven sons (Ruth 4:15), and Elkanah, who valued his own worth as husband of his barren wife Hannah as better than ten sons (1 Sam 1:8), challenged traditional patriarchal and patrilineal ideals.

Ancient Genealogies

Ancient genealogies served a number of purposes. Horizontal or segmented genealogies such as the Table of Nations in Genesis 10 showed how families, clans, and nations were related by means of their common ancestry. Vertical or linear genealogies traced a line of descent from the first person named to the last and often were used to legitimate the rights and the privileges of the last person named for a particular political or religious office.[7] Like the genealogies in Genesis, the genealogy that closes Ruth begins with the formulaic

---

4. Dennis Pardee, "The Widow's Plea," *COS* 3.44:86. Scholars debate its authenticity: see Yuval Goren, Miryam Bar-Matthews, Avner Ayalon and Bettina Schilman, "Authenticity Examination of Two Iron Age Ostraca from the Moussaieff Collection," *IEJ* 55 (2005): 21–34.

5. Younger, *Judges/Ruth*, 474–76.

6. Dennis Pardee, "The Kirta Epic," *COS* 1.102:337. See S. Parker, "The Marriage Blessing in Israel and Ugaritic Literature," *JBL* 95 (1976): 23–30.

7. P. E. Satterthwaite, "Genealogy in the Old Testament," *NIDOTTE* 4:654–63.

expression "these are the generations of" (NIV "This then is the family line of Perez," Ruth 4:18; see also Gen 2:4; 5:1; 6:9; 10:1; 11:10, 27; 25:12, 19; 36:1, 9; 37:2). Ten-member genealogies like the one in Ruth 4 are found in the Babylonian genealogy that legitimates Hammurabi's dynasty, the Assyrian King List, and the genealogies of Noah (Gen 5:1–32) and Abram (Gen 11:10–26).[8]

Women were rarely included in ancient genealogies. The short genealogy introduced by "Naomi has a son!" is unusual. Also remarkable is Matthew's genealogy of Jesus with its inclusion of five women (Matt 1:1–16).

EXPLAIN the Story

Boaz Redeems Ruth (Ruth 4:1–12)

This final chapter moves us away from the very private threshing floor to the public arena of the city gate, away from a world negotiated by women to a world where men take the lead, as Boaz carries out his promise to marry/redeem Ruth if the closer relative refuses his right to be guardian-redeemer. Its first scene is fast-moving and complex as the obstacle to Naomi's plan that Ruth and Boaz marry is faced. When the nearer guardian-redeemer wanders by the city gate where Boaz is sitting, we are reminded of how Ruth "just happened" to choose to glean in Boaz's field at the beginning of the harvest (Ruth 2:3; 4:1). The relative's name, *peloni ʿalmoni*, is a rhyming Hebrew wordplay that is the equivalent of the English "Joe Schmoe";[9] the NIV "my friend" misses the significance of the wordplay. Because *peloni ʿalmoni* later refused to marry Ruth to preserve the name of the dead, it is only fitting that his real name is itself blotted out from history. Like Orpah, who functions as a foil to Ruth, Joe Schmoe makes Boaz's *hesed*-filled actions seem all the more remarkable. Like Ruth, Boaz will be remembered for his acts of generosity and redemption that are tied into God's larger purposes of redemption. In the end, Boaz holds a place of distinction in the book's concluding genealogy (4:18–22).

The prominent and respected landowner Boaz, whom Naomi knew would make good on his word, orders his relative and then the elders of the town to sit down (4:1). The elders would make the legal decision on behalf of the community. Before the ten elders and others who had gathered to witness the proceedings, Boaz invites Joe Schmoe to act as guardian-redeemer of Naomi's land (4:2–4). As Boaz's plan unfolds, the theme of redemption that

8. E. Moore, "Ancient Near Eastern Background," *DOTW* 692–93.

9. Hebrew reads *peloni ʿalmoni*, "a rhyming parody similar to 'Joe Schmoe'"; Davis. *Who Are You,* 97.

was prominent in chapter 3 continues to be significant; the term *go'el* occurs twenty times in various forms in this and the preceding chapter (3:9, 12 [2x], 13 [4x]; 4:1, 3, 4 [5x], 6 [4x], 8, 14; see also ch. 3 and Introduction to Ruth).

While those sitting with Boaz would have known that the destitute Naomi had land that could be redeemed, present-day readers do not. Questions remain for us about Naomi's relationship to the land. If Naomi had inherited the rights to use her husband's property until she remarried or died, at which time the rights reverted to her husband's relatives,[10] she is essentially asking her guardian-redeemer to do what Jeremiah's uncle asked him to do as his nearest relative, namely, to redeem and possess his field (Jer 32:6–12). Alternatively, if Elimelek had sold the rights to the land before he left for Moab, and Naomi had no means to purchase them back, she is asking her guardian-redeemer to buy the land back for her family (Lev 25:25).[11] In either case, Joe Schmoe agrees to take up his responsibilities as a close relative and redeem the land.

What happens next in the story is also difficult to sort out, as the Hebrew scribal tradition has preserved two readings of verse five: the first reads that on the day the land is bought, "you acquire" Ruth, and thus links land redemption with continuing the line of Elimelek; the second reads "I [Boaz] acquire" Ruth, and separates redemption of the land from marriage with the woman whose children would presumably inherit the land. The NIV follows the first, simpler reading: "you also acquire Ruth the Moabite, the dead man's widow, in order to maintain the name of the dead with his property." Boaz's introduction of the issue of the continuance of Elimelek's line by marriage to Elimelek's Moabite daughter-in-law was unexpected. Boaz highlighted the unappealing aspects of the arrangement—namely, marriage to an outsider and limited financial gain, as the child born to the union would inherit the land (4:6). Boaz's strategy to get the closer relative to back out of the deal was brilliant. It joined together the principles of inclusion and restoration to the community that lie behind both the laws of redemption and an expanded version of levirate marriage (see Introduction to Ruth and Ruth 1:1–22: Listen to the Story for other examples of more expansive customs of levirate-like marriage). Like Orpah, Joe Schmoe chooses the route of expediency. He is "willing to participate in the covenant community as long as it involves no risk and no sacrifice. Such action," Waltke suggests, "does not reflect the ethics of God's kingdom community."[12]

Unlike Joe Schmoe, Boaz is willing to enter into this complex land deal that includes marriage to a Moabite. The way he executes the deal suggests

10. See Frederick Bush, *Ruth/Esther*, WBC (Nashville: Thomas Nelson, 1996), 200–43, for a comprehensive discussion of this complex issue; see also Younger, *Judges/Ruth*, 475.

11. Younger, *Judges/Ruth*, 476.

12. Waltke, *An Old Testament Theology*, 860.

that he is highly motivated to gain the support of the community. Boaz's reasons for marrying Ruth are not spelled out, although altruism, duty, *hesed*, and perhaps even attraction may be involved. Because Boaz regards Ruth as an insider in the fullest sense—she is a family member through marriage who has already committed herself to Naomi's people, her God, and even burial in the land—Ruth's ethnicity is not a deal-breaker (1:16–17).

After Joe Schmoe declines the offer, Boaz moves quickly to finalize the details for the redemption (4:6–8). The flow of the narrative is interrupted by a highly symbolic act involving the removal of a sandal, as explained above. After the legal proceedings with the sandal are complete, Boaz calls the growing number of witnesses—now the elders and all the people—to witness that he has acquired both the property of Elimelek and his sons, and Ruth (4:9–10). When Boaz calls his new wife, "Ruth the Moabite, Mahlon's widow," he underscores the noble purpose of his marriage "to maintain the name of the dead with his property, so that his name will not disappear from among his family or from his hometown" (4:10). And yet, ironically, the genealogy at the end of the book does not preserve Mahlon's name but sees Obed as Boaz's son. The land and line, however, stay within the family because Boaz is Elimelek's close relative.

By drawing Ruth into the center of the family circle through land redemption and levirate-like marriage, Ruth's identity as a Moabite becomes secondary; her primary identity becomes one of an insider. A second call to witness this double redemption concludes Boaz's public declaration (4:10c). The upright Boaz is careful to make sure that his marriage to a Moabite is legally sanctioned and supported by the community. Hawk describes Boaz's strategy as "an elaborate and brilliantly executed set-up" that uses Joe Schmoe "as a pawn in [his] plan to marry the Moabite woman and gain the approbation of his fellow townsfolk. . . . By doing what someone else in the community has refused to do, [Boaz] ensures that the community remains intact."[13]

The citizens of Bethlehem invoke a triple blessing (4:11–12; see Listen to the Story, above). The first blessing of Boaz honors Ruth, signaling her full acceptance into their community. It associates Ruth with Israel's matriarchs Rachel and Leah who, together with their maidservants, gave birth to the progenitors of Israel's twelve tribes (Gen 29–30).[14] The second blessing, thought by some to be a common blessing for a groom, consists of parallel lines: the first line is, "May you have *hayil*" (lit., "wealth," "prosperity," "power" or with the NIV, "standing," the word used earlier to describe the characters of both Boaz and Ruth); the second line asks that a name be proclaimed in Bethlehem

13. Hawk, *Ruth*, 129, 131.
14. Sasson, *Ruth*, 151–57.

(NIV: "be famous"). In light of the thematic concern for remembering the dead, this prayer asks that Boaz live on through his children in Bethlehem.[15] The third blessing focuses again on "the woman" with a prayer that Ruth's God-given seed will make Boaz's house like that of Perez, son of Tamar, the widowed outsider whose story bears many likenesses to Ruth's (Gen 38; see Introduction to Ruth). These blessings, which support Boaz in his marriage to an outsider, also underscore one of the countercultural declarations of this concluding chapter, namely, that women's roles in building tribes and dynasties and restoring families and communities should not be forgotten, in spite of women's omission from most genealogical lists.

The marriage of Ruth and Boaz is consummated—a detail that adds considerable weight to the view that Ruth and Boaz did not have sex on the threshing floor. For only the second time in the story, God intervenes directly, enabling the previously barren Ruth to conceive a child that will be named as Naomi's son (Ruth 4:13, 17). These events fulfill Naomi's desire that Ruth "find rest in the home of another husband" (1:9). They also answer Boaz's prayer that Yahweh richly reward Ruth for her words and acts of *hesed* toward Naomi (1:16–17; 2:11–12) and fulfill the community's prayer for children (4:11–12).

A Son is Born (Ruth 4:13–17)

As the focus of the narrative turns again to Naomi and her new fullness, it forms a counterpart to the story's opening narrative and its unfolding of Naomi's emptiness. After the birth of the child of promise, the women of Bethlehem who had previously witnessed Naomi's declaration of emptiness (1:20–21) now speak words of hope and encouragement (4:14–15). They praise the Lord who has not left Naomi without a guardian-redeemer. Here the women are not referring to the legal role of Boaz or the baby in redeeming the land or preserving the names of the dead, but rather the baby's role in giving Naomi new life. The women expand the previous blessing that Boaz be famous in Bethlehem to include fame for his son in all Israel (4:11, 14). Their prayer that the life-giving child will renew Naomi's life (lit., "turn," "return," "bring back"—the same verb used in 1:21 "The Lord has brought me back empty") highlights the reversal of Naomi's situation. "Death and emptiness (1:3–5, 21) have given way to life and fullness—a kind or type of resurrection."[16]

Finally, the women speak of Ruth's love for Naomi; they value her as better than seven sons (4:15b; see Listen to the Story, above for discussion of seven

15. Block, *Judges, Ruth*, 722–23.
16. Younger, *Judges/Ruth*, 482.

sons). In a patriarchal culture that placed great value on male offspring and where seven or eight sons was the ideal number, these women declare that Ruth's love for her mother-in-law is more valuable than even the many sons that patriarchal society values so highly. This countercultural expression of the value of faithful, sacrificial love functions as a capstone in this story of an outsider who models for insiders the meaning of such commands as "love the LORD your God with all your heart and with all your soul and with all your strength" and "love your neighbor as yourself" (Deut 6:5; Lev 19:18). Ironically, it is Ruth the Moabite who models for Israel and for God's people today how to live out what Jesus regarded as the greatest of the commandments (Matt 22:35–49; Mark 12:28–34).

The final picture of Naomi taking the child in her arms (lit., "set him in her bosom") and caring for him symbolizes Naomi's acceptance of "the boy" who would replace "the boys" taken from her (the same Hebrew word for boy/s is used in Ruth 1:5 and 4:16–17). Naomi now cares for the child, who will in time care for her. Naomi's emptiness has been replaced by fullness.

The neighborhood women take on the role that is usually the mother's and name "Naomi's" son Obed, "one who serves." Obed is likely a shortened form of Obadiah, "One who serves Yahweh." Obed's opportunities for service will be many: he will serve his parents and Naomi as a son who brings hope, life, and future security, and he will serve the community by carrying on Elimelek's line, by caring for his land, and remembering the names of the dead. Moreover, as Daniel Hawk observes, "given the role of social identities and classes in the book, the name [Obed, "one who serves"] takes on an ironic nuance: the son of the eminent and powerful man and his powerful wife is a servant."[17]

A short genealogy follows the women's declaration that Obed is Naomi's son: "[Obed] is the father of Jesse, the father of David" (4:17). Placing Naomi at the beginning of this abbreviated genealogy of David brings the world of women into the world of men and enhances the clear acknowledgement of Ruth's active part in the birth of this child of promise (4:13). Tamara Eskenazi suggests that Bethlehem's women actually transform "the patriarchal focus of all male genealogies so prevalent in the Bible."[18] They remind us that women as well as men are integral to the story of God, even though women's roles in that story are rarely acknowledged in the Old Testament.

Connecting the Dots (Ruth 4:18–22)

The final ten-member genealogy corresponds to the "ten years" in the prologue (1:4). It begins with Judah and Tamar's son, Perez, who was mentioned

17. Hawk, *Ruth*, 134.
18. Eskenazi and Frymer-Kensky, *Ruth*, 93.

in the earlier prayer for Boaz and Ruth's family. His birth story has many important connections to the book of Ruth (4:12; Gen 38; see Introduction to Ruth). With Judah's strong connections to royalty (Gen 49:8–12), we might expect Judah to begin the genealogy that ends with David (Ruth 4:17). But this genealogy, like those of Noah (Gen 5) and Abram (Gen 11), traces ten generations, with the tenth person entering into a new covenant with God marking, as Davis suggests, "a fresh and redemptive beginning after a long period of history marked by human violence."[19]

The prominence of Perez, the son of a Canaanite mother, and of Boaz, husband of Ruth the Moabite and father of Obed, also signals an openness to foreigners, an acceptance of David's "foreign blood," and perhaps (as some scholars have suggested) the end of the ten generation ban barring the Ammonites and Moabites and their descendants from the assembly of the Lord (Deut 23:3).[20] The placement of Boaz, husband of Ruth, who has just been lauded as better than seven sons (Ruth 4:15) in the significant seventh place in the genealogy, also highlights the theological truth that God uses ordinary people who make extraordinary decisions and live extraordinary lives of *hesed* to bring forth his greater purposes.

Finally, the mention of David ties the book's conclusion to its beginning; Elimelek was an Ephrathite from Bethlehem in Judah (1:2) and David was "the son of an Ephrathite named Jesse, who was from Bethlehem in Judah (1 Sam 17:12). This closing genealogy looks back to Israel's history and forward to the kingship of David. It anticipates "the Lord's anointed, Great David's greater son," who as the hymn writer James Montgomery recognized, "comes to break oppression, To set the captive free, To take away transgression, And rule in equity."[21]

LIVE the Story

How wondrous the mingled web of human events![22]

Living Lives of *Hesed*

This chapter, with its focus on Boaz, the community, and Naomi, brings us face to face with ordinary people trying to negotiate life in a complex world. It provides us with an exciting vision of how individuals and communities

19. Davis, *Who Are You*, 121.
20. Ibid.
21. See James Montgomery, "Hail to the Lord's Anointed," 1821.
22. Balfour, *The Women of Scripture*, 129.

should imitate God's inclusive care for the poor, the destitute, and the marginalized—a vision Jesus enacted and expected his followers to embrace. From Boaz's extravagant provision of food for Ruth and Naomi to his inclusion of an outsider in community meals, from his protection of Ruth from harassment and abuse to his complete acceptance of a Moabite into his community and later into his immediate family, Boaz models God's vision of generous inclusion and acceptance. At the same time, Boaz incarnates the Lord's *hesed* and points us to Jesus, who fed the hungry, ministered to those in need, and embraced the marginalized. As followers of Jesus, we are called to live such lives of *hesed* that integrate faith and life.

While Joe Schmoe was interested in redeeming Naomi's land for financial gain only, Boaz entered into the agreement to purchase land and marry Ruth for reasons that Eunny Lee identifies as "transgressive" acts of *hesed* that "defy convention and cross-cultural boundaries and go beyond the requirements of Torah to ensure the preservation of a family, and by extension the flourishing of a nation."[23] Boaz's human acts of *hesed* benefitted Naomi, Ruth, and the entire community, who learned from Boaz how to live as a community that embraces the outsider and makes counter-cultural decisions about the value of a triply marginalized person: she is a woman, a widow, and a Moabite, and yet "Is she not worth more than seven sons?" (4:15). Boaz's decision models how resources should be used for God's greater purposes of justice and compassion. Individuals and communities who allow themselves to be shaped by texts like this and who make decisions based on the common good are, as Andrew Sloane suggests, "the kind of community that Yahweh, the God and Father of our Lord Jesus Christ, calls us to be (seen in, for instance, the picture of the early Christian community in Acts 2:4)."[24]

Models of Community

The women of Bethlehem also model how community can work as they gather around the grieving Naomi and her faithful daughter-in-law (1:19–21; 4:15). Their embracing of a broken widow, a Moabite outsider, a man who dared to marry her, and a baby whom they recognized would bring healing, restoration, and hope demonstrates true inclusion. Their answered prayer that Obed become famous in Israel reminds us of the importance and power of the prayers of our communities.

---

23. Eunny P. Lee, "Ruth," in *Women's Bible Commentary, Revised and Updated*, eds. Carol A. Newsom, Sharon H. Ringe, and Jacqueline E. Lapsley (Louisville; Westminster John Knox, 2012), 143.

24. Andrew Sloane, *At Home in a Strange Land: Using the Old Testament in Christian Ethics* (Peabody, MA: Hendrickson, 2008), 47.

Hidden Footprints and the Gospel of Ruth

In a story that features questions of identity, the women's naming of Naomi's son reminds us of the important pastoral and spiritual—but usually hidden and unspoken and thus forgotten—roles of women in community life in Israel. Their inclusion in this story reminds us to look for women's hidden footprints in other stories where women are less visible. In her 1884 retelling of the book of Ruth, *An Old Story of Bethlehem: One Link in the Great Pedigree*, Elizabeth Rundle Charles calls attention to the "eternal" significance of Ruth and Naomi. She writes:

> And so this old story of Bethlehem ends, with sweet and sacred joy in a birth, and the name of Ruth, daughter of the outcast nation, and of Naomi, widowed and childless, are engraven in the pedigree of the Son of Man, of Him through whom none are outcasts, and in whom are not desolate hearts.[25]

Charles recognizes the theological importance of the two genealogies that close the book of Ruth. Their significance does not lie in their exclusion of women, but rather in women's inclusion in the story of salvation. Charles reminds us that Ruth and Naomi are permanently and ineradicably inscribed in the lineage of the one who embraced outcasts such as Ruth the Moabite widow and reached out to the desolate and broken to bring healing, restoration, and new life. The book of Ruth truly can be called the gospel of Ruth—a gospel that proclaims good news to women and men and calls us all to bring the good news to the world.

The deliberations at the city gate regarding land and marriage, and even the closing male-focused genealogy in the final chapter, remind us of the distance between the world of the ancient text and our modern world. That distance is rarely captured in illustrated romantic retellings of the story. Margaret Adams Parker captures a different reality in her compelling woodblock illustrations of the book of Ruth, as she finds "the story contains elements that we recognize more readily from the nightly news . . . refugees and widows, the broken and destitute, the foreigner."[26] Her Naomi is old and bent, Boaz's beard is streaked with white, Ruth is tall and muscular, the tattoo on her forehead marking her foreignness. Recognizing differences in social structures and customs should change how we idealize Ruth and Boaz's marriage as the ideal for God's children. "God's purposes for individual

25. Elizabeth Rundle Charles, *An Old Story of Bethlehem: One Link in the Great Pedigree* (London: SPCK, 1884), 31.

26. Davis, *Who Are You*, xvii.

women and men can still happen apart from marriage," South African scholar Madipoane Masenya writes, and "[those] who choose to lead celibate lives should not be marginalized."[27]

Figural Readings

Christians from the time of the early church recognized that the closing scenes of the book of Ruth lend themselves to being read theologically, as pointing to the mysteries revealed in Christ regarding the gentiles becoming "heirs together with Israel, . . . sharers together in the promise" (Eph 3:3–6). Some figural readings are more compelling than others. Understandable, but not very compelling, is the suggestion of Ambrose of Milan (ca. AD 333–397) that the removal of the sandal in 4:8 mystically prefigures John the Baptist's claim to be unworthy to untie the straps of Christ's sandals (Mark 1:6).[28] Ambrose's answer to the question of how Ruth, "an alien," is found in Jesus' genealogy in Matthew is more insightful:

> For this woman who was an alien, a Moabitess, a nation with whom the Mosaic Law forbad all intermarriage, and shut them totally out of the Church, how did she enter into the Church, unless that she were holy and unstained in her life above the Law? Therefore she was exempt from this restriction of the Law, and deserved to be numbered in the Lord's lineage, chosen from the kindred of her mind, not of her body. To us she is a great example, for in her was prefigured the entrance into the Lord's Church of all of us who are gathered out of the Gentiles.[29]

More compelling examples of theological readings are found in the "Argument" or Introduction to the book of Ruth in the Geneva Bible of 1560. The women's journey from emptiness to fullness, from affliction to blessing, and from barrenness to fruitfulness is held out as a message of hope for a struggling church:

> [The book of Ruth . . .] herein also figuratively is set forth the state of the church which is subject to manifold afflictions, and yet at length God giveth good and joyful issue, teaching us to abide with patience till God deliver us out of troubles.[30]

The same authors also endorse the standard figural reading of Ruth, "a Moabite of base condition, and a stranger from the people of God," as a

---

27. Masenya, "Ruth," 90.
28. Irwin, "Ruth 3," *DOTW* 696.
29. Ambrose as cited in Hawkins, "Ruth Amid the Gentiles," 79.
30. Retrieved from www.genevabible.org/files/Geneva_Bible/Old_Testament/Ruth.pdf.

type of the gentiles who "should be sanctified by him, and joined with his people . . . [into] but one sheepfold, and one shepherd."[31]

Luther similarly taught that redemption of the foreigner, Ruth, shows how the divine word attracts and blesses not only members of the church but also outsiders (*Lectures* on Gen 12:4).[32] This more traditional typological reading of Ruth as a symbol of the gentile church reminds us of the importance of evangelism, as the good news of the gospel is shared by word and deed with those inside and outside the church.

31. Ibid.

32. Irwin, "Ruth 3," *DOTW* 698.

Introduction to Esther

Composition, Transmission, and Canonicity

Authorship, Date, and Occasion for Writing

The book of Esther explains the origin of Purim, a popular Jewish festival that celebrates the victory of the Jews over those who tried to annihilate them. The story's hero, Esther, initially hides her Jewish identity and marries a Persian King. She develops character and maturity as she risks her life to save the Jews. When Esther's uncle Mordecai, the story's second heroic figure, refuses to bow down before his anti-Semitic superior Haman, Haman plots to kill all the Jews. Esther's success in reversing this scheme is celebrated in the feast of Purim.

Neither the author of the book of Esther nor the date of its composition in Hebrew is known. Clues within the book—including its retrospective nature (10:2) and the development of Purim celebrations (9:19)—indicate that Esther must have been written sometime after Xerxes's assassination in 465 BC (for a discussion of the identification of Ahasuerus as Xerxes I, see Historical and Ancient Near Eastern Background below). The question of how long after Xerxes's death Esther was written is debated.[1] Scholars who date the book's initial composition to the late fifth or fourth century BC consider the author's intimate knowledge of Susa and the Persian court, its administration and infrastructure, as well as the book's stylistic features as evidence for Esther's composition closer to the time of exile. Those who place the book's composition and final shaping in the third, second, or even first century BC focus their arguments on the circumstances around the book's composition and its language, ideas, and theology.

While scholars argue about the date of the book's composition in Hebrew, they agree that Esther's story was known in the late second and early first centuries BC, because its Greek versions are dated to this period. The colophon that concludes the Septuagint version (LXX) dates the arrival of the book in Alexandria to "the fourth year of the reign of Ptolemy and Cleopatra" (Esther, Addition F:11). However, many Ptolemies and Cleopatras were in power in

1. For a comprehensive discussion of authorship and dating, see Jean-Daniel Macchi, *Le livre D'Esther* (Genève: Labor et Fides, 2016), 12, 51–80.

Ptolemaic Egypt in the second and first centuries BC and thus even this dating formula is imprecise. The top choices for the latest possible date for the Hebrew version of Esther are 142, 114–113, 78–77, and 49–48 BC.[2]

Title, Canonicity, and Textual Witness

The book of Esther is one of two Old Testament books named after women, the other being Ruth. But why the title Esther? Even the book's earliest commentators wondered why the book was named Esther and not Mordecai, given his prominence at the end of the book and the early identification of Purim as the "day of Mordecai" (2 Macc 15:36). The explanation offered by the third-century Christian theologian Hippolytus as to why the book is named after Esther, who "did one thing only" while "Mordecai did many," still has merit: "The reason is that Esther, as queen, offered her life for the protection of the children of Israel who then were persecuted, and on account of her good deed and the faith which she had in God she was held worthy to be honored as the principal accomplisher of the deed. Thus the book is entitled 'Esther.'"[3]

The textual history of the book of Esther is complex and tied to the question of canonicity. The version of Esther found in the NIV is based on the Hebrew Masoretic Text (MT). Three other early versions of Esther are preserved in Greek: the Old Greek or B-text, which is found in the Septuagint (LXX), the Alpha or A-text,[4] and Josephus's retelling found in his *Jewish Antiquities* (11.184–296). The existence of diverse text forms suggests that the story of Esther was passed on in both oral and written forms over the centuries within various faith communities.[5]

The Hebrew version of Esther is the shortest extant version. Its earliest attested text dates from the eleventh century AD. The MT version, in contrast to the Greek versions, lacks religious language: God is not overtly mentioned; nor are prayer, miracles, the covenant, promises of land, blessing, or progeny.

The LXX (B-text) dates from the third or second centuries BC and is preserved in fourth-century AD manuscripts. This longer and more overtly religious version of Esther fills in many of the puzzling gaps in the Hebrew story. When Jerome (AD 347–420) chose the Hebrew version over the LXX

2. Tricia Miller, *Jews and Anti-Judaism in the Book of Esther* (Cambridge: James Clarke, 2015), 39–41, lists seven possible dates and narrows the choice down to 142 and 78–77 BC; Macchi, *Le livre D'Esther*, 543 n70 suggests 114–113, 78–77, and 49–48 BC as the current top choices.

3. Hippolytus, Sykes, *On the Apostolic Tradition* (Crestwood, NY: St. Vladimir's Seminary Press, 2001), 178.

4. The A-text is reprinted in D. J. A. Clines, *The Esther Scroll* (Sheffield: JSOT Press, 1984), 216–47.

5. Debra Reid, *Esther*, TOTC 13 (Downers Grove, IL: InterVarsity Press, 2008), 44–47.

as the basis for what became the authoritative Latin translation of Esther (the Vulgate or Vulg.), he consigned what we now call the "Additions to Esther" to an appendix. Additions A–F remain part of the canon of Eastern Orthodox and Roman Catholic churches and can be found in versions of the Bible that include the apocryphal or deuterocanonical books. The LXX Esther answers many of the theological questions raised by the Hebrew version. Mordecai's apocalyptic-like dream and its interpretation bookend the story. In the LXX, God is present in the story, Esther and Mordecai are pious Jews, and Purim is not the story's primary focus. Esther is also characterized differently in this version: while she is well informed and possesses inner beauty, she also reveals stereotypical female weakness. When she confronts the king, for example, she faints, falls, and needs help to stand. By the end of the story, however, Esther's weakness is transformed into strength.[6]

The Greek Alpha text is shorter than the LXX. It translates what was perhaps an earlier Hebrew form of the story rather than the Hebrew version recognized as canonical. It also differs from the other versions. It makes explicit, for example, what is implicit in the MT and LXX: that God is the help that Mordecai promises will come to the Jews from "another place" (Esth 4:14). According to the A-text, Esther is exceptionally beautiful, intelligent, and self-sacrificing, and acts to bring about justice for the Jews through the use of violence.[7]

A third Greek version of Esther is found in Josephus's first-century AD version of Esther's story. Scholars used to describe it as a paraphrase of the MT. More recently, some suggest that it may be based on a version of Esther that either predates the Hebrew MT or has been lost. Josephus's version is longer than the MT, but shorter than the LXX and A-text, as it does not contain Mordecai's dream and its interpretation. Josephus's account has its own frame and unique details. It is more overtly religious than the MT, as it summarizes Esther's prayer and conveys the message that God looks after his people.[8]

The timing of Esther's acceptance into the canon is unclear and is tied in with questions about how and when Jews and Christians established the canon of the Old Testament. Both Jews and Christians debated Esther's inclusion in the canon. Esther's absence from among the Dead Sea Scrolls, which attest to all the other Old Testament books, is explained either as coincidental or as evidence for the community's negative attitude toward the book because it fails to mention God. Later Jewish writings also suggest some opposition

6. Linda Day, *Three Faces of a Queen: Characterization in the Books of Esther* (Sheffield: Sheffield Academic, 1995), 196–99.

7. Ibid., 194–96.

8. Reid, *Esther*, 47.

to Esther's inclusion in the canon: on one hand, the Mishnah's instructions about how the "Book of Purim" should be read suggests Esther was deemed canonical by the second century AD, while on the other hand, the writings of third-century Rabbi Samuel indicate that resistance to Esther's inclusion in the canon continued into the third century AD. Early Christians, recognizing that Esther was not mentioned in the New Testament, also questioned Esther's inclusion in the canon. Bishop Melito, for example, did not include Esther in his list of canonical books in AD 170. By the time of the North African church councils of Hippo (AD 393) and Carthage (AD 397), however, Esther's canonical status in the West was secure. The debate over Esther's canonical status continued longer in the Eastern Church, where theologians Athanasius, Gregory of Nazianzus, and Theodore of Mopsuestia continued to discuss Esther's inclusion in the canon until the fifth century.

Once Esther's place in the Jewish canon was secure, Jews recognized its importance as a story celebrating the deliverance of the Jews and mandating the celebration of Purim. Christians, by contrast, continued to wrestle with Esther's ongoing significance, and failed to give it the same attention as other Old Testament books such as Genesis, the Song of Songs, and the Psalms. While some early Christian reflections on Esther remain, it was not until the ninth century that the first full commentary was written by Benedictine theologian Rabanus Maurus.

When the Protestant church affirmed the MT version of Esther, questions about this shorter and less religious version of Esther resurfaced. Luther's often cited but overstated opinion about Esther continues to be voiced even today: "I am so great an enemy to the second book of the Maccabees, and to Esther, that I wish they had not come to us at all, for they have too many heathen unnaturalities."[9] Luther was not alone in wondering how to preach and teach a book that features the hiddenness of God, blandly reports the vindictive acts of its main characters, and is so very difficult to tie into the gospel without using allegory or typology. Neither Luther nor Calvin published commentaries on Esther. Not surprisingly, the book has continued to provoke strong reactions from its readers, especially during times when anti-Semitic sentiments obscure the church's ability to appreciate its theological significance.

9. Martin Luther, William Hazlitt, and Alexander Chalmers, *The Table Talk of Martin Luther* (London: H. G. Bohn, 1857), 11. Many recent Esther commentaries cite a slightly different translation of Luther's *Table Talk*, Of God's Word, XXIV: "I am so hostile to this book [2 Maccabees] and to Esther that I could wish they did not exist at all; for they Judaize greatly and have much pagan impropriety." The rendering of this passage has been recently criticized. See https://www.patheos.com/blogs/davearmstrong/2015/09/did-martin-luther-deny-the-canonicity-of-esther.html. For a more positive theological reading of Esther, see his theological reading of the significance of Xerxes's scepter in Explain the Story, Esther 5:2.

A number of contemporary Christian thinkers believe that Esther is a book that deserves fresh attention. According to Lee Beach, Esther is especially valuable to the church today as it wrestles with questions about how to survive and thrive in a post-Christian context resembling that of the exiled Jews in the Persian Empire.[10] Beach finds in Esther "a message of deep encouragement to the Western church as it learns to work from the margins of culture. From such locales God can do his best work. He is able to use marginalization and weakness for his missional purposes, and the church in the post-Christendom age needs to embrace this very Esther-like perspective at its core as it seeks to be the people of God in a foreign culture."[11] I too hope to show that Esther when read within its historical and canonical contexts, with insights drawn from the faithful who have gone before us as well as contemporary voices, is a life-giving book for the church of the twenty-first century.

Literary Analysis

Genre

The book of Esther has been classified most simply as a story, but also has been described as a wisdom tale, a historical short story, a historical novella, historical fiction, an etiology, and even a festive comedy.[12] While Esther may be best described as a historical short story that explains the origins of Purim, it is much more than this. As Elizabeth Rundle Charles explains, it is "a sacred story" and as such "does not merely gossip about the external facts, but penetrates to the divine and human meanings enfolded in these."[13] Questions about the historicity of the story are addressed below.

Style and Structure

As Richard Bauckham observes, "the narrative art of the book [of Esther] is grudgingly admired by its worst enemies."[14] Its complex structure and style complement each other beautifully to produce a story that effectively entertains while it narrates the origins of the festival of Purim. Given its purpose, Esther is fittingly structured around ten paired eating and drinking banquets. The first set of banquets mark the book's beginning and highlight Xerxes's

10. Lee Beach, *The Church in Exile: Living in Hope After Christendom* (Downers Grove, IL: InterVarsity Press, 2015), 69–80.

11. Ibid., 79.

12. See Adele Berlin, *Esther—אֶסְתֵּר: The Traditional Hebrew Text with the New JPS Translation* (Philadelphia: Jewish Publication Society, 2001), xvi–xxii.

13. Elizabeth Rundle Charles, *Sketches of the Women of Christendom* (New York: Dodd, Mead & Co., 1880), 5.

14. Bauckham, *The Bible in Politics*, 119.

extravagance and opulence (1:3–4, 5–8). These are followed by Vashti's banquet for women (1:9) and Esther's wedding banquet (2:18). Haman and Xerxes's drinking party to celebrate the edict of death (3:15) is complemented by the feasting that follows the announcement of the counteredict (8:17). Esther hosts a double set of banquets for Xerxes and Haman (5:1–8; 7:1–9) that form a bracket around chapter 6, which marks the turning point in the story. Finally, Purim is celebrated with feasting, first in Susa on the fourteenth of Adar, and then beyond Susa on the fifteenth of Adar (9:17–19).[15] These thematically important celebratory banquets poignantly contrast with the fasting, lamentation, and mourning that follow the news of the genocidal edict, the three-day fast Esther calls for (4:16), and the fast of Esther that the Jews later commemorate (9:31).

The book of Esther is also loosely structured as a chiasm that has at its center the sudden turn of events reversing the fate of the Jews in general and of Haman and Mordecai in particular. What follows is an adaptation of Jon Levenson's structural analysis of the book's imperfect but highly significant symmetry:[16]

A Greatness of Xerxes (1:1–8)	Greatness of Xerxes and Mordecai (10:1–3) **A'**
B Two Persian Banquets (1:1–8)	Two Jewish Feasts (9:20–32) **B'**
C Esther Identifies as Gentile (2:10–20)	Gentiles Identify as Jews (8:17) **C'**
D Haman is Exalted (3:1)	Mordecai is Exalted (8:15) **D'**
E Anti-Jewish Edict (3:12–15)	Pro-Jewish Edict (8:9–14) **E'**
F Fateful Exchange of and Esther (4:1–17)	Fateful Exchange of **F'** Xerxes and Esther (7:1–6)
G Esther's First Banquet (5:6–8)	Esther's Second **G'** Banquet (7:1–6)

H Royal Procession (6:1–14)

The book's chiastic structure calls attention to the highly ironic and darkly humorous pivotal scene in which Haman parades Mordecai through Susa, after which Haman's wife and advisers prognosticate that Mordecai the Jew will bring him to ruin (6:13). This structure highlights the theme of reversals that the narrator later calls "the turning of the tables" (lit., "the reverse occurred"; 9:1). Leading up to this turning point are a number of seeming coincidences and critical moments such as Esther's decision to risk her life for her people and her request for a three-day fast (4:16). The series of reversals that follow chapter 6 include the reversals of both Haman's and Mordecai's

15. Jon Levenson, *Esther*, OTL (Louisville: Westminster John Knox, 1997), 5.
16. Ibid., 8.

roles in the court (8:1–2) and of the genocidal edict, as rituals of grief and mourning are set aside to celebrate life and deliverance (8:16–17).

The stylistic feature of repetition complements the structural repetitions and reversals. Many repeated details are woven into the story: the threefold mention of the size of Xerxes's empire (1:1; 8:9; 9:30; see also 10:1); three references to an official book of the annals or chronicles at key points in the story (2:23; 6:1; 10:2); and Xerxes's promise of "up to half the kingdom" (5:3, 6; 7:2; see also 9:12) to name a few. The book also overflows with word pairs that reflect Persian "officialese."[17] Chapter one, with its focus on the court and legal procedures, for example, features twenty-four verbal doublets that are sometimes masked in the English translations. The most striking of these are "Xerxes, i.e., the Xerxes" (1:1); "the vast wealth of his kingdom and the splendor and glory of his majesty" (1:4); and "the king became furious and burned with anger" (1:12). Words are also repeated in longer sequences of three and four synonyms: "destroy, kill, and annihilate" (3:13; 7:4; 8:11); and "happiness and joy, gladness and honor" (8:16). The lists of the names of the seven eunuchs, the seven wise men, and Haman's ten sons also reflect the style typical of court records (1:10, 14; 9:7–9).

Although there are many ways to outline the book of Esther, what follows is the structural breakdown used in this commentary:

1:1–9	King Xerxes's Amazing Empire
1:10–22	Vashti's Ousting
2:1–4	The Plan to Replace Queen Vashti
2:5–7	Mordecai and Esther Introduced
2:8–20	Esther's Success
2:21–23	The Assassination Plot Revealed
3:1–6	Haman's Rise; Mordecai's Fall
3:7–15	An Evil Idea Becomes Law
4:1–3	The Fallout
4:4–17	"For Such a Time as This": Esther Responds to Her Call
5:1–8	Putting Life on the Line
5:9–14	Choosing Scarcity over Abundance
6:1–11	Talking Past Each Other
6:12–14	The Fall Begins
7:1–10	Esther's Second Banquet
8:1–8	The Transfer of Property and Power
8:9–17	Mordecai's Counteredict: Vengeance Belongs to Whom?
9:1–16	The Tables Turned: Killing, Rest, Feasting, Joy, and Gifts

17. Ibid., 11.

9:17–19 Celebrating Life
9:20–32 The Inauguration of Purim
10:1–3 The Glorification of Xerxes and Mordecai

Historical and Ancient Near Eastern Background

The book of Esther introduces us to a community of Jews living in the Persian Empire in the fifth century BC. The Jews had been exiled to Babylon in 597 and 586 BC. There they lived in servitude under a number of Neo-Babylonian kings until Cyrus conquered Babylon and founded the Persian Empire (539 BC). Cyrus put policies of religious freedom in place that allowed the Jews to return to their homeland and rebuild the temple (Ezra 1:1–4). However, the vast majority of Jews chose to remain in Babylon or to move further east to Susa, where Nehemiah had resided (Neh 1:1). The book of Esther is set in the Persian king's winter capital city, Susa, where an evil scheme to kill all Jews in the empire was hatched and eventually overturned.

The name of the Persian king who ruled the massive Persian Empire during the time of the events described in the book of Esther is Ahasuerus in Hebrew. Most scholars identify Ahasuerus as Xerxes I (485–465 BC). They base their judgment on a number of arguments: a linguistic argument (that the Hebrew "Ahasuerus" is derived from the Persian "Xerxes" or "Artaxerxes"); literary/historical arguments based on strong affinities between the king described in Esther's story and Herodotus's portrayal of Xerxes as an impulsive, tyrannical king who loved women and alcohol and ruled over the massive Persian Empire; and the mention of an official named "Marduka" in the annals of Xerxes I.

Since the name Ahasuerus has also been identified as Artaxerxes, three other possible identifications have been explored: Artaxerxes I (465–424 BC), Artaxerxes II (404–358 BC), and Artaxerxes III (358–338 BC). The short reign of Artaxerxes IV (338–336 BC) disqualifies him immediately. A fourth possibility that a number of recent scholars have promoted is that Ahasuerus is a completely fictional name of the king featured in a book they classify as historical fiction. These four alternative identifications, however, are not as compelling as that of Xerxes I. Identifying Ahasuerus with Xerxes I raises a number of difficult historical questions that are discussed briefly below.

Reading the book of Esther in its ancient context provides invaluable information that enhances our understanding of the book. The works of the Greek historians Herodotus, Plutarch, Strabo, and Xenophon are particularly helpful, as they provide complementary portraits of Persian rulers and customs. Herodotus's *Histories* is especially valuable as Herodotus devotes about a third of this work to Xerxes's wars with the Greeks, and like the narrator of Esther, views the empire critically and with a satirical edge. Other ancient writings shed light on attitudes, traditions, and customs that concern women, genocide, slavery, castration, and even record keeping. In addition they illuminate practices relating to war, tribute, royal gifts, and the protocols for approaching royals and commemorating the past. Some ancient texts corroborate personal names in Esther, notably Mordecai and a number of other officials, and also attest to loanwords that fit the book's Persian setting.

Comparative texts also open up the ancient world of symbols, as ancient peoples often assigned meanings to colors, accessories, and actions. The texts that illumine Esther vary in terms of type, date, and provenance; they include histories, commemorative inscriptions, letters, poems, and tales. Ancient artifacts such as perfume burners as well as architectural remains of Persian gardens and palaces and reliefs portraying kings and courts add credibility to the story and help situate it in its ancient context.

Many biblical texts also provide relevant commentary on the book of Esther. They fill in some of the blanks in the story about such issues as the presence of Jews in Persia, the background for the animosity between Mordecai and Haman, practices of holy war, rituals of mourning and fasting, and all things related to God and God's relationship with the Jews. Scriptural echoes and allusions, together with Esther's inclusion in the canon, encourage us to read Esther as an important yet unfinished chapter in a larger story. It is this larger context that opens up the rich theological readings of the book that many of our forebears have discerned and that contemporary readers continue to explore.

Although ancient texts and artifacts provide information that enhances our understanding of Esther, a number of historical challenges remain. For example, the book's hero, Esther, is not mentioned in extra-biblical historical sources. To account for this historical anomaly, some suggest that Vashti was a title or nickname for Amestris, who, according to Herodotus, was Xerxes's queen. But this explanation is problematic for several reasons: first, there is no historical evidence that Xerxes's wife had more than one name; second, it would be most unusual for a woman to have another name in the ancient world; third, and more significantly, it does not fit with Herodotus's depiction of Amestris as a woman who was queen into her old age and never deposed.[18]

Others equate Amestris with Esther based on the similarity of their names. This idea also does not fit with Herodotus's depiction of Amestris as a woman who buried fourteen children alive as an offering to the god of the underworld. Alternatively, some suggest that Xerxes married Esther during the period of his reign not covered by Herodotus's *Histories*.[19] This suggestion raises a further

18. Herodotus, *Hist.* 7.114.

19. Karen H. Jobes, *Esther*, NIVAC (Grand Rapids: Zondervan, 1999), 66–67.

historical concern: Persian royalty normally married women from high-ranking families, not young harem girls. But as Plutarch's report suggests, there were exceptions that allowed royals to marry for love, and Xerxes's marriage to an unusually beautiful harem girl may simply have been such an exception.[20]

The narrator's claim that Xerxes ruled over 127 provinces is also flagged as a historical problem, as the number of provinces ruled by Xerxes (1:11) is larger than expected. Historical records from his father's rule divide the empire into smaller units (variously enumerated as 23, 24, 29, and 30) called satrapies. Xerxes is known, however, to have divided many satrapies into smaller "provinces." He separated the Levant from Babylon, for example, creating a new satrapy known as "Trans-Euphrates" which included such "provinces" as Samaria, Judah, Ammon, and Edom. Such divisions help to explain the large number, at least in part. Still, scholars are not agreed on whether this anomalous number 127 should be explained as symbolic, an embellishment, or more helpfully, as smaller divisions to enhance the portrait of Xerxes's power and greatness (see Esther 1:1–22: Explain the Story, in ch. 5, below).[21]

The timing of some of the events in Esther also elicits debate among scholars. Some scholars connect Xerxes's lavish 180-day banquet with preparations for the Greek wars that he undertook in 483 BC (see Esther 1:1–22: Listen to the Story and Explain the Story). Others argue that Xerxes was otherwise engaged at this time in putting down a revolt in Babylon, and suggest that he ventured over to Greece after he sacked Babylon and destroyed the idol of Marduk in 482 BC (compare Jdt 1:16).[22] Similarly, some point out that Xerxes would have been on campaign and absent from Susa at the time Esther was presented to him in Susa.

Also problematic is the claim that Mordecai was among those taken captive and into exile by Nebuchadnezzar in 597 BC (2:5–6). Since Mordecai would therefore have been at least a centenarian during Xerxes's reign, it makes sense to read this notice as the narrator's way of calling attention to Mordecai's connection to Judah and its history by means of his exiled forebears (see Esther 2:1–23: Explain the Story, in ch. 6 below).

While questions about chronology and the veracity of details within the story of Esther remain, many points of historical convergence are acknowledged, even among scholars who regard Esther as a work of fiction. Indeed, when Esther is read in its ancient context, perplexing details such as Xerxes's astonishingly long 180-day banquet and his outrageous offer of up to half the

20. Plutarch, *Art.* 23.3.

21. Jobes, *Esther*, 58–59.

22. Herodotus speaks of Xerxes subduing Egypt in his second year, which is just before the action of this story begins. See Herodotus, *Hist.* 7.7.1.

kingdom are shown to be historically credible (see Genre, above). Perhaps more significantly, reading Esther within its ancient context as "a sacred story [that] . . . does not merely gossip about the external facts" corrects the misguided readings of those who would make Esther into either a Disney princess who finds her Prince Charming or an unfaithful Jewish whore.[23]

Theological Message: Is Esther too "Earthy"?

Christians have always wrestled with the question of Esther's theological message. Even during the millennium and a half when Christians read Greek or Latin versions of Esther that filled in many of the theological gaps in the Hebrew version, the book was not given the prominence it had among the Jews. People of Jewish heritage placed spiritual, liturgical, and cultural importance on the festival of Purim. The influential Jewish scholar Maimonides (1135–1204) even placed Esther next to the Torah in importance.[24]

Christians who did comment on Esther met the challenge of the perceived theological deficiencies by reading it as part of the story of God. They used a variety of interpretive methods to unearth the book's moral and spiritual senses. Clement of Rome (ca. AD 100), one of the few early Christian writers to cite Esther using an exemplary hermeneutic, presented Esther as a model of piety and courage: "perfect in faith, [Esther] expose[d] herself" and the "all-seeing Master of the ages, . . . seeing the meekness of her soul, rescued the people for whose sake she had faced danger."[25]

The early Syrian writer Aphrahat (ca. AD 270–345) more typically read the story of Esther in light of the gospel. He drew extensive comparisons between Mordecai and Jesus: both were persecuted, both prayed for the deliverance of God's people, and both saved God's people. Aphrahat also regarded Esther as a figure of the Church, Xerxes as a figure of God, and Vashti as an outsider: "Because of Mordecai [Jesus], Esther [the church] was well pleasing to the king [God] and went in and sat instead of Vashti [those outside of the church], who did not do his will; and because of Jesus, the church is well pleasing to God and has gone in to the king, instead of the congregation that did not do his will."[26]

---

23. See discussion of genre above, p. 158; see also Rachel Held Evans, "Esther Actually: Princess, Whore. . .or Something More," *Esther Actually, Part 1*, 10 September 2012, http://rachelheldevans.com/blog/esther-introduction-princess-whore.

24. Carey A. Moore, *Esther*, AB 7B (Garden City, NY: Doubleday, 1984), xvi.

25. Clement of Rome, "1 Clement 55.3–6," quoted in Marco Conti and Gianluca Pilara, *1–2 Kings, 1–2 Chronicles, Ezra, Nehemiah, Esther*, ACCS Old Testament 5 (Downers Grove, IL: InterVarsity Press, 2008), 384.

26. Aphrahat, "Demonstrations" 21.20, quoted in Conti and Pilara, *1–2 Kings, 1–2 Chronicles, Ezra, Nehemiah, Esther*, 389.

Athanasius (ca. 296–373) drew theological meaning from the Jews' decision to celebrate their deliverance from death with the feast of Purim (and its coincidence with the feast of Passover) to make a case for the Christian celebration of Easter, which he viewed as a feast that looked beyond time to eternity: "It is a heavenly feast! We do not announce it as a shadow or a picture or a type but as a real thing."[27] Similar figural readings are found in Rabanus Maurus's ninth-century commentary that allegorized Esther to unearth its Christian message: Xerxes is Christ "reigning far and wide"; Vashti the synagogue; Haman the devil; and Mordecai represents Paul and the other apostles.[28]

Figural and exemplary hermeneutics continued to dominate pre-Reformation Christian readings of Esther. Esther became such a popular type and example of a variety of virtues, including wisdom, courage, and female agency, in writings by both men and women, that scholars speak of the "*typos* of Esther."[29] In *The Book of the City of the Ladies* (1405), Christine de Pisan drew attention to what Esther was able to accomplish in negotiating deliverance for her people and the punishment of Haman.[30] Similarly, Lucrezia Tornabuoni (ca. 1427–1482), who was married to the *de facto* ruler of Florence, encouraged Christian noblewomen to use indirect means to persuade their husbands to do what they thought was needed, just as Esther had done. Tornabuoni viewed Vashti's more direct approach as less helpful: "Women, learn nothing from this queen:/ be prudent, and listen to my words/ with great care and discretion."[31]

The Renaissance and Reformation transformed how the book of Esther was read and interpreted. New interest in manuscripts and in the literal and historical meaning of texts shifted the attention of Protestant theologians and scholars away from earlier figural readings of Esther to the book's literal and historical sense. The decision of Protestants to adopt the Hebrew version of Esther as canonical meant that earlier theological readings of the book of Esther based on material found in the Greek additions had to be reevaluated. Many shared Calvin's disdain for those who "seize the occasion of torturing Scripture, in every possible manner, away from the true sense" by "beating out

27. Athanasius, *Ep. fest.*, 4, quoted in Conti and Pilara, *1–2 Kings, 1–2 Chronicles, Ezra, Nehemiah, Esther*, 397.

28. Jo Carruthers, *Esther Through the Centuries* (Malden, MA: Blackwell, 2008), 28.

29. Ariel Clark Silver, *The Book of Esther and the Typology of Female Transfiguration in American Literature* (New York: Lexington Books, 2017).

30. Christine de Pisan, *The Book of the City of Ladies,* trans. Earl Jeffrey Richards, 2nd ed. (New York: Persea Books, 1982; repr., 1998), 145.

31. Lucrezia Tornabuoni d'Medici, *Sacred Narratives,* ed. and trans. Jane Tylus (Chicago: University of Chicago Press, 2001), 177, 193–94.

allegories" lurking "under the outer bark of the letter."[32] The shift away from figural readings was significant, but not absolute, as many preachers today continue to use a figural approach to discern the spiritual sense of Esther.[33]

The antagonism toward the book of Esther expressed by Luther (see above, Textual Witness and Canonicity) was exacerbated by an increase in anti-Semitism in the nineteenth and twentieth centuries. Bernhard Anderson expresses the sentiments of many when he calls attention to "the discordant note which the book strikes in the ears of those accustomed to hearing the Christian gospel." In his words, Esther is

> an emphatically Jewish book whose primary purpose is the authorization and regulation of a purely Jewish festival, Purim. . . . [T]he book is inspired by a fierce nationalism and an unblushing vindictiveness which stand in glaring contradiction to the Sermon on the Mount. Surely this book is of the earth, earthy. As we turn to it from other books of the Bible, 'we fall, as it were, from heaven to earth,' as Ewald once remarked.[34]

Similarly, Bruce Waltke sees little of theological value in the book as he views the Jews in Esther as "only nominal covenant people, . . . physical descendants of Abraham [who] keep the outward signs of the covenant, but they do not keep its true intention from the heart."[35] In his view, the narrator's "lack of prayer, praise, and piety silently drives home his message; these are nominal Jews, not true Israel."[36] According to Waltke, the book of Esther has theological value only insofar as it teaches implicitly that God works providentially to preserve the "'secular,' self-serving Jews . . . of the Diaspora" and even "furthers salvation history through them."[37] Such negative assessments of Esther as "really of the earth, earthy" have discouraged readers from listening to the book of Esther with ears attuned to "hear what the Spirit says to the churches" (Rev 2:7).

New Theological Perspectives on Esther: Esther Is Much More than "Earthy"

New discoveries, approaches, and insights have changed how we read the book of Esther. Although the book still has its critics, it also has many admirers.

32. John Calvin, *Commentaries on the Epistles of Paul to the Corinthians*, Vol. 2., trans. J. W. Pringle (Grand Rapids: Eerdmans, 1948), 125.

33. Examples of modern figural readings are found in Michael Beckett, *Gospel in Esther* (Carlisle: Paternoster Press, 2002) and Samuel Wells, "Esther," in George Sumner and Samuel Wells, *Esther and Daniel* (Grand Rapids: Brazos Press, 2013).

34. Bernhard W. Anderson, "The Place of the Book of Esther in the Christian Bible," in *Studies in the Book of Esther*, ed. Carey A. Moore (New York: Ktav, 1982), 130.

35. Waltke, *An Old Testament Theology*, 768.

36. Ibid., 768.

37. Ibid., 769.

Appreciation for the book's literary artistry elevates Esther in the eyes of many who find that a narrative approach to reading Esther opens up meanings that interpreters who focus on hidden spiritual meanings miss or lost sight of. An appreciation of the literary artistry in Esther involves an appropriation of allusions and canonical readings that set up illuminating inner-biblical dialogues tying her story into the larger story of God. In addition, today there are easily accessible online translations of ancient texts that allow us to read Esther in its ancient context. Similarly, images of ancient sites such as Susa and wall murals depicting Persian court scenes and perfume burners like those used by the girls in Xerxes's harem remind us that we are reading an ancient story, not watching a contemporary television romance or reading a Cinderella story. New, accessible textual studies of the ancient versions of Esther lead to new appreciation of the early history of the book and its reception in various faith communities.

Many post-Holocaust, post-modern, and globally aware readers call us to read the story of Esther with fresh eyes to appreciate its relevance for today. We now recognize similarities between Esther's world and ours. We recognize Xerxes in the impulsive egocentric tyrants ruling empires today. We encounter vile Hamans who are bent on destroying God's people. The global "Me Too" movement that emerged in 2017 draws increased attention to issues raised in Esther related to the abuse of power, the objectification of women, and sex trafficking. We empathize with the Jews' responses to Haman's genocidal edict because the Holocaust and subsequent genocides in Cambodia, Rwanda, Bosnia and Herzegovina, Iraq, Syria, Darfur, and most recently, Myanmar, remind us of humanity's capacity to plan and carry out annihilation of those who are racially and religiously different. We recognize in ourselves and others the human capacity for evil, vengeance, and violence. Like the Jews in the story, we often experience our world as a place where God is hidden, and only hindsight allows us to recognize coincidences as signs of God's providence.

Other new approaches to reading biblical texts cast additional light on Esther's story. Reading Esther from a post-colonial perspective and through the lens of disaster and trauma studies, for example, brings new theological insights and challenges. When we regard the doubly-orphaned Esther as a victim and survivor of trauma we appreciate her actions and reactions in new light (see further discussion of grief and trauma in Introduction to Ruth: Reading from the Perspective of the Twenty-First Century).

At the same time, a renewed sense of the value of theological exegesis has spawned a cautious appreciation of figural readings of Scripture. This compels us to read the book with the dead, to borrow the title of John Thompson's book.[38]

---

38. John L. Thompson, *Reading the Bible with the Dead: What You Can Learn from the History of Exegesis that You Can't Learn from Exegesis Alone.* (Grand Rapids: Eerdmans, 2007).

Reading Esther with forgotten dead female interpreters of Scripture proves life-giving and inspiring. Some of their insights deserve our careful consideration and cautious appropriation. While I, for one, find many figural readings unhelpful (e.g., reading Xerxes as a type of God, Mordecai as Jesus, and Esther as the church), I do see Esther as a type of Christ in her willingness to lay down her life for the Jews.

To conclude, reading Esther in the twenty-first century is both challenging and exciting. In this commentary, the book of Esther is read within its ancient context, using both biblical and ancient Near Eastern texts. Each chapter is explained using a variety of interpretive methods, drawing on insights from commentators, historians, social scientists, theologians, and preachers as well as students and church friends who have joined me in studying this deeply challenging and life-giving book.

I invite you to pray with me a prayer that renowned nineteenth-century poet Christina Rossetti included in her commentary on the book of Revelation, acknowledging the theme of God's hiddenness in Esther and reminding us to ask Jesus, who is both Truth and Wisdom, to draw near to us as we seek to draw near to him through the study of Esther:

> O Lord Jesus Christ, who art Truth and Wisdom, reveal Thyself unto us, we beseech Thee. Thou art not far from every one of us. Grant us goodwill to draw nigh unto Thee, Who deignest to draw nigh unto us.[39]

---

39. Christina G. Rossetti, *The Face of the Deep: A Devotional Commentary on the Apocalypse*, 2nd ed. (London: SPCK, 1893), 11.

Resources for Teaching and Preaching

Many excellent commentaries on the book of Esther are cited in this commentary. Most helpful for teaching and preaching Esther are the commentaries of Jobes, Levenson, Firth, Reid, Clines, and Goldingay. Anthony Tomasino's commentary on Esther in the third volume of Zondervan's Illustrated Bible Backgrounds Commentary series edited by John H. Walton also provides very useful background information for teaching and preaching not found in other commentaries.

Additional resources include Yairah Amit's wonderful introduction to reading biblical narratives, *Reading Biblical Narratives: Literary Criticism and the Hebrew Bible* (Philadelphia: Fortress, 2001).

For those who know Hebrew, a very helpful resource is Peter Screnock and Robert Holmstedt, *Esther: A Handbook on the Hebrew Text* (Waco, TX: Baylor University Press, 2015).

Jo Carruthers's *Esther Through the Centuries* (Malden, MA: Blackwell, 2008) is a wonderful resource that opens up the long and rich history of interpretation of the book of Esther. Additional help for studying the history of the interpretation of the book of Esther from the end of the New Testament era to AD 750 may be found in Marco Conti and Gianluca Pilara's edited volume *1–2 Kings, 1–2 Chronicles, Ezra, Nehemiah, Esther* (ACCS).

Eliza Lanesford Cushing's drama based on Esther, which is easily accessed on Canadiana online, provides much food for thought (*Esther, A Sacred Drama: With Judith, A Poem* (Boston: Joseph Dowe, 1840).

CHAPTER 5

Esther 1:1–22

LISTEN to the Story

1This is what happened during the time of Xerxes, the Xerxes who ruled over 127 provinces stretching from India to Cush: 2At that time King Xerxes reigned from his royal throne in the citadel of Susa, 3and in the third year of his reign he gave a banquet for all his nobles and officials. The military leaders of Persia and Media, the princes, and the nobles of the provinces were present.

4For a full 180 days he displayed the vast wealth of his kingdom and the splendor and glory of his majesty. 5When these days were over, the king gave a banquet, lasting seven days, in the enclosed garden of the king's palace, for all the people from the least to the greatest who were in the citadel of Susa. 6The garden had hangings of white and blue linen, fastened with cords of white linen and purple material to silver rings on marble pillars. There were couches of gold and silver on a mosaic pavement of porphyry, marble, mother-of-pearl and other costly stones. 7Wine was served in goblets of gold, each one different from the other, and the royal wine was abundant, in keeping with the king's liberality. 8By the king's command each guest was allowed to drink with no restrictions, for the king instructed all the wine stewards to serve each man what he wished.

9Queen Vashti also gave a banquet for the women in the royal palace of King Xerxes.

10On the seventh day, when King Xerxes was in high spirits from wine, he commanded the seven eunuchs who served him—Mehuman, Biztha, Harbona, Bigtha, Abagtha, Zethar and Karkas—11to bring before him Queen Vashti, wearing her royal crown, in order to display her beauty to the people and nobles, for she was lovely to look at. 12But when the attendants delivered the king's command, Queen Vashti refused to come. Then the king became furious and burned with anger.

13Since it was customary for the king to consult experts in matters of law and justice, he spoke with the wise men who understood the times

[14]and were closest to the king—Karshena, Shethar, Admatha, Tarshish,
Meres, Marsena and Memukan, the seven nobles of Persia and Media who
had special access to the king and were highest in the kingdom.
[15]"According to law, what must be done to Queen Vashti?" he asked.
"She has not obeyed the command of King Xerxes that the eunuchs have
taken to her."
[16]Then Memukan replied in the presence of the king and the nobles,
"Queen Vashti has done wrong, not only against the king but also against
all the nobles and the peoples of all the provinces of King Xerxes. [17]For
the queen's conduct will become known to all the women, and so they will
despise their husbands and say, 'King Xerxes commanded Queen Vashti
to be brought before him, but she would not come.' [18]This very day the
Persian and Median women of the nobility who have heard about the
queen's conduct will respond to all the king's nobles in the same way.
There will be no end of disrespect and discord.
[19]"Therefore, if it pleases the king, let him issue a royal decree and let
it be written in the laws of Persia and Media, which cannot be repealed,
that Vashti is never again to enter the presence of King Xerxes. Also let
the king give her royal position to someone else who is better than she.
[20]Then when the king's edict is proclaimed throughout all his vast realm,
all the women will respect their husbands, from the least to the greatest."
[21]The king and his nobles were pleased with this advice, so the king did
as Memukan proposed. [22]He sent dispatches to all parts of the kingdom, to
each province in its own script and to each people in their own language,
proclaiming that every man should be ruler over his own household, using
his native tongue.

Listen to the Text in the Story: Biblical and Apocryphal Texts: Leviticus 22:24–25; Deuteronomy 23:1; 2 Kings 20:12–19; Ezra 7:14; Proverbs 31:4–5; Ecclesiastes 2:4–11; Isaiah 39:2–8; Daniel 5:2; Judith 1:1–16; Ancient Near Eastern Texts: DSf inscription; Herodotus, *Histories* 1.133.4; 3.31.3; 3.67–88; 3.92; 3.95.2; 5.52.1; 6.32; 7.8; 8.98.1–2; Strabo, *Geography* 15.3.9, 19–20; Plutarch, *Moralia* 140B.16; *The Persepolis Fortification* Table 1795; Xenophon, *Cyropaedia*, 8.8.9–10.

The first chapter of Esther invites us into the grandiose world of powerful and inept King Xerxes, whose Hebrew name is Ahasuerus. The writings of Greek historians about life in the Persian Empire, a number of biblical texts, and archeological finds shed considerable light on the world of Esther and correct common misreadings of the story.

Ancient Banquets, Feasts, and Drinking Parties

The book of Esther is built around a series of paired banquets or feasts that provide structure for the book and represent one of its key themes (see Introduction to Esther above). Descriptions of banquets in other ancient texts suggest that the excesses of Xerxes's banquets are not exaggerations but rather reflect royal extravagance and overindulgence. Ancient royals hosted pretentious banquets to flaunt wealth and power, celebrate personal and military successes, and garner support for future military undertakings. The book of Judith, like the book of Esther, begins with an account of the greatness of a king and a kingdom as Nebuchadnezzar hosts an impressive one-hundred-and-twenty-day feast for his troops, who had just subdued a rebellion (Jdt 1:16). King Belshazzar similarly hosts a celebratory banquet that features wine imbibed from gold and silver goblets taken from the temple in Jerusalem (Dan 5:1–4).

Persia's enemies often ridiculed Persian excesses. In his mockery of Persian banqueting excesses, Xenophon of Athens (430–ca. 354 BC) depicts the Persians drinking and eating throughout the day and unable to walk home at night:

> In former times it was their custom also to eat but once in the day, so that they might devote the whole day to business and hard work. Now . . . they begin to eat at the hour when those who breakfast earliest begin their morning meal, and they keep on eating and drinking until the hour when those who stay up latest go to bed, . . . they drink so much that . . . they are themselves carried out when they are no longer able to stand straight enough to walk out.[1]

Greek historian Strabo (64/63 BC–ca. AD 24) similarly portrays Persian parties as pretentious, featuring, among other things, excessive amounts of food and drinks served in gleaming gold and silver cups to guests lounging on gold and silver couches:

> [The Persians] set upon their table entire animals in great number, and of various kinds. Their couches, drinking-cups, and other articles are so brilliantly ornamented that they gleam with gold and silver.[2]

Persian royalty was also renowned for making important decisions while drunk, although, unlike Xerxes in Esther 1, they usually re-evaluated them the next day. Herodotus claims "any decision [Persians] make when they are

1. Xenophon, *Cyr.* 8.8.9–10.
2. Strabo, *Geogr.* 15.3.19–20.

drunk, is reconsidered afterwards when they are sober."[3] By contrast, King Lemuel's mother advised that kings should drink neither wine nor beer, "lest they drink and forget what has been decreed, and deprive all the oppressed of their rights" (Prov 31:4–5). Examples of ancients who, like Xerxes, made foolish decisions while inebriated abound; for instance, the orders Belshazzar gave during a drinking feast led to his demise (Dan 5:2).

Royal women sometimes participated in celebratory banquets (Dan 5:2, 10). Greek historian Plutarch (ca. AD 46–120) claimed that "the lawful wives of the Persian kings sit beside them at dinner" until the drinking gets out of hand and the "music-girls and concubines" are called in (see also Mark 6:22).[4] This custom may explain why Queen Vashti, who is neither a showgirl nor a concubine, refuses to appear before an audience of drunken men.

Ancient Women of Power and Influence and the Issues of Shaming

Women of power and influence are sometimes featured in ancient texts. The Persepolis Fortification Tablets reveal that Persian royal women had considerable power and, like Vashti, hosted their own banquets and acted independently of their husbands. One of Darius I's wives owned estates and had servants, and a certain princess, Irtashduna, had large quantities of wine ordered by the king for some special occasion.[5]

In Persia's honor/shame culture, it was dishonoring for a man to be shamed by a woman or to be called a woman. Vashti's refusal to obey Xerxes's command was an act of shaming that triggered a royal decree intended to reassert the traditional patriarchal order so that other men would not be similarly shamed. According to Herodotus, "the greatest of all taunts in Persia [was] to be called worse than a woman."[6] Abimelech expressed a similar sentiment when he asked his armor bearer to kill him with his sword so people would not be able to say a woman had killed him (Judg 9:52–54; see comments below on Esth 9:13 where it is suggested that Esther's final act of revenge shamed Saul, who had disobeyed God's command to destroy the king of the Amalekites).

Lavish Gardens and Palaces

The elaborate description of Xerxes's paradise-like garden is meant to provide yet further evidence of his affluence and power. Royal gardens featured magnificent structures: irrigated gardens complete with exotic animals, plants, and

3. Herodotus, *Hist.* 1.133.4.

4. Plutarch, *Mor.* 140B.16, quoted in Pierre Briant, *From Cyrus to Alexander: A History of the Persian Empire* (Winona Lake, IN: Eisenbrauns, 2002), 277.

5. R. T. Hallock, *Persepolis Fortification Tablets* (Chicago: University of Chicago Press, 1969), PF 1795: 490.

6. Herodotus, *Hist.* 9.107.1.

trees acquired through conquests and alliances. They were meant to impress guests and provide royals with places to rest, think, and pray (Esth 7:8). Xerxes's garden was part of a large royal complex that included a 3.8 hectare structure that housed the king and his "women," administrative offices, the treasury, and a 1.2 hectare pillared audience hall where the king had his throne. Xerxes's magnificent garden could be accessed through the audience hall as well as from the king's residence. Although archaeologists did not find Susa's royal garden, the remains of the royal palace attest to the lavishness of this Persian capital. An inscription written in Old Persian, Babylonian, and Elamite known as DSf describes the magnificent complex that Xerxes's father, Darius, built.[7]

Israel's kings also had gardens. The book of Ecclesiastes describes Persian-style "paradise" gardens that featured exotic fruit trees watered by a technologically-sophisticated irrigation system, yet regards them as "meaningless, a chasing after the wind" (Eccl 2:4–5, 11).

Wealth at the Expense of Others

The materials and monumental structures archaeologists have uncovered at sites in ancient Persia line up with Strabo's descriptions of the treasures Alexander the Great discovered when he marched on Susa and Persepolis in 330 BC:

> Alexander transferred everything that was precious in Persis [better known as Persia] to Susa, which was itself full of treasures and costly materials. . . . They say that, besides the treasures in Babylon and in the camp of Alexander, which were not included in the sum, the treasure found at Susa and in Persis was reckoned to amount to 40,000, and according to some writers to 50,000, talents. But others say, that the whole treasure, collected from all quarters, and transported to Ecbatana, amounted to 180,000 talents, and that the 8,000 talents which Darius carried away with him in his flight from Media became the booty of those who put him to death.[8]

Much of the wealth Xerxes loved to flaunt was acquired at the expense of conquered peoples (Esth 10:1). Herodotus claims that Xerxes's father Darius "collected a yearly tribute of fourteen thousand five hundred and sixty talents."[9] As Jon Levenson observes: "contextualized within the moral universe

---

7. Edwin M. Yamauchi, *Persia and the Bible* (Grand Rapids: Baker, 1990), 293–300, 332–34. For a discussion of the Achaemenid Royal Inscription DSf, see Jona Lendering, "Achaemenid Royal Inscriptions: DSf," *Livius.org*, 20 April 2019 (2004), https://www.livius.org/sources/content/achaemenid-royal-inscriptions/dsf/.

8. Strabo, *Geogr.* 15.3.9. Diodorus Siculus similarly says in his *Bibliotheca Historica* that Alexander "found the treasure in the palace to include more than forty thousand talents of gold and silver bullion" (17.66.1) and that Alexander took possession of 120,000 talents in Persepolis (17.71.1).

9. Herodotus, *Hist.* 3.95.2.

of the Hebrew Bible, especially wisdom literature, this enormous emphasis on wealth and status cannot speak well for the man who holds the world's most powerful office."[10]

More Darkness: Castration of Boys and Men

Xerxes not only obtained wealth at the expense of others but, like many other ancients, also acquired people whom he used and abused. Eunuchs and good-looking boys destined to be castrated were included in lists of tribute paid to Persian kings and celebrated as prizes of war.[11] Herodotus reports that Darius once received "five hundred castrated boys" along with "a thousand talents of silver" from his subject nations.[12] Testosterone-deprived males were often entrusted with positions of great responsibility as royal advisors, messengers, personal attendants, and overseers of the harem (Esth 1:10, 12, 15; 2:3, 14, 15; 4:4, 5; 6:14; 7:9). However, in contrast to other nations, Israel's attitude toward castration was negative. Castration of animals was forbidden, and animals with missing or damaged testicles were not to be used as sacrifices (Lev 22:24–25). Castrated males or men with crushed testicles could not enter the assembly of the Lord" (Deut 23:1).

Laws: Making, Enforcing, Recording, and Disseminating

The book of Esther, like many other ancient texts describing Persian life, is replete with references to laws and legal experts. Laws are made, interpreted, defied, mocked, and challenged. Like his predecessors, Xerxes surrounded himself with legal experts who advised him on all things legal, including personal matters. Cyrus the Great's son, Cambyses, similarly consulted legal advisors on affairs of the heart when he wanted to find a legal loophole for marrying his sister. Herodotus describes these legal advisors as "men chosen out from the Persians to function until they die or are detected in some injustice; it is they who decide suits in Persia and interpret the laws of the land; all matters are referred to them."[13] The group of seven nobles who exposed Cambyses' assassins before electing Darius as king may have been the first group of special royal advisors.[14] A similar group of seven nobles is also mentioned in King Artaxerxes's letter to Ezra (Ezra 7:14).

---

10. Levenson, *Esther*, 45.

11. "When [the Persians] had gained mastery over the [Ionian] cities, they chose out the most handsome boys and castrated them, making them eunuchs instead of men, and they carried the fairest maidens away to the king; they did all this, and they burnt the cities with their temples" (Herodotus, *Hist.* 6.32.1).

12. Herodotus, *Hist.* 3.92.

13. Ibid., 3.31.3.

14. Ibid., 3.70.3–74.

The stated policy that the laws of the Medes and Persians were unchangeable (Esth 1:19; 8:8; Dan 6:8, 12) fits well with what we know about Xerxes's sense of entitlement, power, and control. The notion of immutability is challenged, however, by a number of other ancient sources that contain examples of Persian royals changing laws. Herodotus, for example, tells about how Darius was persuaded by the wife of a man sentenced to death, along with his sons and household, to change his decree and spare her brother and eldest son.[15] The idea of unchangeable laws was likely meant to prevent the king from the disgrace of having "to admit to having made an error, and so once the laws were written down, they would be reasonably immutable."[16]

The Persian Pony Express

Ancient Persia had an incredible pony-express communication system that enabled swift communication of edicts, letters, and other royal communiqués throughout the vast empire. Herodotus praised the Persian roads and postal service that included "road stations and very good resting places"[17] and messengers and horses that did their jobs effectively:

> Now there is nothing mortal that accomplishes a course more swiftly than do these messengers, by the Persians' skillful contrivance. It is said that as many days as there are in the whole journey, so many are the men and horses that stand along the road, each horse and man at the interval of a day's journey. These are stopped neither by snow nor rain nor heat nor darkness from accomplishing their appointed course with all speed.[18]

EXPLAIN the Story

King Xerxes's Amazing Empire (Esther 1:1–9)

Xerxes was most likely Xerxes I, who ruled over the massive Persian Empire that extended from India (modern southern Pakistan) to Cush (modern North Sudan) from 486 until 465 BC, when he was assassinated (see Introduction to Esther above). The number of provinces reportedly ruled by Xerxes (1:11) is larger than expected. Whether the number 127 represents smaller territorial divisions than expected, or is exaggerated, or perhaps symbolic—ten,

---

15. Ibid., 3.119.
16. Anthony Tomasino, "Esther," in *1 & 2 Kings, 1 & 2 Chronicles, Ezra, Nehemiah, Esther*, ed. John H. Walton, *Zondervan Illustrated Bible Backgrounds Commentary* 3 (Grand Rapids: Zondervan, 2009), 479.
17. Herodotus, *Hist.* 5.52.1.
18. Ibid., 8.98.1–2.

twelve, and seven being significant numbers in Scripture—its effect is clear as it underscores the immensity of Xerxes's empire (see Introduction to Esther).[19] In the third year of his reign, Xerxes hosted two magnificent banquets in his winter palace in Susa. Excavations at what is now a UNESCO heritage site in the modern Iranian city of Shush confirm the monumental nature of the Persian royal buildings at Susa and testify to the wealth and power flaunted by Xerxes in this opening scene (see Listen to the Story).[20]

Like other ancient kings who sought to impress their military and administrative dignitaries with their vast wealth and power and to garner support for future military incursions, the self-aggrandizing Xerxes hosts an elaborate 180-day banquet or drinking party that forms the first of ten paired banquets, which some scholars argue provide the structure of the book. Many scholars associate this banquet with the Greek wars that Xerxes undertook, though some question this association (see Introduction to Esther and Listen to the Story above; compare Jdt 1:16).

A second lavish seven-day banquet meant to impress and please all the people who lived in the fortified area of Susa is set in the resplendent courtyard of the garden in Xerxes's magnificent palace complex (1:5–8). We too are invited into the courtyard where white and blue linen hangings are attached to alabaster columns by linen cords and silver rings, and where gold and silver couches adorn a stunning mosaic floor crowded with guests drinking the abundant royal wine from the very finest handcrafted gold vessels (compare Dan 5:1–4). We imagine the debauchery as the king's law—"No restrictions/constraint!"—encourages guests to drink as much as they want. This first mention of the theme of law signals the famed and yet capricious nature of both Persian law and lawmakers that was often mocked by ancient writers.

A third banquet for women hosted by Vashti in Xerxes's royal palace (1:9) is acknowledged but not described, as if to underscore the prevailing view that power resides in men (1:22).

Vashti's Ousting (Esther 1:10–22)

Xerxes's need to impress continues when on the seventh day of excessive drinking he decides to show off his most prized possession. The inebriated king wants everyone to appreciate Vashti's doubly-noted beauty, "for she was lovely to look at" (1:11). The ostensibly powerful Xerxes sends seven named

---

19. Jobes, *Esther*, 58–59.

20. Images of ancient Susa are easily accessed online. The UNESCO heritage website includes pictures of Persian period Susa, at whc.unesco.org/en/list/1455. See also the collection of pictures of palace ruins of the Persian capital, Persepolis, at https://artsandculture.google.com/exhibit/xwJSKSxv_NfpLQ.

eunuchs to command Vashti to come wearing her royal crown or turban—a singular detail that inspired the persistent rabbinic idea that Vashti was to appear naked, wearing only her crown![21] "As a fitting last course—a delicious feast for male eyes," Queen Vashti is "to parade herself like a beauty pageant contestant before a roomful of drunken dignitaries."[22]

Vashti, however, refuses to come (1:12). The narrator does not reveal Vashti's reasons, but most interpreters feel compelled to explain or justify her rebuff. Some view both Vashti and what she did as exemplary; others malign both Vashti and her actions. Reading the story in its ancient context provides a helpful perspective on Vashti; it suggests that the king's request would have shamed and dishonored his queen, as it countered the convention that concubines, musicians, and dancing girls were the only women who were invited to party with inebriated men. Nobles' wives left banquets when the drinking became excessive.

Without knowing what we do now about ancient protocols and Hebrew narratives, nineteenth-century African-American poet Frances Harper intuited that Vashti was shamed by the request to appear unveiled before "crowds of merry men." Harper regarded her act of defiance as a model of courage and strength:

> "Go, tell the King," she proudly said,
> "That I am Persia's Queen,
> And by his crowds of merry men
> I never will be seen."
> "I'll take the crown from off my head
> And tread it 'neath my feet,
> Before their rude and careless gaze
> My shrinking eyes shall meet."
> "A queen unveil'd before the crowd!—
> Upon each lip my name!—
> Why, Persia's women all would blush
> And weep for Vashti's shame!" . . .
> "Go, tell the King," she sadly said,
> "That I would rather die."[23]

By contrast, interpreters who are committed to patriarchal rule in the home and in society fill in the gaps in the story to vilify Vashti's character.

---

21. Esth. Rab. 3:14, b. Meg. 12b. Tg. Rishon and Tg. Sheni also discuss Vashti's situation; see *The Two Targums of Esther*, trans. Bernard Grossfeld, ArBib 18 (Collegeville, MN: Liturgical Press, 1991); Carruthers, *Esther Through the Centuries*, 62.

22. Carolyn Custis James, *Lost Women of the Bible: The Women We Thought We Knew* (Grand Rapids: Zondervan, 2005), 145.

23. Frances E. W. Harper, *Poems* (Philadelphia: George S. Ferguson, 1900), 45.

Like Xerxes and his advisors, they are not impressed with Vashti's defiance. Writing in 1584, German Protestant John Brentius judged Vashti's conceit, pride, and contempt as worthy of punishment, since he believed that women's subjection was "ordained by God himselfe euen from the beginning of the worlde."[24] Iain Duguid is one of the few modern commentators who uses the legislation formulated after Vashti's fall as a platform for reinforcing the notion of male headship today.[25]

Missing from critical readings of Vashti is any appreciation of the satirical nature of the presentation of power in this chapter, as "the king [who] claims great power . . . turn[s] out to be powerless in the matter of convincing his wife to come to the party. Indeed, he is not only powerless; he is a bumbling buffoon who is surrounded by sycophants who convert a trivial domestic dispute into a state of emergency."[26] The creators of the classic VeggieTales animation of Esther pick up on the scene's humor and irony. In their imaginative retelling, the queen is told that her husband wants her to make him a sandwich at 2 AM. She refuses and suggests that the king make his own sandwich; for her disobedience, she is kicked down the stairs.[27]

To convey the intensity of Xerxes's response to his most prized beauty's refusal, the narrator doubly describes his anger: he was "exceedingly angry and his wrath burned within him" (1:12; NIV; "the king became furious and burned with anger"). Not knowing how to respond, the ostensibly all-powerful—but now shamed and drunken—Xerxes asks his seven named and likely also drunken sages "who understood the times" for legal advice (1:13–14).

Suspense grows as the narrator pauses to explain that Xerxes, like his predecessors, surrounded himself with seven nobles who provided the king with advice. Their counsel, at least in part, was self-serving as they sought to bolster the king's sense of power and competence (1:13–14). Memukan immediately refashions Vashti's refusal as an offense, not simply against the king, but against all rulers and citizens, and comes up with an apocalyptic plan to enable the king to save face (1:16). Ironically, Memukan's stratagem actually spreads the news of Vashti's grievous defiance of her "ruler," as an edict is promulgated that "every man should be ruler over his own household, using his native tongue" (1:22).

Memukan's advice is based not on legal precedent but on patriarchal precedent and his irrational and excessive fear that his wife and the wives of the

24. John Brentius, *A Right Godly and Learned Discourse upon the Booke of Ester* [. . .] (London: John Wolfe for John Harrison, 1584), 41, quoted in Carruthers, *Esther Through the Centuries*, 72.

25. Iain M. Duguid, *Esther and Ruth*, REC (Phillipsburg, NJ: P&R Publishing, 2005), 16.

26. David G. Firth, *The Message of Esther: God Present but Unseen* (Downers Grove, IL: InterVarsity Press, 2010), 37.

27. "VeggieTales: Esther: the Girl Who Became Queen" (Chicago: Big Ideas, 2000), Video.

other nobles will "[t]his very day" defy their husbands leading to "no end of disrespect and discord" (1:18). Memukan's counsel, as David Firth suggests, is "as ripe with folly as his suggested chain of events that would follow news of Vashti's refusal, because every attempt at shoring up power and prestige that does not really exist shows how vacuous it is."[28]

Xerxes does not follow Persian protocol and wait until the next day when he and his advisors are sober to reconsider Memukan's advice. Instead, he enacts an unchangeable law written in the language of each people group in the massive empire, and quickly sends it out using the renowned Persian pony express (1:19–22; see Listen to the Story above). The notion that Persian laws were unchangeable underscores the power of the king. It also hints at the uncertainty and instability experienced by those living under Xerxes's kind of irascible leadership (1:19, 8:8; Dan 6:8, 12; see Listen to the Story above).

The excessive edict also reinforces the story's recurrent theme of obedience/disobedience. It calls us to consider how gender relations play out in the rest of the story: we witness Esther's development from a young, obedient niece and harem-girl to a judicious, thoughtful, and authoritative queen, and we are introduced to Haman's wise, prophetic, and domineering wife. Recognizing the satirical nature of this royal edict relating to husband-wife relations, the rabbis of the Talmud commented: "What sort of decree that is sent unto us, that every man should show himself ruler in his own house? Even the weaver is master in his own house. So, when the decree came to destroy Israel they took it also as a joke."[29] Indeed, the entire first chapter pokes fun at everything about the Persian Empire and its inept leadership.

LIVE the Story

"All That Glitters Is Not Gold"

The opening chapter of Esther features excesses of every kind—the size of Xerxes's empire, the length of the first banquet, the elaborate setting of the second banquet, the amount of wine imbibed, and the reactions to Vashti's defiance. By flaunting his material wealth, Xerxes hopes to draw attention to the magnificence of his empire and his personal greatness. At one level, he succeeds, but his reactions to the Vashti incident show that he is a flawed character: he privileges his need to impress others with his most prized possession, Vashti, over protocol (wives were not present at drinking parties) and over

28. Firth, *The Message of Esther*, 44.

29. b. Meg. 12b, quoted in David J. Clines, *Ezra, Nehemiah, Esther*, NCB (Grand Rapids: Eerdmans, 1984), 283.

her needs and personhood. It is clear that he is unable to control his anger, manage conflict, or make independent decisions.

The story of God in Scripture has much to say about individuals and empires that focus on pleasure, possessions, and power. Ecclesiastes features a king who, like Xerxes, lived a life focused on pleasure and excess—buildings, gardens, silver and gold, treasures, slaves, and beautiful women. When this king looked back over this life, he valued it as "all so meaningless—like chasing the wind. There was nothing really worthwhile anywhere" (Eccl 2:4–11, paraphrased in NLT). Personal and political empires that are focused on this present world leave little or no room for God. Jesus, in fact, taught that a person cannot serve God and money (Matt 6:24). Before the rich young man could follow Jesus, he had to disentangle himself from his possessions and give it all to the poor; sadly, he was not willing to give up his earthly treasures for treasure in heaven (Matt 19:16–22). "What good is it for someone to gain the whole world, yet forfeit their soul?" (Mark 8:36).

Xerxes's feasts for the eyes and bellies came at a high price. He placed a high value on appearances and power. He was willing to use any means to acquire wealth, control those around him, and get what he wanted. It is not hard to imagine that Amos would have preached a message of judgment in Xerxes's court similar to the one given to the pampered rich darlings of Bashan: "Hear this word, you cows of Bashan on Mount Samaria, you women who oppress the poor and crush the needy, and say to your husbands, 'Bring us some drinks!' . . . 'The time will surely come. . . .'" (Amos 4:1, 2). The theme of oppressive and unjust structures of empire built on the backs of others is ever present in the book of Esther. God's attitude toward such unjust empires and privileged leaders is encapsulated in Psalm 2, which reveals the Most High's attitude of laughing derision toward unjust empires led by inept leaders such as Xerxes, and points prophetically to a very different kind of kingship under Jesus.

What about Vashti?

Vashti's defiance and its fallout have elicited comments from interpreters throughout history. As noted above, following the lead of Memukan and in line with traditional cultural expectations of women's subjection to men, many have endorsed the truth and propriety of the royal edict that "every man should be ruler over his own household" (1:22). They also share Memukan's hope that "all the women will respect their husbands, from the least to the greatest" (1:20).

Italian poet writer Lucrezia Tornabuoni (ca. 1427–1482), like Brentius, cited above, was critical of Vashti, suggesting that "Women learn nothing from this queen." However, in her poetic retelling of Esther's story, Tornabuoni recasts the royal decree's directive about men being rulers in the home to read: "All wives and any women who wish to marry must be courteous, wise, and respectful, so that their husbands have no reason to leave them."[30] As a careful reader of the story, Tornabuoni sensed that the lesson drawn from Vashti's defiance was not that women should be subject to men, but rather that they should please their husbands if they want to stay married.

More positive readings of Vashti as an example of self-respect, courage, and nobility became popular in the nineteenth century, when Vashti became a model for those advocating for human rights. Citing the motto (likely penned by Benjamin Franklin) that Thomas Jefferson used on one of his seals, Elizabeth Cady Stanton suggested that Vashti modeled how "Resistance to tyrants is obedience to God."[31] In a British Women's paper in 1890, a certain C. E. B. declared: "Vashti, the noble champion of the right over her own person, in defiance of the unlimited power a drunken despot has ever been one of the noblest of women in my eyes. How gladly must she have put the crown of her shameful wifehood from her noble head and gone down to a chaste, lonely life!"[32]

Recent Christian social justice activists have similarly been inspired by the example of Vashti, arguing that there are oppressive individuals, traditions, and structures in life that need to be opposed—even if it costs everything. Mmapula Diana Kebaneilwe encourages African women to use "the Vashti paradigm" of resistance as a strategy for finding "strength and courage to say 'no' to being infected with HIV by controlling and oppressive husbands who think they own [their wives'] bodies."[33] Ruth Tucker's disturbing account of receiving counsel from her pastor to remain in a physically and emotionally abusive marriage similarly reminds us that New Testament texts about submission and mutuality in marriage such as 1 Corinthians 7:4 should never be used to imprison women in abusive relationships.[34] Christian marriage, in contrast, should be a haven predicated on love, care, and mutual respect between a couple.

The Vashti model or paradigm can be extended far beyond justice issues related to gender to embrace other situations involving injustice and

30. Tornabuoni, *Sacred Narratives*, 177, 176.

31. Elizabeth Cady Stanton, *The Woman's Bible. Part 2 Joshua to Revelation* (Boston: Northeastern University Press, 1898), 83.

32. C. E. B., *Women's Penny Paper* [renamed as] *The Woman's Herald*, 2.104 (1890): 622.

33. Mmapula Diana Kebaneilwe, "The Vashti Paradigm: Resistance as a Strategy for Combating HIV," *The Ecumenical Review* 63.4 (2011): 379.

34. Ruth E. Tucker, *Black and White Bible, Black and Blue Wife: My Story of Finding Hope after Domestic Violence* (Grand Rapids: Zondervan, 2016).

compromise similar to the ones faced by Esther, Mordecai, and many others in Scripture. In my own life, Vashti's story emboldened me not to give in to my defiant three-year old son who was demanding yet again that he sit in the front seat of the double-stroller, meaning that his sister had to ride in the back; and to say no to a student who attached a note to a paper that threatened that if I didn't give him an A on the paper, he would not get into a doctoral program and thus would be shamed by his family. Vashti's courage, like that of Joseph when he stood up to Potiphar's wife (Gen 39), calls us to stand our ground and say, "No! I cannot compromise on this core principle and belief."

As the story of Esther unfolds, the complex issue of compromise will again surface as Esther is instructed by Mordecai to hide that she is a Jew. The question of when to disobey and stand your ground and when to obey and compromise is complex. It was relevant to the first readers of Esther who lived under foreign domination, and it continues to be relevant to Christians living in a post-Christian culture. Reinhold Niebuhr's "Serenity Prayer" reminds us of the need for God's help in negotiating life's many challenges: "God grant me the serenity to accept the things I cannot change, courage to change the things I can, and wisdom to know the difference."[35]

35. Chad Napier, "What is the Serenity Prayer? Is it Biblical?" 6 June 2019, https://www.christianity.com/wiki/prayer/what-is-the-serenity-prayer-is-it-biblical.html.

CHAPTER 6

Esther 2:1–23

LISTEN to the Story

[1]Later when King Xerxes' fury had subsided, he remembered Vashti and what she had done and what he had decreed about her. [2]Then the king's personal attendants proposed, "Let a search be made for beautiful young virgins for the king. [3]Let the king appoint commissioners in every province of his realm to bring all these beautiful young women into the harem at the citadel of Susa. Let them be placed under the care of Hegai, the king's eunuch, who is in charge of the women; and let beauty treatments be given to them. [4]Then let the young woman who pleases the king be queen instead of Vashti." This advice appealed to the king, and he followed it.

[5]Now there was in the citadel of Susa a Jew of the tribe of Benjamin, named Mordecai son of Jair, the son of Shimei, the son of Kish, [6]who had been carried into exile from Jerusalem by Nebuchadnezzar king of Babylon, among those taken captive with Jehoiachin king of Judah. [7]Mordecai had a cousin named Hadassah, whom he had brought up because she had neither father nor mother. This young woman, who was also known as Esther, had a lovely figure and was beautiful. Mordecai had taken her as his own daughter when her father and mother died.

[8]When the king's order and edict had been proclaimed, many young women were brought to the citadel of Susa and put under the care of Hegai. Esther also was taken to the king's palace and entrusted to Hegai, who had charge of the harem. [9]She pleased him and won his favor. Immediately he provided her with her beauty treatments and special food. He assigned to her seven female attendants selected from the king's palace and moved her and her attendants into the best place in the harem.

[10]Esther had not revealed her nationality and family background, because Mordecai had forbidden her to do so. [11]Every day he walked back and forth near the courtyard of the harem to find out how Esther was and what was happening to her.

[12]Before a young woman's turn came to go in to King Xerxes, she had to

complete twelve months of beauty treatments prescribed for the women, six months with oil of myrrh and six with perfumes and cosmetics. [13]And this is how she would go to the king: Anything she wanted was given her to take with her from the harem to the king's palace. [14]In the evening she would go there and in the morning return to another part of the harem to the care of Shaashgaz, the king's eunuch who was in charge of the concubines. She would not return to the king unless he was pleased with her and summoned her by name.

[15]When the turn came for Esther (the young woman Mordecai had adopted, the daughter of his uncle Abihail) to go to the king, she asked for nothing other than what Hegai, the king's eunuch who was in charge of the harem, suggested. And Esther won the favor of everyone who saw her. [16]She was taken to King Xerxes in the royal residence in the tenth month, the month of Tebeth, in the seventh year of his reign.

[17]Now the king was attracted to Esther more than to any of the other women, and she won his favor and approval more than any of the other virgins. So he set a royal crown on her head and made her queen instead of Vashti. [18]And the king gave a great banquet, Esther's banquet, for all his nobles and officials. He proclaimed a holiday throughout the provinces and distributed gifts with royal liberality.

[19]When the virgins were assembled a second time, Mordecai was sitting at the king's gate.

But Esther had kept secret her family background and nationality just as Mordecai had told her to do, for she continued to follow Mordecai's instructions as she had done when he was bringing her up.

[21]During the time Mordecai was sitting at the king's gate, Bigthana and Teresh, two of the king's officers who guarded the doorway, became angry and conspired to assassinate King Xerxes. [22]But Mordecai found out about the plot and told Queen Esther, who in turn reported it to the king, giving credit to Mordecai. [23]And when the report was investigated and found to be true, the two officials were impaled on poles. All this was recorded in the book of the annals in the presence of the king.

Listen to the Text in the Story: Biblical Texts: Exodus 17:14–15; Leviticus 20:2, 14; Numbers 14:41–45; Deuteronomy 21:22–23; 1 Samuel 9:1–2; 15:1–9; 2 Samuel 11, 13; 21:9; 1 Kings 1:2–4; 11:3; 2 Kings 15:6, 11; 1 Chronicles 10:8–10; 2 Chronicles 16:11; Ezra 4:11–16; Psalms 45:8; Proverbs 31:30; Song of Songs 4:11–7; Daniel 2:5; 6:8; Ancient Near Eastern Texts: Herodotus, *Histories* 7:33; 9.108.1–2; *KTU* 1.3. 1–5; Plutarch, *Artaxerxes* 27.2.

Royal Sexual Alliances and Beauty

This chapter focuses on the plan and process by which Esther replaces the deposed Queen Vashti, and the uncovering of an assassination plot meant to kill Xerxes. It introduces yet another portrait of Persian excess and exploitation. Royal marriages in the ancient world were normally arranged through family or political connections.[1] Kingdom-wide searches were sometimes undertaken to find additional women to indulge a king's every desire, and to entertain and impress guests. Such a search was made for a beautiful young virgin to meet the needs of the aged King David (1 Kgs 1:1–4), and for a replacement queen for Xerxes (Esth 2:2). While queens had their own living quarters, concubines, who were neither married to the king nor given the same privileges and duties, lived in the harem. Some harems housed hundreds of women, many living as virtual widows. Solomon had seven hundred wives of royal birth and three hundred concubines (1 Kgs 11:3); Persian King Darius I had "three hundred and sixty concubines selected for their beauty," in addition to his wife Atossa, whom he passionately loved.[2]

A number of ancient stories and love songs describe beautifying preparations that were thought to awaken the senses for love making, or in the case of the warrior goddess, Anat, for combat. Anat's pre-battle spa treatment was elaborate, and like that of Esther, involved seven attendants:

> Seven Slaves rub the skin of Anat with cream,
> They tint her hands and feet with henna.
> Slaves scent the body of Anat with coriander perfume,
> They drape her in a purple robe,
> Anat locked the doors of her sanctuary.[3]

Part of the prenuptial spa experience in Susa likely involved sitting before cosmetic burners that produced fragrant smoke that was absorbed by the skin, hair, and clothes (Ps 45:8).[4]

Beauty was both elaborately enhanced and celebrated by the ancients. The Greek poet Sappho linked goodness and beauty: "the beautiful—its beauty is already visible. Soon also the good will turn into beautiful."[5] Goodness

1. According to Herodotus, King Darius agreed, among other things, that his wife should be chosen from seven noble families (Herodotus, *Hist.* 3.84. See Introduction to Esther, Historical and Ancient Near Eastern Background).

2. Plutarch, *Art.* 27.2.

3. *KTU* 1.3. 1–5 cited in Victor Harold Matthews and Don C. Benjamin, *Old Testament Parallels: Laws and Stories from the Ancient Near East* (New York: Paulist Press, 2006), 228.

4. Tomasino, "Esther," 486.

5. Michael Avioz, citing Sappho's fragment 50 in "The Motif of Beauty in the Books of Samuel and Kings," *VT* 59 (2009): 343.

and beauty are not always coupled in the Old Testament, however, as the encomium to the woman in Proverbs 31:30 warns, "Charm is deceptive, and beauty is fleeting." Many texts about beautiful women associate beauty with seduction and danger (2 Sam 13; Prov 5–7). Esther's beauty put her in danger, but it was also an asset that she used to survive in the harem and to negotiate the deliverance of the Jews. Xerxes's attraction to women was memorialized by Herodotus, who tells of Xerxes's pursuit of his brother's wife whom he later passed over for her daughter:

> Being then at Sardis he became enamored of Masistes' wife. . . . Xerxes found no other way to accomplish his purpose than that he should make a marriage between his own son Darius and the daughter of this woman and Masistes, for he thought that by doing so he would be most likely to win her. So he betrothed them with all due ceremony and rode away to Susa. But when he had come and had taken Darius' bride into his house, he thought no more of Masistes' wife, but changed his mind and wooed and won this girl Artaynte, Darius' wife and Masistes' daughter.[6]

Susa's Gate Complex

Susa's massive gate complex (130 ft. × 90 ft.), excavated in the 1970s, included a number of side rooms where formal and informal business and judicial meetings took place and where troops were stationed.[7] Mordecai's residence in Susa's citadel and his presence at the gate (Esth 2:21) suggest he worked in administration in the service of the king (see also Neh 1:11). His position brought him close to the affairs of state and enabled him to regularly communicate with Esther (Esth 2:11, 22; 4:5–17).

Record Keeping and Royal Gifts

The ancients kept records of military campaigns as well as such day-to-day matters as the plot to kill Xerxes reported by Mordecai. The value of royal records was recognized by Ezra, who requested that Artaxerxes "search . . . in the books of the records of your fathers" to learn the history of relations between Judah and Persia (Ezra 4:11–16 ESV). Xerxes was especially concerned about record keeping. Herodotus speaks of the presence of scribes on the battlefield recording the names and actions of brave warriors who were generously rewarded for their heroism and loyalty:

---

6. Herodotus, *Hist.* 9.108.1–2.
7. Yamauchi, *Persia and the Bible*, 298–300.

> Whenever Xerxes . . . saw one of his own men achieve some feat in the battle, he inquired who did it, and his scribes wrote down the captain's name with his father and city of residence.[8]

The ancients promptly and generously rewarded exceptionally loyal and brave warriors and citizens. Court benefaction was so important to the Persians that they had a special word to designate the king's heroes ("orosangae").[9] For their fearless acts of capturing enemy ships, one Samian captain was made ruler of Samos and another given a large estate.[10] Similarly, Herodotus records that Xerxes I rewarded the man who courageously saved the life of his brother Masistes in ca. 479 BC by making him "ruler of all Cilicia."[11] Given this practice of benefaction, readers expect a notice of Mordecai's reward for reporting the assassination plot (Esth 2:21–23), but they have to wait until chapter 6, as Xerxes forgets to honor Mordecai.

Execution Practices

Ancient practices of execution included stoning (Lev 20:2), death by fire (Lev 20:14); dismemberment (Dan 2:5) and being eaten by animals (Dan 6:7); impalement on pointed wooden stakes (Esth 2:23; 5:14), and crucifixion.[12] Hanging by rope was not practiced. Impaled or suspended bodies or body parts were sometimes displayed as a means of public shaming and warning (Deut 21:22–23; 1 Chr 10:8–10). Royal assassinations were common; Xerxes was eventually killed by the commander of his bodyguard.

EXPLAIN the Story

The Plan to Replace Queen Vashti (Esther 2:1–4)

The undisclosed amount of time that passes between chapters one and two likely coincided with Xerxes's unsuccessful Greek campaign (see Introduction to Esther). Upon his return, Xerxes—a renowned lover of stunning and

8. Herodotus, *Hist.* 8.90.4.

9. Orosangae is the Persian word for benefactors. "The king's benefactors are called "orosangae" in the Persian language." Herodotus, *Hist.*, 8:85.

10. Ibid.

11. Ibid., 9.107. 3.

12. Ibid., 7:33; LXX uses several verbs including "*staupoō*" "to crucify," with regards to Haman. Josephus's Haman prepared a cross on which to crucify Mordecai and was himself crucified on the same cross. (Josephus, *Ant.,* 11.246, 261, 266, 267, 280). Not surprisingly, a number of early interpreters associate Haman's crucifixion with Christ's. See also Kristin De Troyer, *Rewriting the Sacred Text* (Atlanta: Society of Biblical Literature, 2003), 185–86. T. Thornton, "The Crucifixion of Haman and the Scandal of the Cross," *JTS* 37 (1986): 419–26.

inaccessible women—remembers Vashti and her defiance and his coached response that had set in motion her permanent banishment (see Listen to the Story). Eliza Cushing's idea (1794–1886) that the king blamed Memukan for pushing him to get rid of his beautiful wife has some merit:

> Ay, with most cruel haste,
> Thou [Memukan] dids't the deed. Thou fearest lest I [Xerxes]
> should change;
> Lest in a cooler hour, my angry mood
> Should pass. And love return. Full well thou knowest
> That the inebriate wine had fired my blood,
> And paralyzed my brain,—else my words
> Fallen powerless to the ground, as they deserved.[13]

Xerxes's remembering, which opens this chapter, contrasts his forgetting to reward Mordecai, which closes the chapter (2:1, 23). Only later would he remember that he should have rewarded Mordecai (see Listen to the Story, above; see also Esther 6:1–14: Explain the Story). Both acts of remembrance are woven into the grand scheme that saves God's people and is memorialized in the festival of Purim (9:28).

Xerxes's attendants, who are well-acquainted with his hedonistic tendencies, redirect his remorseful thoughts to their scheme. They urge him to replace one "lovely [lit., "good"] to look at" but defiant woman (1:11) with a young virgin who is also described in Hebrew as "good to look at" (2:2). This plan seems to be literally "good in the eyes of the king" (1:21 and 2:4). Like Joseph's masterful plan to have Pharaoh's commissioners gather grain to store for the imminent famine (Gen 41:34–37), the attendants' scheme involves sending commissioners to gather commodified virgins to be used by the king. The girls brought into Xerxes's harem (lit., "house of women") lived under the care of eunuchs who supervised their care. The eunuchs prepared them for sex with the king, who then used and disposed of them (2:3, 8–9; see Esther 1:1–22: Listen to the Story). This "perfected institutionalization of rape, in which the king's will is the only will," effectively restored the king's sense of control.[14]

Mordecai and Esther Introduced (Esther 2:5–7)

Mordecai is introduced as a Jew, a term describing all Hebrews in this period (Esth 2:5; 3:4; 5:13; 6:10, 13; 8:7; 9:29, 31; 10:3). His name is the Hebraized

---

13. Eliza Lanesford Cushing, *Esther, A Sacred Drama: With Judith, A Poem* (Boston: Joseph Dowe, 1840), 16.

14. Yoram Hazony, *God and Politics in Esther* (Cambridge: Cambridge University Press, 2015), 18.

form of Marduka, a common name derived from Marduk, the Babylonian chief god. The narrator links Mordecai geographically to the citadel of Susa where the virgins are being gathered. He also notes Mordecai's connection with the tribe of Benjamin, King Saul (who was also a son of Kish; 1 Sam 9:1–2), and the exile. Mordecai's association with Saul, who failed to destroy completely the city of Amalek and its king, Agag (1 Sam 15:1–23), helps to explain Mordecai's conflictual relationship with Haman the Agagite that unfolds in chapter 3 (see Esther 3:1–15: Listen to the Story and Explain the Story). Mordecai's connection with the exile (mentioned 4 times in the Hebrew of v. 6) was real but distant, because it was his forebears and not Mordecai himself who had been exiled from Judah (2 Kgs 24:8–17; see Introduction to Esther). This repeated mention of exile is highly significant as it provides the book's only explanation of the Jewish presence in Susa. Mordecai was one of many Jews who decided to settle permanently in Persia, even though Cyrus had allowed their return (Jer 29:5–7). Although Mordecai and other diaspora Jews prospered in Persia, they faced many challenges living under the rule of the despotic Xerxes. The allusions to the exile also recall the broken covenant that prompted God's judgment and the promise of a remnant and future restoration (Jer 29:10–14; Ezek 11:14–20). This retrospective link to the past encourages us to read the book in light of the story of God, both past and present, and to look for clues of God's presence in this episode of salvation history.

Esther is introduced by her Hebrew name, Hadassah (myrtle), a name found only in Esther 2:7. Her Babylonian name, Esther, may come from the Persian noun "star," but it is more likely derived from Ishtar, the name of the renowned Babylonian goddess of love and war. Esther's strong associations with both love and war lend weight to the idea that her name is derived from Ishtar. Also appealing is the rabbinic tradition that associates Esther's name with hiddenness by linking the consonants in her name with the verb "hide" in Deuteronomy 31:18, where God declares that he "will certainly hide [his] face" because of his people's wickedness. Esther's association with hiddenness raises the issue of Esther's concealed Jewish identity, the related problem of Persian anti-Semitism (Esth 2:10), and the larger theological puzzle of God's hiddenness in the story. Is God absent in this story because of his people's sin, or has the narrator recounted the story using only subtle allusions to God and the story of God to remind readers that God's hiddenness is not to be equated with God's absence?[15]

15. Reid, *Esther*, 79–80. See also Carruthers, who cites the rabbinic tradition that fleshes out the association of Esther and hiddenness in b. Meg. 13a and Tg. Rishon; Carruthers, *Esther Through the Centuries*, 106.

Esther's identity as an orphan is mentioned twice, as are her family ties with Mordecai (2:7). She was first orphaned when her parents died, and she is orphaned again when she is taken away from Mordecai and placed under the care of Hegai (2:8). As Samuel Wells explains, like orphaned and exiled Israel, "Esther epitomizes the pathos of the Jewish people: she has **neither father nor mother . . .** [and] no home. . . . [her] identity is the identity of the Jewish people."[16] The orphan motif is tied into the larger scriptural theme of God's compassion for orphans, which provides hope that God will abandon neither Esther nor her people forever (Ps 10:14; Hos 14:3). Between the double identification of Esther as an orphan is the double description of Esther's beauty: she is both shapely and good looking—features that foreshadow Esther's being rounded up in the search for beautiful virgins (2:8).

Esther's Success (Esther 2:8–20)

Esther is one of the beautiful girls chosen to gratify the desires of the self-indulgent king in his search for a "better" queen (1:19). Esther thrives in her new surroundings. She pleases Hegai, the eunuch in charge of women, and wins his favor (lit., *hesed*; 2:8–9). She also wins the king's grace and favor (*hesed* 2:17). Hegai's favor includes the provision of beauty treatments and special, though non-kosher, food or "portions," a translation of the Hebrew word used again for the "presents" and "presents of food" given to others at Purim (9:19, 22). Esther is also given seven of the best royal attendants, who move with her to the best place in the harem (2:9). The favor Esther finds recalls the God-given favor experienced by Joseph and Daniel, and hints that the seemingly hidden God is with Esther in the harem (Gen 39:4; Dan 1:8–10). Esther differentiates herself from Joseph and Daniel however, in that she conceals her Jewish identity following the directive of Mordecai, and fails to comply with Torah laws as she prepares to sleep with the pagan king (Esth 2:10; see also Gen 39:8–9; Dan 1:8).

The extravagance that characterizes every aspect of Xerxes's kingdom continues as the young virgins are prepared for their night of involuntary sex with the king. Their elaborate spa experience includes six months of beauty treatments that involve exfoliation and moisturizing with imported aromatic oil of myrrh and another six months of treatment with a variety of spices and cosmetics (Esth 2:12; see Listen to the Story, above). The sexual innuendo present in the fivefold repetition of the Hebrew verb "to go" or "go into" as in intercourse reminds us again of the end goal of the process (vv. 12, 13, 2x in v. 14—only 1x in the NIV—and v. 15). After sex with the king, the girls

16. Wells, "Esther," in Sumner and Wells, *Esther & Daniel*, 38, emphasis in the original.

are moved to a second harem where they wait to be summoned again (2:14). The twelve-month regimen, literally "the law of women," reminds us of other odd laws in Esther, such as drinking without compulsion (1:8) and dealing with disobedient wives (1:15, 21–22). These unconventional laws, together with the later irrevocable decree of genocide, reveal both Persia's legal system and the king who authorizes them as ridiculous. This particularly eccentric "law of women" sounds "a note of contempt for the luxury of the foreign court and its narcissistic and grossly self-indulgent body culture."[17]

Before he describes Esther's night with the king, the narrator reminds readers of Esther's real but hidden Jewish identity—she is "the young woman Mordecai had adopted, the daughter of his uncle Abihail" (2:15). Esther will only reveal her full self as both Jew and Queen of Persia later in the story (7:4; 9:29). The theme of hidden national and family identity, introduced in the narrative about Esther's harem and spa experiences, is repeated following the account of her marriage (2:10–11, 20). Both in the harem and in the king's bed, Esther complies with Mordecai's instructions to hide her identity, which grew out of his concern for her survival as a Jew in an empire he experienced as anti-Semitic (4:7).

When it was Esther's turn to "go to the king," she requested only what Hegai, the eunuch preparing the girls for sex with the king, suggested (2:15). Esther's calculated request is the only active choice she makes while in the harem, and anticipates her later considered demands that lead to the reversal of the genocidal edict, the deaths of Haman and his sons, and a second day of killing (5:6; 7:2; 8:5–6; 9:12–13). The repeated notice of the positive reactions Esther receives from everyone before she is taken to the king (2:9, 15b) prepares us for the statement that the "king was attracted to Esther more than to any of the other women, and she won his favor and approval more than any of the other virgins" (2:17).

Within the frame of the positive notices about "favor" (2:15b, 17) is a formal dating formula that specifies that Esther was brought "to go to the king" four years after Vashti's banishment (v. 16). The significance of this date has been explained in different ways: it grounds the consequential union historically by referencing the unsuccessful Persian wars with the Greeks; it underscores the extravagant wastefulness of the process, as perhaps as many as 1460 girls have been used by the king before it was Esther's turn;[18] and it highlights the importance of the event and how Esther is able to use her royal position to save her people from genocide (2:16). This date also highlights

17. Levenson, *Esther*, 61.

18. Lewis Bayles Paton, *A Critical and Exegetical Commentary on the Book of Esther*, ICC (Edinburgh: T&T Clark, 1908; repr., 1976), 183.

one of the historical problems with the book's chronology, as this date does not match other historical records, which place Xerxes elsewhere at this time (see Introduction to Esther).

After Xerxes chooses Esther as queen, she is given the royal crown that the defiant Vashti had refused to wear (2:17). The marriage is celebrated with a banquet that recalls both Xerxes's first banquet for nobles and officials and the second that led to Vashti's demise (1:3, 5–12). As part of the wedding celebrations, Xerxes proclaims a "rest"—a term usually translated as "holiday" (NIV), but also as a remission of taxes (ESV)—and Xerxes gives gifts (2:18). The commemorative "rest" and "gifts" anticipate the Jews' final feasting in celebration of rest from their enemies, which similarly involves gift-giving (9:16–19, 22). It may additionally point ahead to what is possibly the reversal of this remission of taxes by Xerxes in the book's epilogue (10:1).

The notice of the second gathering of the virgins is puzzling (2:19). This may refer either to what John Goldingay calls "the gathering of the next batch of potential victims for Xerxes" who seems to "need women to bolster [his] position"[19] or to the moving or release of the virgins following the king's marriage (2:19). The note about Mordecai's position at the gate reminds us of his presence near Esther and prepares us for the vignette that follows.

The Assassination Plot Revealed (Esther 2:21–23)

Mordecai is well positioned at the king's gate to overhear plans to assassinate Xerxes (see Listen to the Story, above). Mordecai proves his loyalty to Xerxes when he passes on the information to Esther who in turn reports it to the king, giving credit to Mordecai. After the truth of the report is verified, the conspirators are publicly executed by being attached to a tree or wooden pole. The translation, "impaled on poles" (NIV) is to be preferred to "hanged on gallows" (ESV), which implies the use of a rope around the neck, something that was not done in the ancient world. As convention demanded, the incident was recorded in the royal annals (2:23). Convention also demanded that Mordecai be immediately and generously rewarded for his loyalty (see also Esther 6:1–14). The report of Haman's promotion and not Mordecai's in chapter 3 is therefore surprising. In any case, Mordecai's saving action foreshadows Mordecai and Esther's efforts to save the lives of the Jews by reversing Haman's murderous plan to kill the Jews.[20]

---

19. John Goldingay, *Ezra, Nehemiah & Esther for Everyone* (Louisville: Westminster John Knox, 2012), 166.

20. Levenson, *Esther*, 64.

LIVE the Story

Esther Was Taken: Sex Trafficking

In presenting us with an ever more detailed portrait of a self-indulgent king whose "needs" are met at the expense of others, this chapter reminds us that the Bible does not hide the dark side of life. The plan to find a new queen who is better than Vashti involved the elaborate preparation of young virgins for sex with the king. Although many commentators glamorize Esther's Cinderella-like rags-to-riches story and imagine that all girls want to be queen, it is important to pause and reflect upon the sexual violation of the "voiceless" girls herded into the king's harem where they were cared for by men whose boyhood castration signified another form of sexual violation.

Nineteenth-century evangelical justice advocate Josephine Butler believed that Old Testament stories featuring victims of sexual abuse, such as the horrific gang rape of the Levite's concubine in Judges 19, reveal human depravity. The story of the herding together of girls who were used and discarded by Xerxes also reveals human depravity. Butler's poignant question, "Where is God in the story of the Levite's concubine?" is a question we also need to ask about Esther's story and other stories of terror in Scripture. Butler believed that Jesus was present with the concubine in her suffering, as he is with other victims of exploitation. Her call to her contemporaries and to us is to listen to the silenced cries of victims of sex trafficking and abuse and respond as Jesus would: with compassion, care, and healing.[21] We can become the voices of silent and traumatized victims by being active in advocacy against human trafficking and by supporting organizations committed to ending human trafficking and other forms of human commodification.

Esther Was Taken: What Her Critics Say

The repeated use of the passive voice in this chapter reminds us that Esther did not chose to enter a beauty contest to become Xerxes's next bachelorette. Rather she *was brought* to the citadel and *was placed* under Hegai's care and eventually she *was brought* to the king. Esther's behavior, especially her compliance and passivity, is often criticized. Mark Driscoll, one of her most vicious critics, suggests that Esther "allows men to tend to her needs and make

21. Josephine Butler, "The Lovers of the Lost," *Contemporary Review* 13 (1870): 16; "Christian people! There is a weak and prostrate figure lying at our door; to this door she turns for help. Though it be but in her dying fall; her hands are upon the threshold—dead hands flung forward in mute and terrible appeal to the God above, who, looking down from heaven, sees not the prostrated form alone, but on the one side the powers of hell, on the other, in their safe dwelling-place, the selfish sleepers to whom the pale cold hands appeal in vain. That night is far spent."

her decisions" including her "sinful" behavior of "spend[ing] around a year in the spa getting dolled up to lose her virginity with the pagan king. . . . She's simply a person without any character until her own neck is on the line, and then we see her rise up to save the life of her people when she is converted to a real faith in God."[22] Nicole Duran's criticisms of Esther are equally harsh: "Esther comes in willingly to do what Vashti would not. Esther is, in effect, the scab undermining the impact of the striking worker's sacrifice."[23] Such criticisms tell us more about the authors' views on women than the story, which, when read within its ancient context and using insights from trauma and disaster studies, suggests instead that Esther was a victim of sex trafficking who used an adaptation strategy for survival fitted to the realities of her circumstances.

To survive in the palace, Esther uses "the arts of alternative resistance"—what Yoder calls "revolutionary subordination."[24] She hides her true identity and, like other victim survivors, adopts "a posture of submissiveness" and "represse[s] her spontaneity and replace[s] it with the studied grace and charm taught by her elders."[25] Esther uses all available resources, including the human resources offered by those with experience and power, such as Hegai and Mordecai, to survive and thrive in the situation in which she finds herself. She knows what had happened to Vashti when she defied Xerxes, and she chooses rather to survive and thrive. In this way Esther models survival for all the Jews living in an alien empire and for all readers of her story who find themselves trapped in political, military, or economic systems of oppression and violence.

Esther Was Taken: "My God, My God, Why Have You Forsaken Me?"

The narrator does not reveal Esther's inner thoughts and feelings. However, when we read Esther's story in the context of the rest of Scripture, we can imagine that her response to trauma was similar to Jeremiah's and others who faced losses and sensed abandonment by God. An eleventh-century Midrash on the Psalms suggests that Esther uttered the words of anguish, questioning, and longing found in Psalm 22 during her three-day fast before she approached Xerxes (4:16).[26] I suggest that Psalm 22 also gives voice to the

---

22. Mark Driscoll as quoted in Evans, "Esther Actually: Princess, Whore."

23. Nicole Duran, "Who Wants to Marry a Persian King? Gender Games and Wars and the Book of Esther," in *Pregnant Passion: Gender, Sex and Violence in the Bible*, ed. Cheryl Kirk-Duggan (Atlanta: SBL, 2003), 78, 81.

24. John Howard Yoder, *The Politics of Jesus: Behold the Man! Our Victorious Lamb*, 2nd ed. (Grand Rapids: Eerdmans, 1999), 162–92, quoted in Wells, "Esther," 39.

25. Joshua Berman, "*Hadassah bat Abihail*: The Evolution from Object to Subject in the Character of Esther," *JBL* 12.04 (2001): 649.

26. Esther M. Menn, "No Ordinary Lament: *Relecture* and the Identity of the Distressed in Ps 22," *HTR* 93 (2000): 301–41.

pain and anguish Esther would have experienced as a double-orphaned, traumatized teen being prepared to sleep with the intemperate womanizer, Xerxes.

> "My God, my God, why have you forsaken me?
> Why are you so far from saving me,
> so far from my cries of anguish?
> My God, I cry out by day, but you do not answer,
> by night, but I find no rest.
> [. . .]
> From birth I was cast on you;
> from my mother's womb you have been my God.
> Do not be far from me,
> for trouble is near
> and there is no one to help." (Ps 22:1–2, 10–11)

The New Testament identifies Jesus as the one who speaks in Psalm 22. Indeed, "My God, my God, why have you forsaken me?" are among Jesus' last words on the cross (Matt 27:46; Mark 15:34), and a number of other motifs from this psalm, including the dividing of clothing and the jeering enemies, are woven into all the gospels' recounting of Jesus' suffering and death. If we assume that Esther's response to being herded into the harem was one of great anguish and despair, then her association with Psalm 22 and with Jesus is appropriate. Similarly, the use of the passive voice and comparable terminology in the descriptions of Jesus' arrest, trial, and execution in the gospels suggests reading Esther here as a type of Christ. Further associations of Esther and Jesus will be made later when Esther, like Jesus, is willing to die to save God's people (Esth 4).

Esther Was Taken: Is God Behind the Scenes Even Here?

This scene raises a number of difficult questions: Where was God when the beautiful young orphaned Esther gets pulled into the center of a world controlled by the few who exercise ultimate control over everyone else? Why was Esther not protected, as Sarah was when she was taken into the house of Pharaoh (Gen 12:15–19)? Was Esther's inclusion in the harem a coincidence or an act of providence? If we believe that God placed Esther in a position where she could influence the king and save the Jews, we must also reflect upon what this means. This incident, John Goldingay suggests, "most scandalously invites us to assume God is involved in this world, even in its wickedness."[27]

When faced with the kind of situation Esther faced, belief in a good and

27. Goldingay, *Ezra, Nehemiah & Esther for Everyone*, 164.

all-powerful sovereign (though often hidden) God is comforting. In a letter written in 1938, Edith Stein, a converted German Jew gassed at Auschwitz, testifies to the comfort she finds in Esther's story: "I am confident that the Lord has taken my life for all [Jews]. I always have to think of Queen Esther, who was taken away from her people for the express purpose of standing before the King for her people. I am the very poor, weak, and small Esther, but the King who selected me is infinitely greater and more merciful."[28] The theology of the book of Esther affirms our belief in such a God.

Esther and Hadassah: Who Are You?

Nineteenth-century dramatist Alexander Buchan raises the critical question of how Esther and, by extension, all Jews can survive and thrive as Jew(s) and Persian(s) living in Persia:

> Hadassah, under Mordecai's lov'd roof,
> Esther, king-mated upon Persia's throne,
> Art thou the one same person?[29]

This question is not unique to Jews living in Persia; Christians in post-Christendom face this question daily as they confront ethical and moral situations that demand considered and faithful responses. How can we be both Christians and citizens of secular post-Christian or anti-Christian empires? Esther's story presents more than one way of negotiating life in the empire: hiding one's identity for a time, like Esther, is one option; owning one's Jewish identity and standing up to confront the enemy, as both Mordecai and Esther did later, is another; and timely compromise is what Mordecai models in the final chapter, as he uses his position of power and influence in the empire to seek the welfare of all Jews. Christians do not have to agree upon best practices for negotiating life in the empire, but we can agree that God's wisdom is needed when we find ourselves having to choose among these different approaches.

---

28. Sylvie Courtine-Denamy, *Three Women in Dark Times: Edith Stein, Hannah Arendt, Simone Weil, or Amor Fati, Amor Mundi,* trans. G. M. Goshgarian (Ithaca, NY: Cornell University Press, 2000), 200.

29. Alexander Winston Buchan, *Esther, A Drama in Five Acts* (Glasgow: Thomas Murray and Son, 1873), quoted in Carruthers, *Esther through the Centuries*, 105.

CHAPTER 7

Esther 3:1–15

LISTEN to the Story

1After these events, King Xerxes honored Haman son of Hammedatha, the Agagite, elevating him and giving him a seat of honor higher than that of all the other nobles. 2All the royal officials at the king's gate knelt down and paid honor to Haman, for the king had commanded this concerning him. But Mordecai would not kneel down or pay him honor.

3Then the royal officials at the king's gate asked Mordecai, "Why do you disobey the king's command?" 4Day after day they spoke to him but he refused to comply. Therefore they told Haman about it to see whether Mordecai's behavior would be tolerated, for he had told them he was a Jew.

5When Haman saw that Mordecai would not kneel down or pay him honor, he was enraged. 6Yet having learned who Mordecai's people were, he scorned the idea of killing only Mordecai. Instead Haman looked for a way to destroy all Mordecai's people, the Jews, throughout the whole kingdom of Xerxes.

7In the twelfth year of King Xerxes, in the first month, the month of Nisan, the *pur* (that is, the lot) was cast in the presence of Haman to select a day and month. And the lot fell on the twelfth month, the month of Adar.

8Then Haman said to King Xerxes, "There is a certain people dispersed among the peoples in all the provinces of your kingdom who keep themselves separate. Their customs are different from those of all other people, and they do not obey the king's laws; it is not in the king's best interest to tolerate them. 9If it pleases the king, let a decree be issued to destroy them, and I will give ten thousand talents of silver to the king's administrators for the royal treasury."

10So the king took his signet ring from his finger and gave it to Haman son of Hammedatha, the Agagite, the enemy of the Jews. 11"Keep the money," the king said to Haman, "and do with the people as you please."

12Then on the thirteenth day of the first month the royal secretaries

were summoned. They wrote out in the script of each province and in the language of each people all Haman's orders to the king's satraps, the governors of the various provinces and the nobles of the various peoples. These were written in the name of King Xerxes himself and sealed with
his own ring.
13Dispatches were sent by couriers to all the king's provinces with the order to destroy, kill and annihilate all the Jews—young and old, women and children—on a single day, the thirteenth day of the twelfth month, the month of Adar, and to plunder their goods.
14A copy
of the text of the edict was to be issued as law in every province and made known to the people of every nationality so they would be ready for that day.

15The couriers went out, spurred on by the king's command, and the edict was issued in the citadel of Susa. The king and Haman sat down to drink, but the city of Susa was bewildered.

Listen to the Text in the Story: Biblical Texts: Genesis 39:11–21; 41:37–42; 48:23–31; Exodus 12:18 (see Lev 23:5); Exodus 17:8–15; Numbers 27:21; 28:16; Deuteronomy 25:19; 1 Samuel 15:1–23; 28:6; Nehemiah 10:34; 11:1; Isaiah 10:5–7; 45:23; Daniel 3:5–6; Ancient Near Eastern Texts: The Stela of Pharaoh Merneptah; The Stela of King Mesha; "The Lot of Yahali"; Amarna Letter 254:1–40; Herodotus, *Histories* 9.107.

Haman the Agagite, King Agag, and the Amalekites

Clues scattered throughout the book of Esther suggest it is intended to be read as the final episode in the ancestral war between the Israelites/God and the Amalekites whom Israel was mandated to destroy (Deut 25:19). The conflict began during the wilderness wanderings and continued under King Saul, who defied God's three-fold command to completely destroy the city Amalek, take no plunder, and destroy Agag, King of the Amalekites (Exod 17:8–15; 1 Sam 15:1–23). Haman's introduction (Esth 3:1) connects him to Agag and the Amalekites.

Links to the Joseph Story and Passover

The stories of Esther and Joseph share several themes and linguistic features that draw Esther into the greater story of God. The "day by day" harassment of Mordecai by the officials recalls the "day by day" sexual harassment of Joseph by Potiphar's wife, and their defiance similarly imperiled their lives and became part of the story of the deliverance of God's people (Esth 3:2–6; 9:5–16; 10:3; Gen 39:11–21; 41:41–42; 47:23–31). The celebratory drinks shared by Haman and Xerxes after they had sealed the fate of the Jews echo the meal shared by Joseph's brothers after they had thrown him into a pit to die (Esth 3:15; Gen 37:25). Haman and Xerxes, like Joseph's brothers, were interested in profiting financially from the demise of their enemy (Esth 3:8–9; Gen 37:26–28). Other elements linking the book of Esther to the Joseph story include parallels between Mordecai and Joseph, who were both made second-in-charge in an alien empire (Esth 8:2; 10:3; Gen 41:37–42; 50:20).

The correlation between the genocidal order sent out on "the thirteenth day of the first month" and the eve of Passover, the festival that celebrated life and liberation that began "at twilight on the fourteenth day of the first month" provides a further link to Israel's past (Esth 3:13; Exod 12:18; Lev 23:5; Num 28:16). This "back to back" association of Passover and Haman's genocidal edict and, by extension, the festivals of Passover and Purim (see ch. 13: Esther 9:1–32) testifies, as Barry Webb suggests, "to two complementary aspects of a single reality: the election of Israel, which had its beginning historically in the call of Abraham."[1]

Ancient Etiquette and Customs

Kneeling (prostration or bowing down) symbolized deference, respect, allegiance, and even worship in the ancient world. In his letter to Pharaoh, the so-called "ruler of the heavens and earth," Labayu, Governor of Shechem, showed his allegiance, deference, and respect by figurally bowing down:

> I am your slave, who is less than the dust under your feet, and I renew my covenant with Pharaoh by bowing before you seven times seven times.[2]

Similarly, the Jews in Persia would have regularly shown respect to Xerxes and other superiors by bowing down or kneeling. However, as Shadrach, Meshach, and Abednego's refusal to kneel before Nebuchadnezzar's golden statue illustrates, kneeling before a person or object could also signify worship (Dan 3:5–6). Although a number of early interpreters named idolatry as the reason Mordecai refused to kneel before Haman, it is unlikely that Xerxes would have permitted "religious" adoration of his second-in-command (see fuller discussion of Esth 3:2 in Explain the Story, below).

---

1. Barry G. Webb, *Five Festal Garments: Christian Reflections on the Song of Songs, Ruth, Lamentations, Ecclesiastes and Esther*, NSTB 10 (Downers Grove, IL: IVP Academic, 2000), 127.

2. Amarna Letter 254:1–40 in Matthews and Benjamin, *Old Testament Parallels*, 148.

Casting the Lot to Select the Date of the Genocide

One of many forms of divination ancients used to determine the future was the casting of a lot. A terracotta cube inscribed with an official's name, title, and prayers dating from the reign of the Assyrian King Shalmaneser III provides a useful parallel to the cube or lot used to determine the date of the genocide (Esth 3:7; 9:26). This particular Assyrian cube, used centuries earlier, was cast to determine the year to be named after the official who was being honored and included a prayer that "his *puru*-lot [might] fall in front of the gods Ashur and Adad."[3] Although lots were sometimes cast in Israel (Neh 10:34; 11:1; see also the high priest's lot-like "Urim and Thummin," 1 Sam 28:6; Num 27:21), "every decision," including the ones made when "the lot is cast into the lap," was believed to be controlled by God (Prov 16:33). This underlying theology of God's sovereignty, together with the association of the genocide with Passover, suggests the superintendence of God in the casting of the lot Haman used.

Genocide

The ancients regularly tried to annihilate their enemies. The commemorative Stela of Pharaoh Merneptah (1209/8 BC) praises Merneptah's actual and exaggerated military victories in Palestine, including his alleged annihilation of Israel:

> The (foreign) chieftains lie prostrate, saying "Peace." Not one lifts
> his head among the Nine Bows.
> Libya is captured, while Hatti is pacified.
> Canaan is plundered, Ashkelon is carried off, and Gezer is captured.
> Yenoam is made into non-existence; *Israel is wasted, its seed is not;*
> and Hurri is become a widow because of Egypt.
> All lands united themselves in peace, Those who went about are
> subdued by the king of Upper and Lower Egypt . . . Merneptah."[4]

The ninth-century Moabite Stone similarly regards genocide as a good thing:

> Kemosh [the god of Moab] said to me. "Go, take Nebo from Israel!" And I went in the night, and I fought against it from the break of dawn until noon, and I took it, and I killed [its] whole population, seven thousand male citizens and aliens, and female citizens and aliens, and servant girls;

---

3. *Assyrian Rulers of the Early First Millennium BC, ii 858–745 BC*, trans. A. K. Grayson and Albert Kirk (Toronto: University of Toronto Press, 1996), 179, quoted in Stephanie Dalley, *Esther's Revenge at Susa: From Sennacherib to Ahasuerus* (Oxford: Oxford University Press, 2007), 159 (my emphasis).

4. James K. Hoffmeier, "The (Israel) Stela of Merneptah," *COS* 2.6:41.

for I had put it to the ban for Ashtar Kemosh. And from there I took th[e ves]sels of YHWH, and I hauled them before the face of Kemosh.[5]

By contrast, Isaiah criticizes the practice of genocide. He reproaches the nation that was used to punish Israel for their desire to completely annihilate Israel and other nations:

Woe to the Assyrian, the rod of my anger,
  in whose hand is the club of my wrath!
I send him against a godless nation,
  I dispatch him against a people who anger me,
to seize loot and snatch plunder,
  and to trample them down like mud in the streets.
But this is not what he intends,
  this is not what he has in mind;
his purpose is to destroy,
  to put an end to many nations. (Isa 10:5–7)

EXPLAIN the Story

Haman's Rise; Mordecai's Fall (Esther 3:1–6)

The narrator does not explain Xerxes's unexpected promotion of Haman to the position of highest honor and responsibility in Persia—a reward readers would have expected Mordecai to have received for uncovering the plot to murder the king (2:21–23). Also unexplained is Xerxes's curious command that other officials should honor Haman, since honoring superiors was normal etiquette (3:1–2; see also Esther 2:1–23: Listen to the Story). The narrator's interest lies elsewhere, as he moves quickly to the conflict between Haman and Mordecai that escalates into a plan to destroy all the Jews (3:3, 6).

The officials anticipate our next question: Why does Mordecai disobey the king and refuse to honor Haman (Esth 3:3)? Possible reasons include: (1) Mordecai is jealous over Haman's promotion, given Xerxes's failure to reward him for exposing the assassination plot (2:21–23); (2) Mordecai regards bowing down to Haman as an idolatrous act; or (3) Mordecai has a clear sense of his identity as a Benjaminite descendant of Saul and has the courage to stand up to his ancestral enemy and accept the consequences of his actions.

The back to back placement of these accounts of Mordecai's foiling the assassination attempt and Haman's promotion supports the idea that Mordecai

5. K. A. D. Smelik, "The Inscription of King Mesha," *COS* 2.23:138 (lines 14–18a).

was jealous. However, a considerable amount of time may have passed between these incidents—Vashti was deposed in the third year of Xerxes's reign, Esther was crowned in Xerxes's seventh year, and the date that would be chosen by lot to kill all the Jews was five years later (1:1; 2:16; 3:7). The early interpretive tradition found in the longer LXX version of Esther supports the second reason. In this embellished story, Mordecai explains that he did not act out of "insolence or pride or for any love of glory," but rather refused to "bow down to anyone but you, who are my Lord."[6] The third reason for Mordecai's insolence is most compelling, given the story's many allusions to the unfinished holy war between the Amalekites and God's people, including the repeated motif of plunder (see Listen to the Story, above; 3:13; 8:11; 9:10, 15, 16). Goldingay draws an analogy between Mordecai and Haman and the "Israelis who see the Palestinians as the contemporary embodiment of the Amalekites . . . [and] Arabs who would like to see Israel removed from the map" and by extension all "hate groups . . . who would like to eliminate Jews all over the world."[7] Mordecai's refusal to comply with the royal command also ties into the book's obedience/disobedience theme. It recalls Vashti's defiance, which had consequences for all women, and anticipates the escalation of Mordecai's punishment to include the killing of all Jews (1:12, 20–22; 3:13).

The officials' curiosity about Mordecai's defiance is itself a mystery. It seems unlikely that they would have continued to urge him "day after day" to honor Haman out of their genuine concern for his welfare. That they reported Mordecai to the king following his self-identification as a Jew implies, as Jobes suggests, "a lurking tension between Jews and Gentiles of the court."[8] The echo of Potiphar's wife's "day-by-day" sexual harassment of Joseph suggests that Mordecai's disobedience, like Joseph's and Vashti's, will have dire consequences (Gen 39:10–20; Esth 1:19, 21).

When the self-absorbed Haman becomes aware of Mordecai's defiance (3:5; 5:9), he is "filled with heat," "enraged" (NIV), an emotion the king also frequently exhibits (1:12; 2:1; 7:7, 10). Haman's fury is likely shame driven and inflated by his anti-Semitism. Instead of seeking revenge by blotting out one Jew, Haman decides to eradicate all the Jews in the empire. Mordecai's disobedience becomes an opportunity "to reach into the past and settle old scores," as Amalek now seems "to have the upper hand" (Esth 3:6).[9]

Parallels to Esther chapter one here are striking: both Xerxes and Haman

---

6. LXX Addition C 13.12–14 NRSV. See also: Esth. Rab. 7:6, which explains that Mordecai refused to pay homage because Haman had an idol embroidered on his clothes.

7. Goldingay, *Ezra, Nehemiah & Esther for Everyone*, 169.

8. Jobes, *Esther*, 119.

9. Firth, *The Message of Esther*, 63. Further evidence for anti-Jewish sentiment may also be present in the prophetic declaration of Haman's wife and advisors: "Since Mordecai, before whom

respond to personal challenges with excessive and escalating anger that punishes not only the individual offender but the whole group they represent—namely, all women and all Jews. Life is perilous under the leadership of such madmen. We are left to ponder where God is when his people are living under such threat.

An Evil Idea Becomes Law (Esther 3:7–15)

The enraged evil Haman moves into action and uses an ancient method of divination that involves the throwing of an inscribed cube, called the *pur* or the lot, to determine a divinely-sanctioned day for the proposed genocide (3:7). With the time determined for the massacre of the Jews, Haman moves quickly to gain the king's support. The selection of a date twelve months in the future gives both the Jews and their enemies time to prepare for the genocide. The date's association with Passover strongly hints that the seemingly hidden God of the Jews influenced this decision, and that the Jews will again have a reason for celebrating their rescue from death (Exod 12:1–28; Prov 16:33).

Haman's carefully-crafted speech plays to the king's extravagant need for control, wealth, and power (Esth 3:8–9). Haman contends that Xerxes should not tolerate an ethnic group who follows their own "laws" and keeps disobeying the king's laws. Haman's description of the Jews as scattered, separate, and following different laws suggests that many Jews had resisted assimilation into Persian culture and were living in obedience to Torah.[10] Haman's claim of ongoing disobedience is a gross exaggeration of the insubordination of Mordecai, however, whose allegiance to the king was proven when he exposed the assassination plot (2:22). Haman advises the king to issue a decree to destroy this unnamed people. He sweetens the proposal with an enormous bribe or *bakshish* consisting of the equivalent of two-thirds of Persia's annual gross national product.[11] Given the amount of money involved, Haman was likely not offering to supply all the funds, but rather was thinking that money gained from plundering the Jews would not only pay the men hired to kill the Jews but would also line the king's treasuries (3:13; 4:7).

In an act of great recklessness and misjudgment, the king of Persia entrusts

---

your downfall has started, is of Jewish origin, you cannot stand against him—you will surely come to ruin!" (6:13).

10. Waltke disagrees as he regards the Jews in the diaspora—including Esther and Mordecai—as "nominal covenant people,. . .physical descendants of Abraham [who keep] the outward signs of the covenant, but they do not keep its true intention from the heart." Waltke, *An Old Testament Theology*, 768.

11. Ten thousand talents of silver would weigh over 300 tons and Persia's annual gross national product under Xerxes's father was 14,560 thousand talents. Tomasino, "Esther," 489.

Haman, the Agagite, who is now specifically designated as "the enemy of the Jews," with his signet ring and the power to annihilate an entire people (3:10). This naming of Haman as "the enemy of the Jews" (also in 8:1; 9:10) and later "the enemy of all the Jews" (9:24) points to what many recognize as Haman's typical significance (see Live the Story, above). Haman the Agagite's association with Israel's ancestral enemy, together with Mordecai's association with his ancestor Saul, pushes us to read their conflict as much more than personal. Xerxes's hapless decision contrasts the pharaoh's choice of the wise and honorable Joseph who uses his signet ring to save lives (Gen 41:37–42; see also the stunning reversal in Esth 8:2, 8–15).

Xerxes's literal declaration, "the silver is given to you," may mean either, "Keep the money" (NIV), or its opposite, "dispense the money you get from plundering whatever way you want" (3:11). In favor of the second reading is Esther's later statement that her "people *have been sold* to be destroyed, killed and annihilated" (7:4; emphasis added).

Four detail-laden verses follow, describing how the royal secretaries speedily set in motion Persia's efficient system for disseminating the royal edict of death throughout the vast empire (3:12–15). In the middle of these verses, the Agagite's sordid edict is reproduced: "the order to destroy, kill and annihilate all the Jews—young and old, women and children—on a single day, the thirteenth day of the twelfth month, the month of Adar, and to plunder their goods" (3:13; 7:4). Haman's royally-sanctioned order would essentially reverse the ancient divine command to blot out the memory of Haman's ancestors (Exod 17:16b; Deut 25:19). Like the edict that was formulated by Memucan and agreed to by the angry, inebriated, and irresponsible Xerxes in Esther chapter 1, this edict was orchestrated by Haman, another self-serving official who effectively manipulates Xerxes into authorizing an edict that the king thinks serves his own interests.

The chapter closes as it began in Susa. The dark portraits of Xerxes and Haman continue as Xerxes, still unaware of the full significance of the day's decisions, shares drinks with the triumphant anti-Semite Haman (compare Joseph's brothers' celebratory meal in Gen 37:25). By contrast, both Jews and Gentiles in Susa are confounded or perplexed (a passive form of the verb *bwk*). Joel's use of the same verb to describe the herds of perplexed animals starving because of God's judgment against Judah illuminates the contrast between the morally-blind Haman and Xerxes and those living under their rule (Joel 1:18). This juxtaposition of people and animals communicates the sense of terror experienced by those living in this unstable and unpredictable regime. English commentator Sarah Trimmer (1741–1810) correctly assessed the threat posed by Persia's foolish and inattentive king:

Ahasuerus [Xerxes] was very unjust to consent that a whole people, who were under his protection, should be massacred without any inquiry into their fault, only because his favourite [sic] had said that they were enemies to his state. No wonder that the city of Shushan should be perplexed, for it must grieve every humane or loyal person to see the king [act] so absurd[ly], and the innocent condemned to destruction. Observe, from this chapter, how dangerous it is to listen to detractors, and that we ought never to credit evil reports till we have first inquired into the truth of them.[12]

LIVE the Story

Haman's Fake News

Sarah Trimmer's warning about the dangers of listening to fake news presented by those we trust is very timely. In our world of misinformation and disinformation, of fake news and fraudulent websites seeking political and/or financial gain, we need to check out all our sources and make sure we make our decisions based on true and reliable information. Trimmer's labelling of the king as "absurd" is also correct and timely, as many of us live in empires that are led by those whom we judge to be similarly absurd, misinformed, impulsive, and irresponsible. The Anglican Collect for the Second Sunday in Lent is a particularly appropriate prayer in this regard: "Almighty God, who seest that we have no power of ourselves to help ourselves: Keep us both outwardly in our bodies, and inwardly in our souls; that we may be defended from all adversities which may happen to the body, and from all evil thoughts which may assault and hurt the soul; through Jesus Christ our Lord. Amen."

When Madmen Rule: A Call to Action and Prayer

The vengeful and manipulative enemy of the Jews, Haman, takes advantage of his position and the king's ineptitude to orchestrate a genocide of his ancestral enemies. Readers have always regarded Haman as more than a historical figure; he "belongs to no one age or nation."[13] Ninth-century commentator Rabanus Maurus recognized Haman's archetypal significance and regarded him as a symbol of the arrogance of "the powerful of this world who take advantage of the benefits conceded to them by divine mercy."[14] He even reads

12. Sarah Trimmer, *A Help to the Unlearned in the Study of the Holy Scriptures: Being an Attempt to Explain the Bible in a Familiar Way* (London: T. Bensley, 1805), 263.

13. Arthur C. Lichtenberger, "Esther," *IB* 3:849, quoted in Carruthers, *Esther Through the Centuries*, 139.

14. Rabanus Maurus, "Explanation on the Book of Esther 6," quoted in Conti and Pilara, *1–2 Kings, 1–2 Chronicles, Ezra, Nehemiah, Esther*, 381–82.

Psalm 138:6 in reference to Haman: "For though the LORD is high, he regards the lowly, but the haughty he knows from afar" [ESV]. American Preacher Harriet Livermore, writing more than a millennium later, goes further and associates Haman with the evil one himself—he is as "an instrument of the foul serpent," an "artful, unhappy man! [whose] contemplated mischief shall reverberate upon [him], and [his] violent dealing bruise [his] malicious pate."[15]

Generations of readers have also associated Haman with a wide variety of evil figures. None fit better than Adolf Hitler who, together with the Nazi party, orchestrated the murder of nearly six million Jews who were similarly looked upon as strangers and a threat to the empire. This particular association with Hitler was recognized as early as 1935 by Wilhelmina Stitch who wrote: "here is a man called Hitler whose temperament seems much akin to the villain of this piece."[16] Hitler exploited both anti-Jewish readings of the book of Esther that were popular among Christians during this period, and the popularity of Esther's story among the Jews. He made reference to the book of Esther in a speech he gave January 30, 1944 in which he took on Haman's role as the vile indicter and enemy of the Jews. Specifically, Hitler portrays the Jews as "enemies of the state, destructive and dangerous, and appeals to self-defense in order to justify attack."[17] Hitler's genocidal tendencies further underscore his likeness to Haman. His actions contributed to the United Nations' formal acknowledgement of genocide as a crime during times of war and peace in 1948.[18]

The poisoned spirit, pride, and vindictiveness of these two Hamans and countless other maniacal villains throughout history call us to reflect on the utter darkness of human sin and our propensity to hatred, prejudice, and callous indifference. Such awareness brings us to our knees with thankfulness that Jesus paid the price for our sins, "the righteous for the unrighteous, to bring [us] to God" (1 Pet 3:18). It also pushes us to ponder the source of Haman's intense hatred of the Jews. Had he learned from his family to hate "the other," or from other anti-Semites in Persia? Nelson Mandela reminds us: "No one is born hating another person because of the color of his skin, or his background, or his religion. People must learn to hate, and if they can

---

15. Livermore, *Scriptural Evidence*, 52, 57.

16. Wilhelmina Stitch, *Women of the Bible* (London: Methuen & Co, 1935), 250, quoted in Carruthers, *Esther Through the Centuries*, 157.

17. Jo Carruthers, "Esther and Hitler: A Second Triumphant Purim" in *The Oxford Handbook of the Reception History of the Bible*, ed. Michael Lieb, Emma Mason, Jonathan Roberts, and Christopher Rowland (Oxford: Oxford University Press, 2011), 521.

18. For the full proceedings, see "Australia, Bulgaria, Cambodia, Ceylon, Czechoslovakia, etc.: Convention on the Prevention and Punishment of the Crime of Genocide. Adopted by the General Assembly of the United Nations on 9 December 1948." treaties.un.org/doc/publication/unts/volume%2078/volume-78-i-1021-english.pdf.

learn to hate, they can be taught to love, for love comes more naturally to the human heart than its opposite."[19] Since hatred is taught, we all need to teach others—children and adults—not to hate "the other," but rather to love. We need to point them to the good news of the gospel, which is the ultimate hope for and solution to the problem of hatred, prejudice, and other forms of human sin.

The genocidal edict the king authorizes confounds both Jews and Gentiles in Susa, and raises issues that resonate with so many in our world: the seeming triumph of evil, the hiddenness of God, and the often inexplicable hostility directed toward the people of God. When we read this chapter of Esther's story within the context of the larger story of God that features many other stories about God's people under threat, we are reminded that God's faithful often cry out to God when facing crises, asking: Where are you God? How long will this suffering go on? and Why is this happening? Like the prophet Habakkuk, we find encouragement to hold on and carry on by faith: "Though the fig tree does not bud and there are no grapes on the vines, though the olive crop fails and the fields produce no food, though there are no sheep in the pen and no cattle in the stalls, yet I will rejoice in the Lord, I will be joyful in God my Savior" (Hab 3:17–18). Faith, as defined by Benjamin Warfield, is "the distinctive feature of the righteous [person], . . . [it] is a profound and abiding disposition, an ingrained attitude of mind and heart toward God which affects and gives character to all the activities."[20]

We need to pray for believers living today in empires ruled by leaders like Haman and Xerxes and allied with "the spiritual forces of evil in the heavenly realms." We need to pray against such evil powers, "put[ting] on the full armor of God" as we prepare to "stand against the devil's schemes" (Eph 6:10–12). Together we must trust in God's sovereignty, believing that "neither death nor life, neither angels nor demons, neither the present nor the future, nor any powers, neither height nor depth, nor anything else in all creation, will be able to separate us from the love of God that is in Christ Jesus our Lord" (Rom 8:38–39).

As Christians, we are not only called to pray, wrestle, and live by faith, we are also called to act, as Mordecai and Esther did, when Haman-like perfidious leaders take advantage of their position and power to destroy others. Today we might see Haman in the extremists associated with groups such as ISIS and Boko Haram who delight to murder "a certain people," and we need to

19. Nelson Mandela, *Long Walk To Freedom: The Autobiography of Nelson Mandela* (Boston: Back Bay Books, 1995), 622.

20. Benjamin B. Warfield, "Faith," in *Dictionary of the Bible*, ed. James Hastings (Edinburgh: T&T Clark, 1936), 827.

stand up to such Hamans. Gerald McDermott writes, "God is calling men and women in this crazy political season to speak up and not be passive. [God] might seem hidden while ISIS and Boko Haram rampage, but he is calling his people, in ways that are often invisible to outsiders, to act. And yes, he might be calling some to use force to stop radical evil."[21] Others agree that genocide is an evil that continues in our world and must be stopped, but stand against the use of force to stop radical evil and look for other ways to eradicate evil. Whatever our position on violence and war, we need to listen to McDermott's concerns and respond. Doing nothing is not an option. The failure of Christians to take a stand against Hitler has cast a long shadow over the Christian Church.

The dire consequences of Mordecai's actions remind God's people living in unstable, post-Christian or anti-Christian empires today to carefully weigh the costs of challenging individuals and government policies directly. At the same time, as the book of Esther unfolds, more indirect and even subversive approaches emerge to challenge individuals and empires and influence the world in the direction of God's shalom and kingdom purposes (see ch. 14: Esther 10:1–3). Indeed, Esther and Mordecai show how God's people can critically engage an ambivalent or hostile empire for the good of God's people.[22]

---

21. Gerald McDermott, "Reading Esther in the Shadow of ISIS: A Jewish philosopher's perspective on how God delivers his people from radical evil," review of *God and Politics in Esther*, Yoram Hazony, *Christianity Today*, 7 April 2016, www.christianitytoday.com/ct/2016/april-web-only/reading-esther-in-shadow-of-isis.html.

22. Whether Esther compromised too much when she asked for a further day of killing (Esth 9:13) and whether Mordecai went too far in initiating or agreeing to Xerxes's taxation plan (10:1) are questions that are raised by the final chapters of the book of Esther.

CHAPTER 8

Esther 4:1–17

LISTEN to the Story

1When Mordecai learned of all that had been done, he tore his clothes, put on sackcloth and ashes, and went out into the city, wailing loudly and bitterly. 2But he went only as far as the king's gate, because no one clothed in sackcloth was allowed to enter it. 3In every province to which the edict and order of the king came, there was great mourning among the Jews, with fasting, weeping and wailing. Many lay in sackcloth and ashes.

4When Esther's eunuchs and female attendants came and told her about Mordecai, she was in great distress. She sent clothes for him to put on instead of his sackcloth, but he would not accept them. 5Then Esther summoned Hathak, one of the king's eunuchs assigned to attend her, and ordered him to find out what was troubling Mordecai and why.

6So Hathak went out to Mordecai in the open square of the city in front of the king's gate. 7Mordecai told him everything that had happened to him, including the exact amount of money Haman had promised to pay into the royal treasury for the destruction of the Jews. 8He also gave him a copy of the text of the edict for their annihilation, which had been published in Susa, to show to Esther and explain it to her, and he told him to instruct her to go into the king's presence to beg for mercy and plead with him for her people.

9Hathak went back and reported to Esther what Mordecai had said. 10Then she instructed him to say to Mordecai, 11"All the king's officials and the people of the royal provinces know that for any man or woman who approaches the king in the inner court without being summoned the king has but one law: that they be put to death unless the king extends the gold scepter to them and spares their lives. But thirty days have passed since I was called to go to the king."

12When Esther's words were reported to Mordecai, 13he sent back this answer: "Do not think that because you are in the king's house you alone of all the Jews will escape. 14For if you remain silent at this time, relief and deliverance for the Jews will arise from another place, but you and your father's family will perish. And who knows but that you have come to your royal position for such a time as this?"

15 Then Esther sent this reply to Mordecai: 16 "Go, gather together all the Jews who are in Susa, and fast for me. Do not eat or drink for three days, night or day. I and my attendants will fast as you do. When this is done, I will go to the king, even though it is against the law. And if I perish, I perish."

17 So Mordecai went away and carried out all of Esther's instructions.

Listen to the Text in the Story: Biblical Texts: Genesis 37:34; 2 Chronicles 20:1–4; Ezra 8:21, 23; Nehemiah 2:2; Joel 2:12–15; Jonah 3:5–8; Ancient Near Eastern Texts: Herodotus, *Histories* 1.99.1; 1.118.1; 3.68–69; 3.84; 3.119.3–4.

Reading this chapter alongside other ancient texts about mourning rites, public protests, access to royalty, and vocational callings deepens our understanding of this game-changing episode.

Rituals of Mourning, Fasting, and Repentance

Israel shared with her neighbors grief and mourning rituals that expressed pain and anguish and in some cases, even caused physical pain. These rituals included tearing clothes, wearing coarse sackcloth woven from goat or camel hair next to the skin, rubbing ashes into the skin, and sleeping on a bed of ashes. These symbolic rituals were often accompanied by tears, wailing, lamenting, and prayers for help and forgiveness. Jacob's acts of tearing his clothes and putting sackcloth on his loins as he mourned the loss of his favorite son (Gen 37:34) were similar to those of the king of Nineveh who commanded people and animals to fast and wear sackcloth, and who instructed citizens to call earnestly on God and repent of their evil and violent ways (Jonah 3:5–8). Similarly, God's people in Israel fasted and prayed in times of personal or national crisis in hope that God would intervene and reverse their circumstances (2 Chr 20:1–4; Ezra 8:21, 23). These texts, together with such related texts as Joel 2:12–15, which calls God's people to "return to me with all your heart, with fasting and weeping and mourning," suggest that the Jews facing genocide would have been calling out to God for help in their despair. (See Explain the Story, below and the discussion of complaint and trauma in Ruth 1:1–22: Listen to the Story and Live the Story.)

Public Protests

Stories of citizens publicly demonstrating to get the attention of the king abound in ancient literature. They suggest that Mordecai's public display of grief was meant to attract the attention of Esther as well as other Persians. Herodotus writes about a woman whose relentless weeping and lamenting at the palace gates was communicated to King Darius, who acted on her behalf:

> Then Intaphrenes' wife began coming to the palace gates, weeping and lamenting; and by continuing to do this same thing she persuaded Darius to pity her; and he sent a messenger to tell her, "Woman, King Darius will allow one of your imprisoned relatives to survive, whomever you prefer of them all." After considering she answered, "If indeed the king gives me the life of one, I chose from them all my brother."[1]

The law that forbade mourners wearing sackcloth from entering the king's gate, mentioned in Esther 4:2, is not attested elsewhere. But intolerance of public displays of emotion and sorrow by troubled or uncooperative citizens fits with what we know about Xerxes's need to be surrounded by order, beauty, and luxury (see Haman's arguments for killing the Jews in Esth 3:8). Nehemiah's fear that King Artaxerxes would be disturbed by expressions of sadness over the plight of the Jews suggests that Xerxes was not the only king to be protected from the pain of others (Neh 2:2).

Access to the King

Limiting direct access to royals was another way of restricting their exposure to problems and danger. Herodotus recounts a number of stories that suggest that access to the king was severely restricted. Indeed, he claims that the Median king, Deioces, "was first to establish the rule that no one should come into the presence of the king, but everything should be done by means of messengers."[2] The Persians also limited direct access to the king to members of seven noble families[3] and individuals whose requests were screened ahead of time by an official.[4] Even then those with access to the king were denied such when the king was engaging in sexual intercourse: "With regard to all of them they decreed that any one of the seven should, if he wished, enter the king's palace unannounced, except when the king was sleeping with a woman."[5]

1. Herodotus, *Hist.* 3.119.3–4.
2. Ibid., 1.99.1.
3. Ibid., 3.72.
4. Ibid., 3.77.
5. Ibid., 3.84.2.

Even royal wives like Esther had restricted access to their husbands and the other wives and concubines. Herodotus tells a story of a certain well-born Otanes whose daughter Phaedyme, like Esther, had been taken as a royal wife. Otanes asked her to put her life on the line for the greater good to find out if her husband was an imposter. Her responses show striking parallels to Esther's and underscore again the isolation of royal women:

> Otanes sent to this daughter, asking at what man's side she lay. . . . She sent back a message that she did not know. . . . Otanes sent a second message, . . . "find out from Atossa who it is that she and you are living with; for surely she knows her own brother." To this his daughter replied: "I cannot communicate with Atossa, nor can I see any other of the women of the household; for no sooner had this man, whoever he is, made himself king, than he sent us to live apart, each in her own appointed place." . . . [H]e sent her this third message: "Daughter, your noble birth obliges you to run any risk that your father commands you to face. . . . Now, then, when he lies with you and you see that he is sleeping, feel his ears." . . . Phaedyme answered by messenger that she would run a very great risk by so doing; for if it should turn out that he had no ears, and she were caught feeling for them, he would surely kill her; nevertheless she would do it. So she promised to do this for her father; . . . she came to his bed and felt for the Magus' ears while he slumbered deeply; and having with no great difficulty assured herself that he had no ears, she sent and told this to her father as soon as it was morning.[6]

Call Narratives

Stories of formal and informal calls abound in Scripture. Using Gideon's call as his model, Norman Habel identified six elements shared by the formal call narratives: the divine confrontation, the introductory word, the commission, the objection, the reassurance, and the sign.[7] The calls of such renowned figures as Moses, Jeremiah, and Isaiah share a number of these elements. God called others—Elisha, Deborah, Jael, and many prophets—in less direct and predictable ways. Esther's call to deliver God's people is similar to Moses's call. Like Moses, she sets out a number of objections, but it is Mordecai, not God, who introduces and delivers her commission. Esther receives no signs or assurances. She has to draw on inner resources and experience and presumably, she also called upon God for help.

---

6. Ibid., 3.68–69.

7. Norman Habel, "The Form and Significance of the Call Narratives," *ZAW* 77.3 (1965): 297–323.

EXPLAIN the Story

The Fallout (Esther 4:1–3)

In response to the royal decree to kill the Jews, Mordecai tears his garments, dons sackcloth and ashes, and wails loudly and bitterly throughout the city. He stops at the king's gate as public expressions of grief and protest are unwelcome in the palace complex (4:1–2; see Listen to the Story, above). As the catastrophic news of the edict spreads, Jews throughout the empire similarly express their great sorrow with fasting and weeping as they lay in sackcloth and ashes (4:3). Missing from all the reports of their reactions to the news of genocide are explicit references to God and prayer. While some conclude that the Persian Jews were ethnic or secular Jews,[8] others argue that God's hiddenness in the story does not mean God's absence. On the contrary, the clues of God's presence are found in the story when it is read in its ancient context.

Many have wondered what was behind Mordecai's ritualized and yet unusually public response to the crisis that he himself had inaugurated. The unfolding story strongly supports the idea that Mordecai staged his public response to garner the support of Esther and the Persians who were already confused by the genocidal edict (3:15). Mordecai's staged public actions assume a theology of human-divine cooperation that presupposes that humans facing dire straits not only need to participate in recognized rituals of mourning, protest, and prayer, but also to initiate game plans to save themselves—plans that are later recognized as God's plan. Such a theology encourages us to recognize God's hand behind the surprises, coincidences, and reversals that are part of God's larger plan to save the Jews.

At the same time, whispers of Joel 2:12–16, in which the prophet calls God's people to "return . . . with fasting and weeping and mourning," invite us to interpret Mordecai's actions as much more than a calculated stratagem or empty ritual (4:1). Rather, his actions, and those of the Jews throughout the empire, express their hope that God will hear and answer their prayers for deliverance. Indeed, reading the ritualized responses of the Jews in the context of the ancient world, and especially of Scripture, presses us to include God in this scene of suffering, distress, and hope. Mordecai's use of the prophet's hopeful expression "who knows?" in his challenge to Esther to risk her life for the sake of her people later in the chapter may also be an expression of Mordecai's expectation that God might intervene to bring deliverance and life (Joel 2:14; Esth 4:14).

---

8. See Ronald W. Pierce, "The Politics of Esther and Mordecai: Courage or Compromise?" *BBR* 2 (1992): 88–89.

Esther's subsequent call for all the Jews in Susa to fast on her behalf (4:16) may also be heard as a call to prayer and repentance, as one further echo of the final command of Joel's oracle suggests: "Blow the trumpet in Zion, declare a holy fast. . . . Gather the people" (Joel 2:15–16).[9] The rituals surrounding death in this chapter contrast with the earlier celebrations of life through banqueting and feasting, and anticipate the great reversal of death to life that Purim celebrates (see ch. 13: Esther 9:1–32).

"For Such a Time as This": Esther Responds to Her Call (Esther 4:4–17)

Esther, who knows nothing about the genocide, responds to the news about Mordecai with "great distress" (4:4). The intense form of the verb *hyl* ("to writhe or tremble") that characterizes Esther's emotional state also describes the extreme distress that the wicked deserve (Job 15:20), and that Jeremiah's bones experience ("trembling") when his heart is being broken in response to the Lord's words about false prophets (Jer 23:9). Confused by Mordecai's mourning attire and concerned that his public display might expose their relationship and her hidden identity as a Jew, Esther sends Mordecai non-mourning clothes that he can wear to gain access to the king's gate so they can communicate directly. Intrigued by Esther's lack of knowledge of the crisis, Iain Duguid, who is certainly not a fan of Esther's life choices, fantasizes: "Perhaps she didn't have time between her manicures, pedicures, and other beauty treatments to keep up with the local coffee klatch about the fortunes of her people."[10] Surely the narrator's point, rather, is that Esther knows nothing of the impending disaster because of her isolation from family and community (see Listen to the Story, above).

Because Mordecai refused the clothing, Esther sends her most trusted eunuch to gather information so that she might finally "know" what Mordecai "knows" (NIV: "learned," v. 1) and what he needs Esther to "know" (NIV: "find out," v. 5) if his plan is to move forward. Mordecai and Hathak meet in the busy open square (v. 6), where Mordecai will later be honored and will wear royal robes in place of his sackcloth and ashes (6:9, 11). In contrast to the traitorous eunuchs, Bigthana and Teresh (2:21), Hathak effectively mediates communication between Mordecai and Esther. As the negotiations intensify, Hathak and the other messengers who made sure ("Esther's words were reported to Mordecai," 4:12) fade into the background as Esther's and Mordecai's words are subsequently delivered with direct speech.

Mordecai's use of a perfective form of the verb to recount "everything that

9. Jobes, *Esther*, 135–37.
10. Duguid, *Esther and Ruth*, 47.

had happened to him" (v. 7) is judged by some to be self-centered.[11] Mordecai's casting of himself as a victim rather than the cause of the crisis suggests that he does not feel responsible for what has happened. Rather he identifies with his people: "He is their representative, even their personification, and what happens to them happens to him for ill, as here, or for good, as at the end of the tale."[12]

The ever well-informed Mordecai, who knew about the attempt to assassinate Xerxes (2:22) and "all that had been done" regarding the planned genocide (4:1), now provides Esther with precise information about the exorbitant amount of money that Haman was willing to pay to kill the Jews (4:7b). As Jon Levenson suggests, as "a master tactician," Mordecai knows that this information will give Esther "a chilling sense of the degree of Haman's hatred" and push her into action.[13] To underscore the severity of the crisis, Mordecai also provides Esther with written proof of the threat of destruction (v. 8).

Finally, in this book that does not mention God explicitly, it is her uncle Mordecai who presents Esther with her "call" to action. Treating Esther more like a daughter than a queen, Mordecai "instructs" NIV (lit., "commands") her to use her position, power, and influence over Xerxes to convince the king to act on behalf of her people (v. 8). Previously, Mordecai had instructed Esther to hide her Jewish identity; now, as Firth suggests, "in a conflict between the state and her faith and people, identifying with her faith and people must take priority."[14]

Unlike Moses's objections to God's call that were based on his deep sense of inadequacy (Exod 3:11–4:13), Esther's protests are reasoned (4:11). She knows Persian law and the impulsive character of her husband, who had deposed her predecessor (1:16–21) and had recently expressed little interest in her (see Listen to the Story, above). Reacting to Esther's initial reticence, one of Esther's many critics describes her as "a poor blind queen" living in "her little self-centered world" who needs Mordecai to shame her out of her "despicable selfishness."[15] Rather, Esther's hesitation seems quite reasonable—indeed, even wise—given the information she (and we as readers) have about Xerxes and his rule. Esther's initial comeback and the decision she later makes based on further information mark a transition in her character: she is no longer a compliant child; she is an adult capable of making independent, reasoned, and courageous judgments.

11. Carol M. Bechtel, *Esther*, INT (Louisville: John Knox, 2002), 46.

12. Levenson, *Esther*, 79.

13. Ibid.

14. Firth, *The Message of Esther*, 74.

15. W. G. Elmslie, "The Story of Esther" in *Professor W. G. Elmslie, D.D.: Memoir and Sermons*, ed. W. Robertson Nicoll and A. N. MacNicoll (London: Hodder & Stoughton, 1890), 201.

Esther's call is different from the calls of Moses, Jeremiah, and others who were given divine assurance after they protested their calls (Exod 3:12–4:17; Jer 1:7–19). Esther receives neither divine nor human assurance, nor a sign; instead, Mordecai informs her that living in the palace will not protect her from the edict to kill the Jews (Esth 4:13). He threatens that if she fails to act (lit., "is completely silent"), the Jews will find "relief and deliverance" from another place and she and her "father's family" will perish (v. 14).

The theologically pregnant terms "relief" and "deliverance" provide further evidence that we may read Esther's call to save the Jews alongside others' calls: the formal calls of such great leaders and prophets as Moses and Jeremiah, on the one hand, and the informal calls of women like Moses's mother, Miriam, and the Hebrew midwives, who acted with great courage to rescue God's people from destruction and death, on the other (Exod 1:15–2:10). The foreboding idea that Esther will perish along with other Jews if she refuses to accept the call to broker a rescue plan raises the question of who might call her out as a Jew. Would Mordecai or her fellow Jews in Susa, whom Josephus imagines "now despised" her, reveal her identity?[16]

The meaning of Mordecai's striking claim that help will arise "from another place" (4:14) has been debated at length. Some think that Mordecai is threatening that another well-connected Nehemiah-type Jew with royal connections—perhaps even Mordecai himself—would save the Jews if Esther refuses her call. Others suggest Mordecai is using "place" as a covert reference to God, whom he believes will safeguard God's chosen people. This second reading is found in a number of early texts and commentaries that read the story of Esther in the context of the story of God and specifically reference God as the source of relief and deliverance (A-text of Esther 4:5, 9, both Aramaic Targums, and Josephus).[17]

The climax of Mordecai's final appeal to Esther is, for many, the high point of the book: "And who knows but that you have come to your royal position for such a time as this?" (4:14c). The familiar expression, "who knows," is not an expression of skepticism or fatalism, but rather, as Richard Bauckham suggests, "a hopeful working hypothesis" used in life and death situations when the outcome is unclear.[18] If the whispers of Joel 2:12–16 are heard in this context, as suggested above, they intimate that God is very present in this crisis. As Mordecai reminds Esther, it is no accident that she is who she

16. Josephus, *Ant.*, 11.221. Ronald Pierce understands this text to mean that Mordecai himself will step up to the plate to rescue the Jews and even kill Esther if she deserts her people at this critical time. Pierce, "The Politics of Esther and Mordecai," 87.

17. Jobes, *Esther*, 133–34.

18. Bauckham, *The Bible in Politics*, 125.

is and where she is at this time in her life. Samuel Wells expands Mordecai's rhetorical question to include a list of the "givens" in Esther's life that have prepared her to negotiate deliverance for the Jews: "Take your femininity, your long training in the harem, your vulnerability, your membership of the Jewish people—givens that may seem challenging or unjust—and treat them as gifts by incorporating them into the larger story of saving your people. Each of these apparent givens does indeed become a gift in the course of Esther's sequence of banquets for and petitions to the king."[19]

Mordecai's powerful arguments (4:13–14) convince Esther to embrace her call to go to the king, as Moses went before Pharaoh (Exod 7:1–2), and ask him to deliver her people. Unlike Vashti, who risked all by refusing to appear before the king, Esther will risk all for daring to appear before Xerxes (1:12; 4:11). Once she decides to risk her life to lead the mission to save the Jews, Esther calls on others to support her. She commands Mordecai to gather all the Jews in Susa to join her and her maids in a three-day fast on her behalf, as she prepares to break the law by approaching the king unbidden (v. 15).

Reading this text in the context of Scripture as a whole, we can assume that Esther was praying and asking others to pray with her for God's help during those days. Alexandrian bishop Athanasius (ca. 296–373) interpreted the importance of Esther's fast in terms of the outcome of the story when he wrote: "When the whole nation of Israel was about to perish, blessed Esther defeated the tyrant's anger simply by fasting and praying to God. By faith she changed the ruin of her people into safety."[20]

Esther's final words, "If I perish, I perish," echo the words of her forefather Jacob who pragmatically declared, "As for me, if I am bereaved, I am bereaved," after praying that God would grant his sons mercy before Joseph so that they would all return from Egypt (Gen 43:14). Esther now embraces a call that is fraught with danger, a call that will enable her to fully discover herself and embrace her full identity as both Jew and Persian queen. In her defiance of the king's law, Esther stands with both Vashti and Mordecai in their disobedience to the king's orders and rises above the intent of the royal edict that mandates that husbands rule their households (1:20–22).

Chapter 4 ends where it began, with the focus on Mordecai (4:17). But things have changed. No longer in charge of the rescue plan, Mordecai leaves the open square to carry out the orders of the increasingly confident Queen Esther, as he fully expects her to be able to orchestrate his/God's plan.

---

19. Wells, "Esther," 56.

20. Athanasius, *Ep. Fest.*, 4, quoted in Conti and Pilara, *1–2 Kings, 1–2 Chronicles, Ezra, Nehemiah, Esther*, 397.

LIVE the Story

When Life Happens . . . Embracing Spiritual Practices and Action

In the face of crises, Christians past and present have found many of the practices used by the Jews in Persia, who were facing extreme trauma and distress, to be effective means of expressing fear, sadness, and anger and asking for mercy and deliverance. Whether we are open to consider the possibility of gathering a community together to fast and to express our grief, sadness, and repentance is influenced in part by cultural and denominational preferences. Unlike many of the upbeat American cartoon versions of the story of Esther that skip over the ritualized actions that are portrayed in chapter 4, a children's musical production of the book of Esther in Hong Kong includes a very moving scene depicting repentant Jews in torn clothes and ashes, wailing and crying out to God for help.[21] The writers of the script clearly regard the practices of the Jews in Persia as models for children and adults today. Esther's call to the community to fast on her behalf encourages us to embrace, again or for the first time, self-denying spiritual practices. Our brothers and sisters who face persecution every day can teach us much about moving out of routinized and cerebral expressions of faith to embrace wholehearted Christian living that encompasses all of life—the good, the bad, and the ugly.

In addition to embracing traditional spiritual practices that enable those in crisis to express their emotions and recognize their reliance on God's help, the Persian Jews become agents of change. Mordecai moves quickly to bring Esther on board with his plan for her to negotiate the deliverance of the Jews. His actions show that he believes that calamity calls "for faithful (but not foolhardy) action to discover where God will act. It is taking the risk of faith in order to summon others to do the same."[22] This theology of human-divine cooperation operates throughout Esther. It encourages us to recognize the hand of God behind the surprises, coincidences, and reversals in this story and in our own lives.

Mordecai's conviction that Esther use her position and power "for such a time as this" has inspired others to recognize the hand of God bringing together the right persons, at the right time, for the right reasons. When British parliamentarian William Wilberforce was thinking about leaving politics, his friend, converted slave trader John Newton, invoked Esther's story to challenge Wilberforce's reasoning: "God has raised you up for the good of

---

21. "Hadassah." Children's Grand Musical Theater, 611 Bread of Life Christian Church, Hong Kong, 2015.

22. Firth, *The Message of Esther*, 73.

the church and the good of the nation, maintain your friendship with Pitt, continue in Parliament, who knows that but for such a time as this God has brought you into public life and has a purpose for you." Wilberforce listened to Newton's counsel and continued to use his position and power for the next forty-eight years, as he and other Christians worked tirelessly to abolish the British slave trade, free all slaves in British territories, and initiate reforms in education, healthcare, childcare, and prisons.[23]

"For Such a Time as This": Decision Making, Call, and Vocation

Esther's decision to take up the call to save the Jews also raises the larger question of how we make life choices. This question has intrigued thinkers throughout history and has spawned courses such as "How You Decide: The Science of Human Decision Making."[24] The science of how Esther makes her decision to accept her call is unveiled as the narrator walks us through Esther's deliberation process. Esther's reasoned response and ultimate obedience to her call to undertake a perilous mission of deliverance demonstrates her wisdom and courage. It challenges the views of those who stress Esther's self-centeredness, lack of courage, and hesitancy to perform what Clement of Rome (fl. ca. 92–101) calls Esther's "manly deeds." Clement cites Esther and Judith as examples of "women [who] being strengthened through the grace of God have performed many manly deeds" (1 Clem 55:3). Specifically, he underscores Esther's courage and faith as she "expose[d] herself, that she might deliver the twelve tribes of Israel, when they were on the point to perish. For through her fasting and her humiliation she entreated the all-seeing Master, the God of the ages; and He, seeing the humility of her soul, delivered the people for whose sake she encountered the peril" (1 Clem 55:5–6).[25]

Esther's discernment process should also be regarded as exemplary. According to Oliver O'Donovan, "when we look to find a 'way' or a 'path' . . . we set off into the future with a purpose and a degree of anticipation, but though we may, and must, form anticipation and purposes, we know that these are projections only and that we have no clear sight of the actual future where our action will fetch up a *fait accompli*."[26] However, repeatedly in the story of God, we are shown that in order to discern whether we have come

---

23. Steve Monsma, *Healing for A Broken World: Christian Perspectives on Public Policy* (Wheaton, IL: Crossway, 2008), 13–14.

24. Professor Ryan Hamilton from Emory University teaches this course for The Teaching Company's Great Courses series, 2016.

25. *First Epistle of Clement to the Corinthians*, trans. J. B. Lightfoot, *The Apostolic Fathers, First Part, Volume II* (London: MacMillan, 1890), 299–300.

26. Oliver O'Donovan, *Finding and Seeking: Ethics as Theology Volume 2* (Grand Rapids: Eerdmans, 2014), 218.

to a particular place, position, or vocation "for such a time as this," prayer is essential: "Lead me, Lord in your righteousness because of my enemies—make your way straight before me" (Ps 5:8).[27] Esther's vocational call was presented by Mordecai, as most of our calls to service are; like Esther, we must ask questions and listen to those who play a role similar to Mordecai's in our own lives. Although Esther embraced her own call before asking others to join her in a prolonged fast, part of our discernment process should involve the disciplines of prayer, fasting, and meditation on Scripture as we ask the Lord to make his way straight before us.

Providence

In her poem "Esther," nineteenth-century American poet Frances M. Caulkins uses Esther's story to cast light on the mysteries of God's providence:

> Imperial Jewess, thy sweet story sheds
> A light on heaven's deep ways;
> Shows Providence inweaving golden threads
> Amid life's dubious maze.
> From varying shades of good and ill
> One beauteous whole is wrought,
> While all man's erring paths fulfil
> Eternal Wisdom's thought.[28]

Esther's willingness to embrace her full identity as the Jewish wife of the capricious Persian King Xerxes, and her response to the call to risk her life in what seemed to be a divinely-sanctioned plan for delivering the Jews, has inspired many to recognize the hand of God in even the messiest parts of their lives. Jewish convert Edith Stein, who was put to death at Auschwitz, identified herself closely with Esther. Like Esther, Stein embraced the idea of God's superintending providence over her life:

> Things were in God's plan which I had not planned at all. I am coming to the living faith and conviction that—from God's point of view—there is no chance and that the whole of my life, down to every detail, has been mapped out in God's divine providence and makes complete and perfect sense in God's all-seeing eyes.[29]

---

27. Ibid, 221–22.

28. Frances M. Caulkins, "Esther," *Eve and her Daughters of Holy Writ, Or, Women of the Bible* (New York: American Tract Society, n.d.), 121.

29. Julie Onderko, *Discover Your Next Mission from God; Saints Who Found God's Will—and How You Can Too* (Manchester, NH: Sophia Institute Press, 2015), 83.

Esther's willingness to embrace her call gives witness to her vulnerability, uncertainty, and courage to risk all as God's agent of deliverance for her people. "Courage," as researcher Brené Brown explains, "starts with showing up and letting ourselves be seen."[30]

In her willingness to face death, Esther can be seen as a type of Christ, who "when the days drew near for him to be taken up, he set his face to go to Jerusalem" (Luke 9:51 ESV). Also like Jesus, who fully identifies with his people as he "became flesh and made his dwelling among us" (John 1:14), Esther uses her position and fully embraces her Jewishness to carry out her salvific mission.

Read Globally

Like the Jews in Persia, many Christians endure persecution under oppressive regimes that are antagonistic to faith. Reading Esther's story in the light of the heinous atrocities of ISIS and Boko Haram, Gerald McDermott asks the disturbing question: "What if God calls and too few listen, so that a Christian genocide ensues?"[31] McDermott challenges us, as Mordecai challenged Esther, to consider using our positions and power "for such a time as this." Whether or not we agree with the idea of using force to stop radical evil, the call to strategize, speak up, and not be passive is one that God extends to all of us. Mordecai listened very well and knew how to use his connections to save the life of the king and, later, to save the Jews from extinction—and so should we.

Many easily-accessed media resources can unite us with our persecuted brothers and sisters so that we can pray and act. The Voice of the Martyrs blog invites us to hear the stories of the persecution and martyrdom of our brothers and sisters and to respond.[32] By experiencing the dramatic stories of those who have given up everything to proclaim that they are followers of Christ, we become part of the ministry described in Hebrews 13:3—"Continue to remember those in prison as if you were together with them in prison, and those who are mistreated as if you yourselves were suffering."

30. Brené C. Brown, *Daring Greatly: How the Courage to Be Vulnerable Transforms the Way We Live, Love, Parent, and Lead* (New York: Gotham Books, 2012), 30.

31. McDermott, "Reading Esther in the Shadow of ISIS."

32. See the "Persecution Blog" at www.persecutionblog.com.

CHAPTER 9

Esther 5:1–14

LISTEN to the Story

[1]On the third day Esther put on her royal robes and stood in the inner court of the palace, in front of the king's hall. The king was sitting on his royal throne in the hall, facing the entrance. [2]When he saw Queen Esther standing in the court, he was pleased with her and held out to her the gold scepter that was in his hand. So Esther approached and touched the tip of the scepter.

[3]Then the king asked, "What is it, Queen Esther? What is your request? Even up to half the kingdom, it will be given you."

[4]"If it pleases the king," replied Esther, "let the king, together with Haman, come today to a banquet I have prepared for him."

[5]"Bring Haman at once," the king said, "so that we may do what Esther asks."

So the king and Haman went to the banquet Esther had prepared. [6]As they were drinking wine, the king again asked Esther, "Now what is your petition? It will be given you. And what is your request? Even up to half the kingdom, it will be granted."

[7]Esther replied, "My petition and my request is this: [8]If the king regards me with favor and if it pleases the king to grant my petition and fulfill my request, let the king and Haman come tomorrow to the banquet I will prepare for them. Then I will answer the king's question."

[9]Haman went out that day happy and in high spirits. But when he saw Mordecai at the king's gate and observed that he neither rose nor showed fear in his presence, he was filled with rage against Mordecai. [10]Nevertheless, Haman restrained himself and went home.

Calling together his friends and Zeresh, his wife, [11]Haman boasted to them about his vast wealth, his many sons, and all the ways the king had honored him and how he had elevated him above the other nobles and officials. [12]"And that's not all," Haman added. "I'm the only person Queen Esther invited to accompany the king to the banquet she gave. And she has invited me along with the king tomorrow. [13]But all this gives me no satisfaction as long as I see that Jew Mordecai sitting at the king's gate."

[14]His wife Zeresh and all his friends said to him, "Have a pole set up, reaching to a height of fifty cubits, and ask the king in the morning to have Mordecai impaled on it. Then go with the king to the banquet and enjoy yourself." This suggestion delighted Haman, and he had the pole set up.

Listen to the Text in the Story: Biblical Texts: Genesis 22:4–19; 31:22–33; Ruth 4:15; 1 Samuel 1:8; Proverbs 11:2; 16:5, 18; Hosea 6:2; Jonah 1:17; 2:10; Matthew 12:40; Mark 6:23; 1 Corinthians 15:4; Ancient Near Eastern Texts: Herodotus, *Histories*, 1.136; 5.24.4; 9.109–113; "The Descent of Ishtar."

The Resplendent World of Symbols: More than the Literal Sense

This chapter brings us again into the symbolic world of Xerxes's court; it moves us out to the gate where actions symbolize attitudes and spawn emotions; and finally, it takes us into Haman's home where the symbolic meanings of wealth, sons, and promotion are discounted and a pole symbolizing death and revenge is embraced.

The Third Day

Esther's decision to make her perilous approach to the king on the third day sets up resonances with other biblical stories involving mortal danger and deliverance on the third day. It was on the third day when Abraham offered up Isaac as a sacrifice, but was stopped by an angel (Gen 22:4–19). Three days after Jacob had fled from Laban, Laban set out to do him harm but was stopped by a divine word in a dream (Gen 31:22–32). After three days and nights in the belly of a fish, Jonah was delivered (Jonah 1:17; 2:10). Hosea's promise of restoration on the third day "that we may live in his presence" anticipates Jesus' resurrection on the third day (Hos 6:2; Matt 12:40; 1 Cor 15:4) and whispers a positive outcome to Esther's approach on the third day.[1]

Royal Clothing and Accessories

The mention of clothing and accessories worn by humans and animals in ancient texts often carries meaning that goes beyond simple description. As Ishtar, the Mesopotamian goddess of sex, procreation, war, and power,

1. Karen Jobes also discusses the significance of the third day in Jewish Midrash. Jobes, *Esther*, 146.

descends into the underworld, she is stripped of her clothing and accessories and loses her powers, suggesting that her clothing is symbolic:

> After Ishtar went down to the netherworld
> The oxen would not mount the cow, the donkey would not
> impregnate the she ass
> The young man laid in his chamber
> The young woman laid on her side.
> ("The Descent of Ishtar," lines 76–80)[2]

Unlike the naked Ishtar, Esther is royally attired as she enters into "battle" to deliver the Jews. Her royal apparel is not described, but we can assume it was an absolutely breathtaking version of the very long, colorful, and richly-adorned full and broad-sleeved belted dresses that Persian noble women wore.[3]

The Number of Sons

Ancient societies placed a very high value on sons—the more the better! The women in Bethlehem challenged the longstanding view that sons were more important than daughters when they declared that Ruth was more valuable to Naomi than seven sons (Ruth 4:15; see Ruth 4:1–22: Listen to the Story). Haman was very proud of his ten sons. According to Herodotus, the king of Persia sent yearly gifts to the man with the most sons:

> After valor in battle it is accounted noble to father the greatest number of sons: the king sends gifts yearly to him who gets most. Strength, they believe, is in numbers.[4]

The Pole

While the suggestion that Mordecai be impaled on a pole (Esth 5:14) fits with Persian practices of execution and post-death humiliation, the pole's proposed height of fifty cubits (22.86 meters or 75 feet) seems exaggerated in light of what we know about the relative heights of ancient Persian structures. The 36 colossal columns which supported the roof of the great audience hall at Susa, for example, were 45.9 cubits high (21 meters or 68.9 feet).[5] The idea of a

2. As cited in Shawn W. Flynn, "The Function of Divine Clothing in the Israelite Religion and Mesopotamia," a paper given in the Hebrew Bible Research Group on Clothing 2014–2016, Society of Biblical Literature Pacific Northwest Regional Meeting, University of Calgary, May 9, 2014.

3. Maria Brosius, *Women in Ancient Persia, 559–331 BC* (Oxford: Clarendon Press, 1996), 85–6; see also Carl Köhler, *A History of Costume*, ed. Emma von Sichart, trans. Alexander K. Dallas (New York: Dover, 1963).

4. Herodotus, *Hist.*, 1.136.1.

5. For a picture of the columns and a discussion of the architecture at Susa, see Catherine Giraudon, "Capital of a column from the audience hall of the palace of Darius I," *Louvre Curatorial Departments*, www.louvre.fr/en/oeuvre-notices/capital-column-audience-hall-palace-darius-i.

pole so tall that all Susa would see the impaled body of Mordecai was surely what appealed to Haman, who so desperately wanted to shame, humiliate, and kill his nemesis. (See Esther 2:1–23: Listen to the Story for a discussion of ancient methods of execution; see also Esth 2:23; 6:4; 7:9–10; 8:7; 9:13, 25.)

Ancient Idioms of Generosity

In the ancient world, Xerxes's lavish offer to Esther of half the kingdom (5:3) would have been understood as generous rather than exact. It recalls Darius I's offer to a man he was trying to recruit: "Leave Miletus and your newly founded Thracian city and follow me to Susa, where you will have all that is mine, sharing my table and my counsels."[6] Herodotus also recounts a story of Xerxes's generous offer to a lover who audaciously asked for the robe Xerxes's wife had given to him. Realizing his lover had trapped him, Xerxes upped his offer to include cities, gold, and even an army. The outcome of Xerxes's sordid affair precipitated the disfigurement of the mother of Xerxes's mistress and his own brother's death:

> Being pleased with her too, he asked her what she wanted in return for her favors, for he would deny nothing at her asking. Thereupon—for she and all her house were doomed to evil— . . . she asked boldly for his mantle. Xerxes tried to refuse her, for no reason except that he feared that Amestris might have clear proof of his doing what she already guessed. He accordingly offered her cities instead and gold in abundance and an army for none but herself to command. Armies are the most suitable of gifts in Persia. But as he could not move her, he gave her the mantle; and she, rejoicing greatly in the gift, went flaunting her finery.[7]

Pride

Scripture discusses pride at length and Haman provides a great case study. The book of Proverbs teaches that pride is followed by disgrace (Prov 11:2), punishment (16:5), and a fall or destruction (16:18), and foreshadows Haman's humiliation and ultimate destruction (Esth 6:10–13; 7:10).

EXPLAIN the Story

Putting Life on the Line (Esther 5:1–8)

The narrator invites us to witness Esther's perilous, unbidden entrance into Xerxes's magnificent, 350 square-foot audience hall that contained the inner

---

6. Herodotus, *Hist.*, 5:24.4. Compare also Herod Antipas's offer to Herodias's daughter, Salome of "up to half [his] kingdom," which led to the beheading of John the Baptist (Mark 6:23).

7. Ibid., 9:109.

court where guests stood in the sightline of the king seated on his throne.[8] As an ancient relief depicting an enthroned Persian king holding a long gold scepter and guarded by a soldier brandishing a large axe reminds us, Esther bravely risked her life when she approached the king before he had extended his scepter.[9]

Esther's approach follows three days of communal fasting (see Esther 4:1–17: Listen to the Story). Its timing, "on the third day," echoes other third days associated with deliverance in Scripture and hints that Esther's mission to save the Jews will succeed (see Listen to the Story, above). Her unsolicited entry following the publication of Haman's edict on the thirteenth day of the first month also propitiously coincides with Passover, a feast that commemorates freedom and rescue from death by God (3:12; see Esther 3:1–15: Listen to the Story).[10] Esther's much anticipated encounter with Xerxes, whose foibles and preferences Esther knows firsthand, contrasts with her first rendezvous with the king that followed twelve months of beauty treatment and private instruction (2:12–16). Queen Vashti's earlier defiance of the king's orders casts an additional long and ominous shadow over Esther's bold, unsolicited, law-defying approach to the king (1:12; see Esther 4:1–17: Listen to the Story).

Since Xerxes would *see* Esther standing in the inner court before he talked to her (5:1–2), Esther would have thought very carefully about what to wear. She needed to command the attention of a man who loved beautiful and compliant wives, women and girls, and, if Herodotus is to be trusted, even women married to other men—like his brother's wife (see Listen to the Story, above). The NIV, like most English translations, renders the Hebrew as "Esther put on her royal robes," but the more literal translation "she wore a kingdom" suggests that her magnificent eye-catching finery carried deep symbolic meaning. Esther dressed to challenge Persian law as well as the king who upheld it and who supported Haman. Her bold act initiated her battle against Haman and his supporters, whom the narrator associates with the Jews' ancestral enemies, the Amalekites. Missing from this plot-altering and tension-filled scene is any description of Esther's emotion. She presents herself as a confident, courageous, and determined woman on a mission; her initial reticence about the plan (4:11) is nowhere to be seen.

The narrator uses repetition to convey the palpable tension in the *royal* palace as the *royally*-attired Esther risks all to approach the *king* sitting on his

8. Tomasino, "Esther," 493.

9. Ibid., 491; see also archival photographs of another of Xerxes's capital cities, Persepolis, at "Persepolis: Images of an Empire," *Google Arts & Culture*, https://artsandculture.google.com/exhibit/xwJSKSxv_NfpLQ.

10. Levenson, *Esther*, 89.

kingly throne in the *king's* hall (5:1). Words related to "king" and all things royal (Hebrew *mlk*) are repeated six times (one refers to the king himself and five are used as adjectives describing Esther's attire, the palace, the throne, and the hall; the NIV omits the first mention of "royal" before "palace"). The repeated adverbial particle "opposite" (Hebrew *nokah*) as in "opposite" or "in front of" the king's hall and "opposite" or "facing" the entrance, underscores the spatial distance and power differential between Esther and all things kingly.

"In all the splendor of her queenly robes," writes nineteenth-century American Christian educator Leigh Norval, "[Esther] stood before him. He was a capricious tyrant, and it might be that her daring would deeply offend him, and instant death would still her beating pulses. He looked; she found 'favor in his sight.'"[11] The favor Esther found in Xerxes's eyes (5:2) was like the favor she had found earlier with everyone who saw her in the harem (2:15) and with Xerxes, who had shown her favor and kindness after he had spent one night with her (2:17). Esther's favorable reception also recalls the favor the Israelites received from their Egyptian neighbors who gave them gold, silver, and clothes (Exod 12:36), and provides yet another link to the Exodus. According to Wells, this association, together with the calendar association to Passover noted above, is an "improvisation" on the Passover; but this Persian Passover deliverance "takes place not [directly] by hand of God but by the attention to detail of one woman."[12]

Xerxes formally signals his pleasure by extending the golden scepter for Esther to touch. This ritual act suggests that Esther's mission will go well. Some readers also regard this gesture as a not-so-subtle sexual symbol. Wells, for example, suggests that Xerxes is helpless in the hands of Esther, "a queen in terms of sexual prowess."[13] Luther, by contrast, interprets Xerxes's life-giving act in light of the gospel of Christ. In Luther's commentary on Psalm 2:9, he associates the scepter the Lord's Son will use to "break . . . and dash them in pieces like a potter's vessel" with Xerxes's life-and death-delivering scepter.[14]

Impressed that Esther risked her life by approaching him (see 4:11 and Esther 4:1–17: Listen to the Story), Xerxes asks Esther—whom he now addresses as Queen Esther—what she wants. Using an expression of liberality flaunted by ancients who possessed means and power, he promises her "up to half the kingdom" (5:3; see Listen to the Story above). The repeated use of Esther's name together with her royal title from this time onwards in the story

11. Leigh Norval, *Women of the Bible: Sketches of All the Prominent Female Characters in the Old and the New Testament* (Nashville: Publishing House of the M. E. Church, South, Sunday-School Department, 1889), 198.

12. Wells, "Esther," 62.

13. Ibid, 63.

14. *LW* 14:346.

marks a change in her character and role that is recognized by those around her as she increasingly appropriates her double identity and vocation as Persian queen and deliverer of the Jews (5:3, 12; 7:1, 2, 3, 5, 7; 8:1, 7; 9:12).

Esther's reply is both unexpected and suspense creating (5:4). She postpones her answer and asks the king and Haman to join her for a banquet that she has already prepared. Esther's reply is clearly part of her strategy to find the right moment to discuss Haman's planned genocide with Xerxes, who had earlier agreed to the plan (3:10–11). From this point onward, we watch Esther's tactics as she deals with Xerxes and Haman, who both need to feel important and love to party.

To begin, Esther hosts Xerxes and Haman in her own quarters, thereby gaining power and control. In this way, she shifts the real and symbolic center of power away from the king in the throne room and toward herself. She also uses an indirect and subtle approach to communicating her desires and goals that dramatically contrasts with Vashti's direct and defiant style (1:12). Her refined plan includes lulling Haman into thinking that she respects and honors him and perhaps even has some affection toward him. She seems to be planting a seed of jealousy in Xerxes that accounts, at least in part, for his explosive reaction to Haman's alleged assault of Esther during their second banquet together (7:8).

Xerxes responds favorably and quickly to Esther's desires, ordering that Haman be brought quickly "to do the word of Esther" (5:5a YLT). This order and both men's immediate compliance dramatically contrast with Xerxes's earlier edict that every man be master in his own house (1:22). "And to add irony to irony," Patricia Tull observes, "Haman not only obeys a woman, but delights in being hosted by a Jew passing as a Persian so splendidly that she puts the lie to all he said about her people's disruptiveness" (5:9).[15]

In contrast to Xerxes's elaborately depicted banquets in chapter one, the details about the venue and fare at Esther's intimate first and second banquets are scant—the focus is instead on the dialogue (5:5b–8; 7:1–10). While drinking wine, the king repeats his query about what Esther wants and his generous offer of "even up to half the kingdom" (5:6; see Listen to the Story, above and in Esther 1). Although Esther's plan seems to be working, the notice of the king's wine consumption introduces a possible threat in light of his earlier wine-and anger-induced decisions related to Vashti's defiance. Haman's inebriation will also impact the unfolding story (5:9–14).

Esther's drawn-out response to the king creates suspense (7–8). Following her initial statement, "my petition and my request is this," Esther adds two

---

15. Patricia K. Tull, *Esther and Ruth* (Louisville: Westminster John Knox, 2003), 26.

deferential conditional clauses, which, for the moment, place the power the king had given to her when he promised to grant her request back in his own court: "If the king regards me with favor and if it pleases the king to grant my petition and fulfill my request" (5:8). Esther's next move is again unexpected as she defers her answer until the next night at a second banquet, where she promises to "do according to the word of the king" (v. 8). Against the view that Esther's delaying tactics are a sign of weakness is the more compelling interpretation that her strategies are part of a carefully-crafted plan to bolster the egos of both the king and Haman before blindsiding them by exposing Xerxes's second-in-command, Haman, as the manipulative and malevolent enemy of the Jews (7:6).

Choosing Scarcity over Abundance (Esther 5:9–14)

The narrator, who invites us to witness Esther's law-defying entrance into the throne room but effectively conceals Esther's inner thoughts and feelings, now exposes the tumultuous emotional life of Haman. Between Haman's euphoric moments that begin and end this scene (5:9, 14), Haman exposes his rage toward Mordecai, who has prevented him from experiencing the joy, gratitude, and contentment that he knows he should experience, based on all the good things in his life (5:9–13; see Listen to the Story, above).

The incident that provokes Haman's mood swing is his encounter with Mordecai, who once more refuses, on the third day of the fast invoked by Esther, to rise or show fear in Haman's presence (5:1, 9). Given that it was Mordecai's refusal to obey the king's command to bow down and pay homage to Haman that had prompted the series of events that led to the genocidal edict in the first place (3:1–6), it is surprising that Mordecai again and even more brashly disrespects both Haman and the law (3:2). His unexplained insolence prompts us to wonder why Mordecai would risk publicly disrespecting his ancestral enemy once again. Is he confident that Esther will be able to negotiate the plan to save the Jews and dispose of Haman? Or does Mordecai trust that God will deliver the Jews?

Haman's reactive rage (5:9) recalls his earlier outrage that had escalated into the genocidal edict (3:5–6); it also echoes Xerxes's response to Vashti's disobedience that had prompted the edict meant to control wives (1:12, 22). This time, Haman contains his anger until he reaches his home where, like Xerxes before his advisors, he unleashes his inner turmoil, indecision, excessive pride, and egotism (1:13–21; 5:9–13). Haman enumerates his many accomplishments before his inner circle—the glory of his riches (perhaps an allusion to his exceedingly generous offer to fund the genocide in 3:9); his large family (see Listen to the Story, above); his professional achievements, including his advancement over other nobles and officials (3:1); and his most recent decoration, his invitation by Queen Esther to a second banquet with the royal couple (5:12). This last prideful announcement is the only fresh news for those in his inner circle. Ironically, the revelation of the things Haman truly values and flaunts—"wealth, recognition and abundance"—prepares us for "the outcome of the story whereby Haman's riches are given to Esther (8:1) and his sons are killed by Jews (9:10)."[16]

In a moment of surprising self-awareness and vulnerability, Haman confesses that the very sight of Mordecai the Jew sitting in the king's gate dispels the satisfaction that his accomplishments and honors should bring (5:13). Haman's "wise counsel" suggests impaling Mordecai on a pole tall enough for all to see in the morning (see Listen to the Story, above and Esther 6:1–14). With a plan in place to kill his irritant, Haman's supporters imagine that he will be able to go to the banquet in good spirits (v. 14). Their very dark suggestion recalls Jezebel's plot to kill Naboth to dispel her husband Ahab's pouting and depression (1 Kgs 21) and Xerxes's attendants' solution to his wistful remembering of Vashti (Esth 2:1).

The vindictive plan to kill Mordecai renews the sense of foreboding that began the chapter as Esther dares to approach the royal throne. The threat of death now looms over Mordecai. Will he be killed before Esther is able to expose Haman for who he really is and before she asks for the redemption of the Jews? Or do the subtle hints of redemption in this and previous chapters offset the sense of impending doom?

LIVE the Story

Exceptional Tactics and Courage

> Beauty is power; a smile is its sword
>
> —John Ray, English Puritan and naturalist (1627–1705)

Interpreters through the ages have imagined what Esther must have looked like and how she felt as she entered Xerxes's court to negotiate the deliverance of the Jews and the condemnation of the evil Haman. Her tactics, which include natural and acquired skills, have also intrigued readers. Clement of Alexandria (AD 150–215) was concerned about Esther's use of beauty, given traditional Christian teachings about the beauty of the soul rather than the body, since "we walk by faith not by sight" (2 Cor 5:7 KJV). He reasoned that

16. Reid, *Esther*, 112.

Esther's use of beauty and ornamentation was exceptional: "As for women, the only one we know of who used ornaments without blame is Esther." Clement gave "mystical significance" to Esther's "action in making herself beautiful" suggesting she was able to obtain the "deliverance for her people by her beauty."[17]

Less concerned with Esther's use of beauty and charm was the fifteenth-century writer and influential political advisor, Lucrezia Tornabuoni de Medici. She thought that Esther's natural and enhanced beauty and her acquired knowledge provided a model that she and other well-born women could adopt to influence public affairs through the powerful males of their families. Tornabuoni suggests that when Esther entered the court "royally dressed, adorned, and graceful," she knew "it was the right moment to give her all." In addition to recognizing the importance of Esther's beauty and attire, which she pictured as including "regal insignia . . . rubies, pearls and infinite treasures," Tornabuoni imagines that Esther prayed for divine wisdom: "Oh my Lord, teach me how to speak, so I will know how to utter words that will persuade."[18]

The freed slave, Sojourner Truth, was inspired less by Esther's tactics than by her courage to risk her life to advocate on behalf of the oppressed. She argued that the women of America, who were asking for much less than Esther, needed to bring their requests courageously before "the king of the United States." She found it ironic that Esther was well received when she asked for the deliverance of her nation, but that American women who ask for much less hear "sons hiss their mothers like snakes, because they ask for their rights; and can they ask for anything less?"[19]

Esther's courage and tactics continue to inspire God's people to risk all to do what is right. It suggests that those who, like Esther, find themselves in situations of power and gender imbalance may have to use all their assets, exceptional tactics, and means to accomplish their ends. But those of us who do not have to confront the kind of power imbalances that Esther faced would do well to take to heart Clement of Alexandria's insight that her tactics were exceptional. Other, better, means of advocacy are usually available.

Esther as a Type of Christ

> Enthroned, prepared, and waiting—born to save
> Arise, fair morning star, and shine,

---

17. Clement of Alexandria, "Christ the Educator 3.2.12," as cited in Conti and Pilara, *1–2 Kings, 1–2 Chronicles, Ezra, Nehemiah, Esther*, 386.

18. Tornabuoni, *Sacred Narratives*, 193–94.

19. Sojourner Truth, "Speech of Sojourner Truth to the Mob Convention, New York, September, 1853," in *History of Woman Suffrage, Vol 1: 1848–1861*, ed. Elizabeth Cady Stanton, Susan B. Anthony, and Matilda Joslyn Gage (New York: Fowler and Wells, 1881), 568.

All royal in array
Let myrtles with thy tresses twine,
And perfumes lead the way.
Come, thou devoted, now thine influence try,
Forth with thy motto, "If I die, I die!"[20]

American poet Frances Caulkins recognized Esther as a Christ figure in this chapter: "Enthroned, prepared, and waiting—born to save" and willing to go forth with her motto, "If I die, I die!" As noted in Listen to the Story, Esther's decision to make her perilous approach to the king on the third day reminds us of other biblical stories involving "the third day" (Gen 22:4–19; 31:22–32; Jonah 1:17; 2:10; Hos 6:2) These anticipatory allusions are supported by the stronger associations between Esther and Jesus found in this and other chapters in the book of Esther that illuminate Christ's person and work. Esther, like Jesus, was born to save her people. Her mission, like Jesus', involved courageously risking her life for the salvation of her people. This scene where Esther undertakes her mission dressed in her finest queenly robes, however, contrasts with the scenes of Jesus' betrayal, trial, and crucifixion when he was stripped of his clothes and humiliated as he overcame his enemies and offered his life to save sinners (Matt 12:40).

Pick Your Friends Wisely

This chapter casts further light on Haman, who might today be described as an egomaniac suffering from self-delusion. It also features the responses of his wife and friends as they indulge him. They try to fix his perceived "problem" instead of challenging his assumptions and invoking the Persian protocol of waiting until the day after to reconsider thoughts and decisions made while drunk (see Esther 1:1–22: Listen to the Story). Like Jezebel, Haman's support team suggests he eliminate the annoyance as the best way of dealing with the problem. Proverbs' teaching about the importance of the company we keep is particularly apt: "Whoever walks with the wise becomes wise, but the companion of fools will suffer harm" (Prov 13:20 ESV). It is interesting to imagine what would have changed if Haman's support group had spoken truth and encouraged reconciliation, not revenge. This of course is not the plot of Esther's story, but, as those of us living in post-colonial contexts recognize, learning to live in peace with diversity is vital; it is what the gospel of Christ demands.

20. Caulkins, *Eve and Her Daughters*, 123.

Haman's Pride and Blindness: The Battle of Scarcity

Haman's hubris illustrates Scripture's teaching about the sin of pride. Early American biblical interpreter Hannah Flagg Gould regarded Haman as a portrait of pride that encourages us to examine our own lives, lest we too fall: "Who [after] observ[ing] the elevation and fall of Haman, will not be afraid of the first indulgence of *pride*, which is the root of all sin, and which brings down God's heaviest judgments?"[21] Samuel Wells goes further and associates Haman with sin and the fall: "Like Adam and Eve, Haman may have the whole world and permission to enjoy it, but all he can think about is one thing he doesn't have."[22] Haman's whole world included great blessings—family, wealth, and position, but his deep hatred and prejudice blinds him to his abundance. While Haman's reaction to Mordecai's disdain is excessive, his lack of gratitude is all too common. Like Haman, many of us focus on the difficult people or circumstances in our lives, and, by so doing, we effectively empower those people or circumstances to take away our sense of enjoyment and gratitude for the good things with which God has blessed us.

Brené Brown describes western society as a "never enough" or "perceived scarcity" culture in which whatever we have, do, or get, it's never enough." But here's the problem. Not only are all of these comparisons discouraging and even debilitating, they distort and hide the tremendous gifts we have been given."[23] Haman also had this blinding disease, but his perceived "never enough" was entwined with his vile anti-Semitism.

The apostle Paul's teaching on contentment speaks to this issue of gratitude: "Not that I am speaking of being in need, for I have learned in whatever situation I am to be content. I know how to be brought low, and I know how to abound. In any and every circumstance, I have learned the secret of facing plenty and hunger, abundance and need. I can do all things through him who strengthens me" (Phil 4:11, 12 ESV). The Samaritan leper, who was the only one out of the ten lepers Jesus had healed to return and thank him, models the counter-cultural attitude of gratitude that we are called to have: "One of them, when he saw he was healed, came back, praising God in a loud voice. He threw himself at Jesus' feet and thanked him—and he was a Samaritan. Jesus asked, 'Were not all ten cleansed? Where are the other nine? Has no one returned to give praise to God except this foreigner?'" (Luke 17:15–18).

---

21. H. F. Gould, *Esther: A Scripture Narrative by a Lady, together with an Original Poem* (New York: D. Appleton & Co., 1835), 68.

22. Wells, "Esther," 63.

23. Michael Hyatt, "Perceived Scarcity in a World of Outrageous Abundance," 18 July 2014, http://michaelhyatt.com/perceived-scarcity-outrageous-abundance/. See also Brown, *Daring Greatly*.

Well-known Christian businessman and author Michael Hyatt describes three spiritual disciplines that have helped him battle scarcity—prayer, thankfulness, and journaling gratitude:

1. I start and end the day with prayer. Instead of bookending the day with what I failed to get—sleep or accomplishments or whatever—I try focusing on the blessings I do have and express them in prayer.
2. I practice thankfulness. Before I get caught in endless comparisons, I express gratitude for the gifts I do have. I find prayer before meals gives me several natural points in the day to do this.
3. I journal my gratitude. Journaling is useful for many things, but expressing and capturing our gratitude is certainly one. Not only do I have the in-the-moment benefit of focusing on the good, I've recorded it for later reflection, for those times when things don't feel like they're going as well as I had hoped.[24]

May we have courage to stand against ingratitude and praise God daily for all that our Creator so generously provides.

24. Hyatt, "Perceived Scarcity."

CHAPTER 10

Esther 6:1–14

LISTEN to the Story

1That night the king could not sleep; so he ordered the book of the
chronicles, the record of his reign, to be brought in and read to him. 2It
was found recorded there that Mordecai had exposed Bigthana and Teresh,
two of the king's officers who guarded the doorway, who had conspired to
assassinate King Xerxes.

3"What honor and recognition has Mordecai received for this?" the
king asked.

"Nothing has been done for him," his attendants answered.

4The king said, "Who is in the court?" Now Haman had just entered
the outer court of the palace to speak to the king about impaling Mordecai
on the pole he had set up for him.

5His attendants answered, "Haman is standing in the court."

"Bring him in," the king ordered.

6When Haman entered, the king asked him, "What should be done
for the man the king delights to honor?"

Now Haman thought to himself, "Who is there that the king would
rather honor than me?" 7So he answered the king, "For the man the king
delights to honor, 8have them bring a royal robe the king has worn and a
horse the king has ridden, one with a royal crest placed on its head. 9Then
let the robe and horse be entrusted to one of the king's most noble princes.
Let them robe the man the king delights to honor, and lead him on the
horse through the city streets, proclaiming before him, 'This is what is
done for the man the king delights to honor!' "

10"Go at once," the king commanded Haman. "Get the robe and the
horse and do just as you have suggested for Mordecai the Jew, who sits at
the king's gate. Do not neglect anything you have recommended."

11So Haman got the robe and the horse. He robed Mordecai, and led
him on horseback through the city streets, proclaiming before him, "This
is what is done for the man the king delights to honor!"

[12]Afterward Mordecai returned to the king's gate. But Haman rushed home, with his head covered in grief, [13]and told Zeresh his wife and all his friends everything that had happened to him.

His advisers and his wife Zeresh said to him, "Since Mordecai, before whom your downfall has started, is of Jewish origin, you cannot stand against him—you will surely come to ruin!" [14]While they were still talking with him, the king's eunuchs arrived and hurried Haman away to the banquet Esther had prepared.

Listen to the Text in the Story: Biblical Texts: Genesis 41:37–45; Exodus 7:5, 17; 9:16, 29; 17:14; 18:9–10; Numbers 22–24; Joshua 2:8–11; 1 Samuel 4:6–8; 1 Kings 1:32–49; Ancient Near Eastern Texts: Herodotus, *Histories* 9.107; Xenophon, *Cyropaedia*, 8.3.23; Xenophon, *Anabasis* 1.2.27; Plutarch, *Themistocles* 29.5.

Rewards for Service and Loyalty

Reading this chapter in the context of the ancient world reveals Haman's expertise in managing protocols of royal benefaction for service to the empire and king. Ancient kings promptly honored, rewarded, publicly acclaimed, and recorded the names of those who performed exceptional acts of service. Failure to honor someone promptly was associated with shame.[1] Benefaction gifts included money, land, and prestigious positions of power symbolized by special clothes and accessories worn before an adoring public. Pharaoh, for example, gifted Joseph with his signet ring, dressed him in fine linen robes adorned by a gold chain, placed him in his second chariot, and put him in charge of the whole land of Egypt. The public recognized Joseph as deserving of honor (Gen 41:37–45). Xenophon also describes the political ramifications of benefaction:

> Cyrus gave [the first man to arrive] one of the horses that were being led in the procession and gave orders to one of the macebearers to have it led away for him wherever he should direct. And to those who saw it, it seemed to be a mark of great honour, and as a consequence of that event many more people paid court to that man.[2]

Animals used in ceremonies honoring loyal heroes or citizens were sometimes decorated. Xenophon's list of gifts of honor is similar to Haman's wish list, as it includes "a horse with a gold-mounted bridle, a gold necklace and bracelets,

1. See Esther 2:1–23: Listen to the Story for background for these events.
2. Xenophon, *Cyr.* 8.3.23.

a gold dagger, and a Persian robe."[3] Archaeologists have uncovered many pictures of decorated horses and ornamented horse figurines in excavations in the ancient Near East. The fifth-century BC sculpture of a horse flaunting a crown made from his mane that was part of the artwork that adorned the massive east staircase of the king's audience hall at Persepolis helps us to visualize what Haman had in mind when he included a decorated horse on his wish list.[4]

Plutarch recounts the story of a Spartan who requested to be rewarded by riding into Sardis wearing a tiara in the same fashion as the king, but was refused. The story suggests that some ancients believed that not only kings, but even what they wore had divine power:

> When Demaratus, the exiled Spartan king who was living in Persia, was ordered to choose a reward for himself, he asked to be permitted to ride in state into and through Sardis, wearing his tiara upright, as the Persian kings do. At this Mithropaustes, the king's cousin, laid his hand on Demaratus' tiara and remarked: "This tiara of yours has no brains to cover and, as for yourself, you will not become Zeus simply by taking hold of his thunderbolt."[5]

Fear of Israel's God

The theme of outsiders recognizing the power of Israel's God recurs throughout the story of God. When the inhabitants in and around Jericho heard about Israel's military successes, they testified: "our hearts melted in fear and everyone's courage failed because of you, for the Lord your God is God in heaven above and on the earth below" (Josh 2:11). When the Philistines learned that the ark of the Lord had come into the camp, they too were afraid:

> "A god has come into the camp," they said. "Oh no! Nothing like this has happened before. We're doomed! Who will deliver us from the hand of these mighty gods?" (1 Sam 4:6–8)

EXPLAIN the Story

Esther 6:1–11: Talking Past Each Other

This highly ironic and darkly humorous chapter follows on the heels of Haman's shaming by Mordecai that had inspired the dark suggestion that

---

3. Xenophon, *Anab.* 1.2.27.

4. See slides 22–55 of "The Apadana," *The Oriental Institute*, http://oi.uchicago.edu/gallery/apadana#1F6_72dpi.png.

5. Plutarch, *Them.* 29.8, quoted in A. Kuhrt, *The Persian Empire: A Corpus of Sources from the Achaemenid Period* (London; New York: Routledge, 2007), 661.

Haman kill his archenemy. Time slows down as we overhear an early morning conversation based on a portentous misunderstanding between Xerxes and Haman.

The opening verses describe a series of seemingly random coincidences that initiate the deeply ironic reversals in the fortunes of Haman and Mordecai. The narrator does not reveal why "the king could not sleep" (lit., "the sleep of the king fled") following Esther's banquet. While some imagine Xerxes was disturbed by Esther's unwillingness to reveal what she wanted, others think God caused his insomnia. This second view is supported by other Old Testament texts that associate insomnia with God.[6] According to the LXX, God caused Xerxes's insomnia; similarly, the A-text explains that "the mighty one" took his sleep way. The king's choice of a sleeping aid is surprisingly not one of the many women in his harem, but rather listening to the ancient equivalent of an audio book, in which was recorded such matters as the assassination plot that Mordecai had thwarted (2:21–23).

When Xerxes finds out that nothing had been done to honor and reward Mordecai for saving his life, he is deeply ashamed (6:3) as he should have promptly, generously, and publicly honored and rewarded Mordecai for his loyalty. An appropriate reward for Mordecai would have been similar to the one Haman had received when he was promoted and given authority over other officials (3:1).

The king acts quickly to rectify his oversight. True to his character, he looks to others to tell him what to do (6:3–5). The juxtaposition of Xerxes's question, "Who is in the court?" with the unexpected early morning arrival of his honor-loving highest official, Haman, creates yet another highly unlikely coincidence. Both Xerxes and Haman have had sleepless nights: Xerxes's antidote for insomnia has left him in a shame storm and Haman has been busy setting up the gigantic pole he plans to use to impale the very man Xerxes plans to honor. Both men are desperate to resolve their pressing issues: Xerxes needs advice and Haman needs permission to kill Mordecai. The irony is intense, as is the inference that God's hand is behind the perfectly-timed series of coincidences that bring Haman and Xerxes together. As Firth suggests, "God's providential care is again in evidence as Haman arrived at exactly the right moment to solve the king's dilemma, but in such a way as to trap himself . . . a trap that is full of divine coincidences. . . . The timing is perfect."[7]

After Haman is allowed to enter the court, Xerxes asks the honor-obsessed Haman: "What should be done for the man the king delights to honor?" (6:6). Haman's fulsome answer is predicated on his erroneous assumption

6. Texts that associate sleeplessness and God include Job 4:12–16; 33:19; Ps 4:4; Dan 2:29.

7. Firth, *The Message of Esther*, 93–94.

that he is the person the king wants to honor. And just as "Pride goes before destruction, [and] a haughty spirit before a fall (Prov 16:18), so the narcissistic Haman inadvertently maps out his own demise. It is at this point in the story that the great reversal of fortune that points to God's superintending providence begins.

Unlike Esther, whose response to Xerxes is deferential and respectful (Esth 5:4), Haman launches immediately into his vainglorious vision of how he should be honored (6:6–9). He begins with an incomplete sentence in Hebrew that repeats the delectable phrase—the man the king delights to honor (6:6, 7). This phrase, Fox notes, "rolls . . . around in [Haman's] mouth four times, beginning and ending his little speech, . . . [words which] once savored will then fill his mouth with gall" as he repeats them over and over as he leads Mordecai around on the royal horse (11).[8]

Haman's list (7–9) begins with royal attire: the honoree is to wear robes previously worn by the king. The robes were likely purple, embroidered, and distinctive in elegance and style. It is possible that Haman believed the king's robes imbued the person wearing them with special kingly powers (see Listen to the Story, above).[9] The royally attired honoree is then to ride a royally crowned horse previously ridden by the king. Whether the horse actually wears a crown or has his mane sculpted into a crown is debated (for a link to a visual of a crowned horse, see Listen to the Story, above). Finally, Haman counsels that one of the king's noblest princes dress the royally-attired honoree and lead him mounted on the king's crowned horse through the streets (lit., "for all to see") while shouting: "This is what is done for the man the king delights to honor."

Haman's vainglorious suggestions are at the same time conventional and exceptional. They echo Pharaoh's gifts of benefaction to Joseph, who was also honored with a robe and mount intimately connected with the pharaoh's person and publicly acclaimed (Gen 41:37–45). Ironically, Mordecai, the person whom Xerxes intends to honor, like Joseph and unlike Haman, is the one deserving of royal benefaction (Gen 41:37–45; Esth 2:19–23).

Haman's counsel is also extraordinary as it reflects his personal obsession with all things royal, including what seems to be his fantasy of being king. As readers of the Hebrew text have long observed, the root word for king (*mlk*) occurs seven times in verses 7–8. Echoes of the transition of power from David to Solomon that included riding on his father's mule and public acclamation also suggest that Haman at least subconsciously wanted to be king

8. Michael V. Fox, *Character and Ideology in the Book of Esther*, 2nd ed. (Eugene, OR: Wipf & Stock, 1991), 76.

9. Jobes, *Esther*, 153.

(1 Kgs 1:32–49). Missing from Haman's wish list is a sexual relationship with the king's wife, which is exactly what the king accuses him of at the banquet that follows (7:8). As Ahithophel counseled Absalom, sleeping with the wife or concubine of a king signaled a challenge to kingly power and authority (2 Sam 16:21). Haman's self-aggrandizing desire to usurp the throne was more fanciful than Absalom's. Had Xerxes thought that Haman was suggesting that he himself should be honored as "king for a day," he might have said to him what was said to Demaratus the Spartan who also aspired to be king of Persia for a day: "you will not become Zeus simply by taking hold of his thunderbolt" (see Listen to the Story, above).

Not surprisingly, Xerxes loves Haman's ideas, as he has all previous suggestions put forward to him (6:10). Xerxes's command to move ahead quickly with the benefaction scheme also fits with the Persian protocol of speed and efficiency. The hustling theme recurs a few verses later, as Haman himself is hurried off to the second banquet and imminent death (v. 14). The contrast between the king's incompetence and the empire's efficiency is one of the ways the narrator continues to satirize the Persian Empire.

At the last moment, the king reveals the identity of the honoree and, to Haman's chagrin, it is his archenemy, Mordecai, the Jew! The king's last words, "Do not neglect anything you have recommended," rubs in the irony of the reversal, since Haman himself must dress, parade around, and publicly acclaim as "the man the king delights to honor" the man he had planned to kill that very day (6:10).

The narrator does not allow us into Haman's mind as he prepares and then leads the public celebration of the king's honoring of Mordecai. "Snared by the work of his own hands," the "wicked" Haman was undoubtedly mortified (see Ps 9:16). "This wretched man," nineteenth-century English commentator Mary Cornwallis writes, "affords a fine lesson to beware of the beginning of pride, ambition, and envy; and to avoid all the intricacies of sin, which are sure, sooner, or later, to bewilder him who ventures into them."[10] The often-repeated rabbinic story that Haman's daughter threw a pot of excrement from the roof on the head of the man she thought was Mordecai but was really her father underscores Haman's deep sense of shame. This story ends when, after Haman told his daughter that she also had embarrassed him, she fell from the roof and died.[11]

10. Mrs. [Mary] Cornwallis, *Observations, Critical, Explanatory and Practical on the Canonical Scriptures*, Vol. 2 (London: Baldwin, Cradock & Joy, 1817), 147.

11. Tg. Rishon, 72, as cited by Carruthers, *Esther Through the Centuries*, 228.

The Fall Begins (Esther 6:12–14)

The narrator passes over the reactions of Mordecai and the crowd and instead focuses on what happens after Mordecai's exaltation (Esth 6:12). Mordecai, along with all the other Jews, still faces death, but returns to his post at the gate. Haman, who has just dressed his enemy in kingly regalia, hurries home with his head covered as a sign of shame and mourning, symbolically foreshadowing his impending death (2 Sam 15:30; Jer 14:2–4). Behind the ironic reversal of expectations and outcomes that the changes in clothing symbolize, many see the hand of God. Medieval commentator Rabanus Maurus suggests: "this is the change caused by the right hand of the Highest: the one who had just boasted about his power and was arrogant toward everyone else becomes viler and weaker than anyone else."[12]

Just as Mordecai had earlier told Hathak "everything that had happened to him" that had led up to the perilous genocidal edict (Esth 4:7), so Haman tells his advisors and wife "everything that had happened to him" (6:13). Haman's loyal supporters, who were expecting to hear that Haman had received Xerxes's permission to carry out their vindictive plan to publicly humiliate and impale Mordecai that very day, are no longer identified as "his wife Zeresh and all his friends" but rather "his advisers and his wife Zeresh." Their response is unexpected: they announce the beginning of Haman's downfall before Mordecai the Jew (5:14; 6:13).

Mary Cornwallis, however, was not surprised by the responses of Haman's supporters. She suggests their "unfeeling" response is typical, because those who are corrupt enough "to incite others to sin are incapable" of the kind of "generous feelings" which are "the essence of true friendship."[13] She assesses Haman's so-called friends as being so self-centered that they are incapable of caring for him and wonders if they might "even rejoice in the misery to which they have been accessary."[14] Perhaps it is not surprising that wicked Haman would surround himself with such depraved people.

The announcement by Haman's advisors of the triumph of the Jew over his enemy recalls Balaam's prophecy of the triumph of Jacob's descendants over their enemies and Daniel's revelation of the demise of Nebuchadnezzar's kingdom (Num 24; Dan 2:36–48). That God is behind the reversals announced by Balaam and Daniel is clear; God's role in the reversals in Esther is whispered much more softly. The LXX (6:13) clarifies that Haman will fall "because the living God is with [Mordecai the Jew]."

---

12. Rabanus Maurus, "Explanation on the Book of Esther 9," quoted in Conti and Pilara, *1–2 Kings, 1–2 Chronicles, Ezra, Nehemiah, Esther*, 389.

13. Cornwallis, *Observations*, Vol. 2, 147.

14. Ibid.

While they were still talking and before Haman had time to digest the substance of his advisors' prognostications, he is hurried off to the banquet and to his death in true Persian fashion (6:14; for other examples of the "hurry" motif, see 3:15; 6:12; 8:14; also 2:9; 5:5; 6:10). As Fox observes: "Haman, the skilled manipulator of the king's will and (he hopes) a people's destiny, is no longer in control of his own life. He is rushed out and taken to a situation that *Esther* has prepared, he has been brought to her territory, and the initiative is now with her."[15]

LIVE the Story

Coincidence or Providence

As Canadian temperance advocate Letitia Youmans recognized, God is strangely absent from this chapter and, indeed, from the entire book of Esther, "and yet God is as legibly written in every chapter as in any other book in the Bible."[16] Also notably absent from this game-changing chapter are the principal players, Mordecai and Esther. Xerxes and Haman are both intent on securing decisions about Mordecai's future. Xerxes wants advice on how to honor the very person Haman needs permission to impale. But as this deeply ironic scene plays out, we observe that the future that Haman unwittingly shapes is one of blessing and life for Mordecai and shame, humiliation, and ultimately death for himself.

In the king's court on the auspicious morning described in this chapter, "there is no room," as David Clines suggests, "for human initiatives such as have been played out so adroitly in the previous scene. Now everything must be providential—or rather coincidental (which is the narrator's cipher for 'divinely arranged')."[17] This chapter's coincidences include the sleeplessness of the king; his decision to have the records of his reign read to him; the reading of the account of the conspiracy to assassinate the king that Mordecai had thwarted and that the king had failed to respond to; the timing of Haman's entrance; and Haman's knowledge of benefaction procedures, including those that elevated the honoree politically. These happenstances worked together to bring about the reversal in the fortunes of the Jew Mordecai and the enemy of the Jews, Haman, and ultimately the deliverance of all the Jews from genocidal

15. Fox, *Character and Ideology*, 81 (Fox's italics).

16. Letitia Youmans, *Campaign Echoes. The Autobiography of Mrs. Letitia Youmans, the Pioneer of the White Ribbon Movement in Canada Written by Request of the Provincial Woman's Christian Temperance Union of Canada* (Toronto: William Briggs, 1893), 196.

17. Clines, *Ezra, Nehemiah, Esther*, 306–7.

death. This deliverance ensured the fulfilment of God's promise to bring blessing to all nations through Abraham's seed, and anticipates the ultimate reversal enacted by Christ's death and resurrection (Gen 12:1–3; Rom 6:23).

Esther chapter six describes a series of seeming coincidences that together provoke a momentous reversal of fortunes, suggesting that God is present, though perhaps unseen. He not only upholds the existence and natural order of the universe—what theologians call *conservatio*—but also intervenes more directly in the lives of individuals—what theologians call *concursus*—who act as agents in the larger story of God that moves toward God's final purpose—what theologians call *gubernatio*.[18] The reversal in Haman's and Mordecai's fortunes and, ultimately, the reversal of the genocidal edict and the deliverance of God's people illustrate the concept of God's providence that is implied in such texts as Romans 11:36, "For from him and through him and to him are all things."

John Webster's discussion of a Christian doctrine of providence encourages us to step back and consider such events as the king's insomnia, and even such agents as the inept Xerxes and wicked Haman, in light of God's final purposes:

> A Christian doctrine of providence is . . . a representation of how the Father's plan for the fullness of time is set forth in Christ and made actual by the Holy Spirit among the children of Adam. In other words, the identities of the agents in the history of providence—this God and his creatures—are fundamental to determining its course and character. . . . Again Christian specificity about the ends of providence is crucial to grasping its nature, for providence is not mere static world maintenance but teleological, the fulfilment of the ordered fellowship with God which is the creature's perfected happiness.[19]

In his wisdom, God uses all of his creatures—Xerxes, Haman, Haman's wife and advisors, and of course Mordecai and Esther—as agents in the unfolding story of salvation. The deliverance of the Jews was necessary in the larger plan of salvation when, in the fullness of time, "God sent his Son, born of a woman, born under the law, in order to redeem those who were under the law, so that we might receive adoption as children" (Gal 4:4–5 NRSV).

Where Is God When Bad Things Happen to God's People?

While it is easy to recognize God's hand in our lives when things are going well, it is difficult to discern God's providence when bad things happen to

---

18. Kevin J. Vanhoozer, "Providence," *DTIB*: 641.

19. John Webster, *God Without Measure: Working Papers in Christian Theology: Volume 1: God and the Works of God* (London: T&T Clark, 2016), 131.

good people. In the case of Mordecai and Esther, it would have been difficult to discern God's hand when their little family was ripped apart for the second time: the first trauma being the death of Esther's parents, and the second when Esther was sex-trafficked into the king's harem (2:7–9). But as the story unfolds, we are shown how, "for such a time as this" and in such a place at this (4:14), Esther became a strategic agent in negotiating deliverance for the Jews.

Trusting in God's providence does not take away the pain and trauma Esther would have experienced in being separated from her uncle and friends and in being denied her dreams of a future as a Jewish woman, wife, and mother. Esther did not have the big picture that we as readers of Scripture have in terms of the role she played in God's final deliverance. And neither do we see the whole picture when it comes to the unfathomable tragic and traumatic events in our own lives and the lives of those we love. We do not have all the data. We can't see everything. We don't know what God is doing. Sometimes, we are able to look back on our lives and make sense out of what seemed at the time to be senseless, unnecessary, or even cruel. At other times, the mystery of God's workings remains, and, unlike Job, we are not privy to God's perspective.

The "Hymn of the Hungarian Galley Slaves" addresses the issue of how faith in God's providence allows us to carry on when life seems too much to bear. The hymn commemorates the courage and faith of the forty-one Protestant pastors and teachers who were jailed and eventually sold as galley slaves after refusing to recant during the Counter-Reformation move to reclaim Hungary for the Catholic Church in the late seventeenth century. Near death, these faithful Christians were eventually ransomed and given political asylum in Holland and Switzerland.

> Lift your heads, O martyrs, weeping,
> God our Maker still does reign!
> You are daily in God's keeping,
> God is with you in your pain.
> Rise and be of valiant heart,
> And with courage bear your part;
> Soon again God's arms will fold you
> To God's loving heart and hold you.
> Though the storms may rage and roll
> O'er the vast and fearful sea,
> Though you cry from wretched toil,
> "O my Savior, rescue me!"
> Though it seems that God does sleep,

Hope and trust in God still keep;
Calm your hearts though they be quaking,
God is faithful, none forsaking . . .
Though in chains you now are grieving,
Though a tortured slave you die,
Martyrs, if you die believing,
Heaven's path shall open lie,
Upward gaze and trust anew,
God has not forsaken you;
You are God's own people, surely
God will fold God's own securely.[20]

It is this message of hope that the story of God proclaims. This chapter in Esther's story is one of many stories in Scripture that encourage us to continue to trust God's providence and faithfulness: "[We] are God's own people, surely God will fold God's own securely."

20. The "Hymn of the Hungarian Galley Slaves" is still found in a number of hymn books under the title, "Lift Thy Head, O Zion, Weeping." This updated version is cited in Barbara Brown Zikmund, *The Living Theological Heritage of the United Church of Christ* (Cleveland: Pilgrim, 1995), 641.

CHAPTER 11

Esther 7:1–10

LISTEN to the Story

[1]So the king and Haman went to Queen Esther's banquet, [2]and as they were drinking wine on the second day, the king again asked, "Queen Esther, what is your petition? It will be given you. What is your request? Even up to half the kingdom, it will be granted."

[3]Then Queen Esther answered, "If I have found favor with you, Your Majesty, and if it pleases you, grant me my life—this is my petition. And spare my people—this is my request. [4]For I and my people have been sold to be destroyed, killed and annihilated. If we had merely been sold as male and female slaves, I would have kept quiet, because no such distress would justify disturbing the king."

[5]King Xerxes asked Queen Esther, "Who is he? Where is he—the man who has dared to do such a thing?"

[6]Esther said, "An adversary and enemy! This vile Haman!"

Then Haman was terrified before the king and queen. [7]The king got up in a rage, left his wine and went out into the palace garden. But Haman, realizing that the king had already decided his fate, stayed behind to beg Queen Esther for his life.

[8]Just as the king returned from the palace garden to the banquet hall, Haman was falling on the couch where Esther was reclining.

The king exclaimed, "Will he even molest the queen while she is with me in the house?"

As soon as the word left the king's mouth, they covered Haman's face. [9]Then Harbona, one of the eunuchs attending the king, said, "A pole reaching to a height of fifty cubits stands by Haman's house. He had it set up for Mordecai, who spoke up to help the king."

The king said, "Impale him on it!" [10]So they impaled Haman on the pole he had set up for Mordecai. Then the king's fury subsided.

Listen to the Text in the Story: Biblical Texts: 2 Samuel 16:20–22; 1 Kings 9:21; 2 Kings 2:13–25; Nehemiah 5:5; Joel 3:4–8; Ancient Near Eastern Texts: Herodotus, *Histories* 3.140.5; 6.32; 7.38–39; Plutarch, *Artaxerxes* 26.2; 27.1.

Slavery in the Ancient World: "If We Had Merely Been Sold as Male and Female Slaves"

Scholars estimate that almost half of the people living in urban centers in the ancient Mediterranean world were slaves.[1] Debt often led to slavery even among the Jews, as those experiencing poverty in Jerusalem testified: "Although we are of the same flesh and blood as our fellow Jews and though our children are as good as theirs, yet we have to subject our sons and daughters to slavery. Some of our daughters have already been enslaved, but we are powerless, because our fields and our vineyards belong to others" (Neh 5:5). Prisoners of war and rebellious groups were also enslaved. Solomon's practice of conscripting prisoners of war for his slave labor force was commonplace (1 Kgs 9:21; Joel 3:4–8). So too, the Persians enslaved and sometimes killed rebellious peoples, such as the "certain people" who Haman claims, "do not obey the king's laws" (Esth 3:8–9). Herodotus described the Persian practice of enslaving insurrectionists that Esther alludes to during her second banquet (7:4):

> When [the Persians] had gained mastery over the cities, they chose out the most handsome boys and castrated them, making them eunuchs instead of men, and they carried the fairest maidens away to the king; they did all this, and they burnt the [Ionian] cities with their temples. Thus three times had the Ionians been enslaved, first by the Lydians and now twice in a row by the Persians.[2]

Xerxes's Dark Side and the Challenge of Negotiating with Persian Kings

Stories about Xerxes's cruel and unpredictable behavior remind us of what Esther was up against when she made her request to Xerxes. Herodotus's story of Xerxes's indifference toward a loyal citizen who asked that the eldest of his five sons be freed from active war duty to care for him in his old age reveals Xerxes's dark side:

> "You and four of your sons are saved by your hospitality; but you shall be punished by the life of that one you most desire to keep." With that reply, [Xerxes] immediately ordered those who were assigned to do these things to find the eldest of Pythius' sons and cut him in half, then to set one half of his body on the right side of the road and the other on the left, so that the army would pass between them.[3]

1. M. A. Dandamayev, "Slavery: Ancient Near East, Old Testament," *ABD* 6:58–65; Tomasino, "Esther," 496.

2. Herodotus, *Hist.* 6.32.1.

3. Ibid., 7:38–39.

Sex and Power: "Will He Even Molest the Queen?"

Royal wives and concubines were often used as pawns in male power plays in the ancient world. When Absalom was trying to usurp his father David's throne, Ahithophel counseled him to sleep with his father's concubines as a sign to all Israel that he was serious in his challenge to the throne (2 Sam 16:20–22). Similarly, Solomon interpreted his brother Adonijah's request to marry Abishag the Shunammite as a sign of his desire to seize the throne, so Solomon ordered him killed (1 Kgs 2:13–25). Stories of Persians violating the women attached to the men whose positions they wanted abound. In his account of the life of Artaxerxes, Plutarch tells how Artaxerxes's youngest son tries to position himself in the line of succession by making promises to, and perhaps even sleeping with, the king's wife, Atossa:

> But [Artaxerxes's] youngest son, Ochus, who was of an impetuous and violent disposition, not only had many adherents among the courtiers, but hoped for most success in winning over his father through the aid of Atossa. For he sought to gain Atossa's favour by promising that she should be his wife and share the throne with him after the death of his father. And there was a report that even while his father was alive Ochus had secret relations with Atossa.[4]

Later in the same story, Plutarch raises the issue of the sexual boundaries placed around royal wives and concubines that comes into play when Haman falls upon Esther during the second banquet (Esth 7:8):

> Barbarian folk are terribly jealous in all that pertains to the pleasures of love, so that it is death for a man, not only to come up and touch one of the royal concubines, but even in journeying to go along past the wagons on which they are conveyed.[5]

EXPLAIN the Story

Esther's Second Banquet (Esther 7:1–10)

This chapter follows on the heels of Esther chapter 6, where the shame-faced Haman bestows on Mordecai the honors he thinks belong to him, and where his closest allies predict his demise before he is hurried off to his final banquet with the queen. Esther's second banquet closely mirrors the first, where Xerxes asks Esther what she wants and offers her up to half his kingdom

4. Plutarch, *Art.* 26.2.
5. Ibid., 27.1.

(Esth 5). It also contains striking parallels to Xerxes's second drinking extravaganza when Queen Vashti's defiance precipitated Xerxes's rage, her demise, and Esther's rise (1:7–2:18). At Esther's second banquet of wine, the queen's revelation precipitates Xerxes's rage, and Haman's demise leads to Esther's enhancement, as she is given Haman's property. This banquet also triggers Mordecai's rise, as he is placed over the estate of Haman, whom he replaces as second-in-command (7:3–8:2).

The seven Hebrew words that introduce this chapter convey the sense of urgency felt by all present (7:1: *wayyabo' hammelek wehaman lishtot 'im-'Ester hammalkah*; So the king and Haman went to Queen Esther's banquet). Xerxes's initial words reveal his frustration in not knowing what Esther really wants: "Queen Esther, what is your petition?" Haman is in a liminal state; he is deeply troubled by the ominous prophecy that he will fall before Mordecai the Jew, and yet he is thrilled to party again with the royal pair as he believes they greatly esteem him (6:13). Esther, on the other hand, has a plan for how the evening will progress. She is aware that "for such a time as this" she must use every means at her disposal—her beauty, wisdom, and intimate knowledge of the likes, weaknesses, fears, and obsessions of both Haman and Xerxes—to achieve the seemingly impossible reversal of the edict of death.

While Esther chapter 7 is filled with intense drama and dialogue, it reveals frustratingly little about the inner thoughts of Esther and Xerxes. Ironically, Haman's emotions are palpable as he journeys toward impalement upon the enormous pole he had ordered to be constructed for the public viewing of Mordecai's dead body (7:10). Xerxes's movements are well-defined as he leaves behind his wine to retreat to the garden, only to return and find Haman falling on Esther's couch. Xerxes's actions, however, are open to a variety of interpretations (7:8). Esther's physical movements are not noted, but in her third set of responses to the king's question about what she wants, she continues what has been aptly described as "a gentle spiral" as she "circles round and round the king's repeated promise, and with each turn her prospects rise . . . [and] now fully positioned for a favorable hearing, she unveils her shocking request" (7:3).[6]

The self-indulgent (and now most likely inebriated) king again acknowledges Esther's royal position as queen and asks her for the third time to make her petition and request known, promising her yet again up to half his kingdom (see 5:3, 6; 7:2). Esther's carefully constructed reply (7:3–6) deserves a close analysis as it again shows her mastery of the art of persuasion. She not only exposes Haman as the despicable enemy who has endangered her life and

6. Tull, *Esther and Ruth*, 37.

the lives of her people, but also does so in a way that veils the king's culpability in the genocidal plan he so blindly and irresponsibly signed off on (3:10).

Esther begins her response (7:3) as she did in 5:4, with two formal *if* clauses—the first is personal: "If I have found favor in your sight (ESV)"—favor being something that Esther has always received by those she encounters (2:9, 15, 17). The second clause, "if it please the king (ESV)," underscores Esther's deference to the king whom she knows can be tyrannical, volatile, and callous in terms of the value he places on human life (see Listen to the Story, above). Esther structures the substance of her shocking response around the king's rhetoric: "petition," "request," and "granted." Her petition is that the king grant her life and spare the lives of her as yet undesignated people. At this point in the story it is important to remember that, while we as readers are very aware of Esther's double identity as Persian and Jew, Xerxes seems oblivious to the fact that his wife is a Jew and therefore is also doomed to destruction in the genocidal edict he thoughtlessly supported (3:8–10).

Esther continues her carefully constructed disclosure of the genocidal *selling* of her people, using the same trilogy of terms of destruction found in the actual order that Mordecai had shown her earlier: "to destroy, kill, and annihilate" all the Jews (3:9–11; 4:7–8; 7:4). She cleverly uses economic terms to describe the deal Haman made with the king and alludes to Haman's promise to give Xerxes an enormous amount of money for the destruction of the Jews (3:8–11). Throughout her appeal, Esther uses the passive voice to avoid placing any blame on Xerxes for the edict—guilty though he is.

Esther appeals to Xerxes's sense of importance as she again places herself in a subservient position: "If we had merely been sold as male and female slaves, I would have kept quiet" (7:4). While Esther's assent to the possibility of enslavement may seem shocking to contemporary readers, enslaving individuals and people groups was widespread in the Persian empire (see Neh 5:8 and Listen to the Story, above). Esther's words also obscure the reality that she had already experienced the evils of slavery, when as a young girl she was herded into the king's harem where she joined many other sex slaves (Esth 2:8).

Esther concludes her initial reply to the king (7:4) with a clause that is, as Patricia Tull suggests, "masterfully ambiguous—so ambiguous in fact, that nearly every modern translation renders it differently."[7] The ambiguity begins with the subject, *tsar*, which can mean either "distress" (NIV) or "enemy" (NRSV, KJV). The verb that follows, *showeh*, can be translated as "be equivalent to," "to compare with," or "to compensate for"; the object of the verb is the word *nezeq*, which occurs only here in the Hebrew Bible and has something

7. Ibid.

to do with causing or doing harm, damage, or trouble. The NIV, "because no such distress would justify disturbing the king," makes good sense out of the Hebrew, although the NRSV's choice of "enemy" rather than "distress" ties the clause more specifically to Haman and the harm or loss of income Xerxes would sustain if the Jews were enslaved: "but no enemy can compensate for this damage to the king."

The king's response to Esther's shocking disclosure (lit., "And King Xerxes spoke and said to Esther, the queen"; 7:5) contains the uncommon double use of the verb "to say." The NIV translation, "King Xerxes asked," makes sense in light of the king's questions, "Who is he? Where is he?" But it also masks the narrator's intent to slow down the narrative to create further tension.[8] The irony of this moment is intense: the king of the world's greatest empire has no idea that his second-in-command and trusted drinking companion, Haman, is the one who is about to be exposed. Haman, on the other hand, knows very well that he is the one whom Esther is about to identify.

Esther mirrors the king's double question (7:5) with her double identification of the "adversary and enemy" who is threatening her life and the lives of her people (7:6). As a means of creating further suspense, she intentionally does not name the contemptible Haman until the last possible moment. Dialogue changes to commentary as the narrator reveals Haman's abject fear due to his recognition that Esther and Xerxes are now united against him (7:6).

"Like an angry lion," writes renowned American commentator Harriet Beecher Stowe, Xerxes "rose up in a fury and rushed out into the gardens."[9] We have seen Xerxes's rage before in his response to Vashti's defiance (1:12; 2:1). Some interpreters have imagined that Xerxes ran out into the palace garden because he was feeling guilt for his own involvement in the edict and needed time to come up with a plan to save face. Stowe reads it this way and suggests that "at this moment [the king] perceived the net into which he had been drawn by his favorite [i.e., Haman]"; he had been played and had ordered "the destruction of this people, to whom his wife belongs, and for whom she intercedes."[10] Similarly, early American dramatist Eliza Cushing imagines the king turning toward a "pale and motionless" Haman at this point and soliloquizing:

> Oh, gracious gods! Have I been thus deceived?
> Is this the man, the ingrate vile and base,
> Whom I have raised o'er wiser, better men,
> Crowned with high honors, loaded with vast wealth,

---

8. Bush, *Ruth/Esther*, 428–29.

9. Harriet Beecher Stowe, *Woman in Sacred History*: A Celebration of Women in the Bible (New York: Portland House, 1990), 157.

10. Ibid.

Within his grasp placed power, and laid myself,
Aye, e'en my inmost soul, bare to his gaze ?—
And he has used me thus—bounty repaid
With vile ingratitude—fair truth with lies—
Honor with treachery base, and in the name
Of sacred justice has abused my power,
To make me seem that which I never was—
A cruel tyrant thirsting for the blood
Of a poor nation, who beneath my sway
Lead blameless lives within their quiet homes!
Gods! for your vengeance to reward such deeds![11]

If Xerxes was feeling guilt, he needed time to come up with a plan to save face.

Others imagine Xerxes was incapable of such self-awareness and picture him directing his rage at Haman who, like Xerxes, often experienced rage when things did not go as planned (7:7, 10; 3:5; 5:9). If this is so, the most-likely inebriated Xerxes takes time to get a handle on what has just been revealed in a space meant to provide royals with a place to rest, think, and pray (see Esther 1:1–22: Listen to the Story). All this being said, the reason the raging king leaves his wife with the person who was planning to kill her remains ambiguous, and yet Xerxes's actions provide what Jon Levenson identifies as "a comic touch that reinforces our sense of him as weak, malleable, and devoid of self-control."[12]

Recognizing that he is the object of the king's anger and that his fate is sealed, Haman launches a desperate attempt to save his life. As a great schemer and manipulator himself, he recognizes that the woman who has just presented a compelling case for saving the Jews is the only person who can save his life.

In what is arguably the darkest and perhaps the funniest moment in the book, the king returns to the banquet hall to watch Haman falling on Esther's couch—a literal fall that precipitates the actual demise that Zeresh and his friends had earlier predicted (7:8; 6:13). Haman's fall provides Xerxes with the plan that protects both himself and Esther as well as disposes of Haman, who wanted all things royal and has now crossed the line using what could be construed as a ploy commonly used by usurpers of thrones (see Listen to the Story, above). This comical juncture is seen by some as a moment of divine intervention. Perhaps, as the early rabbis surmised, an angelic push caused Haman's divinely-ordained fall![13]

11. Cushing, *Esther*, 94–95.

12. Levenson, *Esther*, 104.

13. Carruthers, *Esther through the Centuries*, 239, citing b. Meg. 16a, Esth. Rab. x.9, and Tg. Rishon.

Xerxes responds to what appeared to be Haman's crossing of sexual boundaries with the rhetorical question, "Will he even molest the queen while she is with me in the house?" (7:8). Xerxes's misinterpretation of Haman's posture has been construed as either a mistake provoked by intoxication, rage, or fear, or brilliance on the part of the king. Given that Xerxes had just a day earlier been reminded of the plot to kill him and seize power (2:19–23; 6:1–3), and given that royal wives and concubines were often used as pawns in royal power plays, and given Haman's obvious obsession with honor, success, attention, and the idea of being king for a day (3:1–6; see also 5:11–13; 6:6–9), it is not surprising that Xerxes may have believed Haman was intent on usurping the throne. Or perhaps more simply, Xerxes has been effectively drawn into Esther's plan to garner his personal support and is now deeply concerned about his victimized wife; he regards Haman's violation of the protocols about keeping one's distance from royal women as yet another violation of his wife.

Whether Xerxes's misapprehension is real or contrived, it serves as a good reason for condemning Haman. Xerxes's later explanation that Haman was impaled because he plotted to lay hands on the Jews (8:7) suggests that the king condemned Haman for molesting his wife as a means of directing attention away from the pressing issue of his own role in agreeing to Haman's vile idea of genocide. The king's attendants interpret the king's reaction to Haman's actions as a death sentence for Haman and cover his face (7:8).

At this point, Harbona, the opportunistic eunuch who had a minor role earlier in the book (1:10), offers the king information that he should have had but, perhaps alone in all of Susa, did not have (7:9). He discloses that Haman had erected an enormous pole for impaling the very person the king had just honored for saving him (5:14; 6:10). As Hazony suggests, Harbona's move "is a defection from the camp of Haman's supporters to that of the Jews. He recognizes the shift in power that has taken place and determines to place his bet on the ascendant party, the party he believes will soon be in control: Mordechai and Esther."[14]

Not surprisingly, Xerxes, who throughout the book has acceded to the advice of others, agrees that Haman's impaling pole would make an excellent execution device and commands: "Impale him on it!" (7:9). Ironically, Haman was impaled for rape, a crime he did not commit (7:10). As Hamlet quipped, "'tis the sport to have the engineer hoist with his own petard."[15]

---

14. Hazony, *God and Politics in Esther*, 115.

15. Hamlet, 3.4.207–8.

LIVE the Story

Esther's Triumph and God's Triumph

> "I am sending you out like sheep among wolves. Therefore be as shrewd as snakes and as innocent as doves." (Matt 10:16)

Esther's commission to convince the self-centered, impulsive, and irresponsible tyrant Xerxes to spare Jewish lives was much like that of the disciples whom Jesus sent out like sheep among wolves. In this scene, Esther is both sheep and snake as she humbly and shrewdly confronts the wolves, Xerxes and Haman. Bishop Marbod (ca. 1035–1123) of Rennes in Brittany also associated this scene in Esther's story with Jesus' commissioning of his disciples in Matthew. He describes Queen Esther as a courageous woman "married to a cruel tyrant like a lamb to a wolf [who] did not fear to cross the threshold at the risk of her life."[16]

Esther's rhetorical skills, like those of Abraham when he pled for Sodom (Gen 18:25–32) and negotiated land for Sarah's burial (Gen 23:1–20), illustrate the proverbial saying "Through patience a ruler can be persuaded, and a gentle tongue can break a bone" (Prov 25:15). Esther's speech at this second banquet has been justly lauded for its "rhetorical perfection" and used by men and women as "an exemplar of an ideal political speech."[17] Eighteenth-century poet James Maxwell praised Esther for her rhetoric and prudence, but also used her example to shame other prattling female tongues:

> O *Esther*! I admire thy *matchless* prudence:
> How prudently didst thou thy cause present!
> Let all thy sex a lesson learn from thee,
> Not to be rash and hasty with their words.
> How many righteous causes have been lost
> By over hasty prate of female tongues.[18]

While many have lauded Esther's speech, some of her most vicious critics disdain her "manipulative" behavior in this scene. They are especially bothered by how she uses her knowledge of the king's affection toward her to

16. Lois L. Huneycutt, "Intercession and the High-Medieval Queen: The Esther Topos," in *Power of the Weak: Studies on Medieval Women*, ed. Jennifer Carpenter and Sally-Beth Maclean (Urbana: University of Illinois, 1995), 141.

17. Carruthers, *Esther through the Centuries*, 234.

18. James Maxwell, *Another Display of the Wonders of Divine Providence, Exemplified in the History of Queen Esther: or, a Poetical Paraphrase on the Whole Book of Esther, to which is added, The Virtuous Woman; or a Paraphrase on Proverbs 31:10–31* (Glasgow: printed for the author, 1784), 21, quoted in Carruthers, *Esther through the Centuries*, 235.

her own advantage in her quest to get him on her side in the battle against Haman. But given the time and place and Esther's experience as a victim-survivor of trauma, she instinctually uses all means available for survival; we should join the company of witnesses throughout history who have been inspired by Esther's courage, tenacity, and wisdom as she comes face-to-face with the impetuous and self-serving Xerxes and the equally self-serving anti-Semitic Haman.

Empowering the Weak, Marginalized, and Vulnerable

Esther has inspired God's people throughout history to step into perilous arenas to use their influence to make a difference. Ninth-century Pope John VIII appealed to Charles the Bald's wife to advocate for the imperial church in the same way that Esther spoke up for her people.[19] Similarly, Esther's courageous and yet judicious example inspired Matilda, queen to Henry I of England (1100–1118), to use her power and influence over her husband for good.[20] As well, Christine de Pizan [Pisan] (ca. 1364–ca. 1430) thought that when Esther convinced her husband that Haman was the author of the plot to kill the Jews, she proved that women have the power to bring good to the world.[21]

Esther's importance as a role model for Christian men and women who find themselves in a minority position in a dominant culture continues today in our postmodern world. As Esther's comments about slavery (7:4) remind us, Esther—and indeed all God's people—faced enormous challenges living in an empire whose values conflict with Scripture. Even when the Jews were saved from genocide, their future was precarious at best. Their freedom to keep themselves separate and live according to distinctive laws could be challenged again at the blink of an eye. Today, many Christians face similar challenges from the world's great empires. We need to be wise and use all our resources and knowledge as we negotiate with those who do not share our values. Like Esther, we need to battle evil, advocate for justice, and plead for the deliverance of those whose lives are in peril.

What about Forgiveness?

Historically, this chapter has raised and continues (for some) to raise the issue of (un)forgiveness. Even though Esther was not given a chance to respond to Haman's plea for mercy, her silence on the matter has bothered readers

19. Huneycutt, "Intercession and the High-Medieval Queen," 129.

20. Ibid., 127.

21. Josette A. Wisman, "Christine de Pizan," in *Handbook of Women Biblical Interpreters*, ed. Marion Ann Taylor (Grand Rapids: Baker, 2012), 128–29.

who assume that Esther should have been compassionate and offered mercy and forgiveness to her enemy Haman. Eighteenth-century dramatist Thomas Brereton imagined that Haman specifically asked Esther, as a follower of the compassionate and forgiving God of the Jews, to forgive him: "I find 'tis vain to fight your God and live: / But does he teach you never to forgive?"[22] The influential Esther scholar Lewis Paton shares this frustration with Esther's lack of compassion, declaring that "her character would have been more attractive if she had shown pity toward a fallen foe."[23] But such interpretations fail to appreciate the complexities of the conflict between Haman and the Jews. After all, the man seeking forgiveness had orchestrated the destruction of God's people. Moreover, while begging for his own life, Haman showed no remorse for condemning all Jews to death. Haman was, as Harriet Livermore suggests, "an instrument of the foul serpent."[24] Eliza Cushing goes further and regards Esther as a vehicle of God's justice:

> **Haman:** Mercy! Great Queen!
> I do implore thee in the name of Him,
> Thou call'st thy God.
> **Esther:** He is a God of justice, wretched Man!
> And his commands writ on eternal stone
> Thou hast defied, and dared to violate,
> When thou didst falsely swear, and rashly seek
> The guiltless blood of those whom He protects.[25]

The conflict between Haman and Esther was neither personal nor between equals. As the Kairos theologians commenting on the political crisis in South Africa in 1985 recognized:

> There are conflicts where one side is a fully armed and violent oppressor while the other side is defenseless and oppressed. There are conflicts that can only be described as the struggle between justice and injustice, good and evil, God and the devil. To speak of reconciling these two is not only a mistaken application of the Christian idea of reconciliation; it is total betrayal of all that Christian faith has ever meant.[26]

---

22. Thomas Brereton, *Esther, or Faith Triumphant: A Sacred Tragedy* (London: for J. Tonson, 1715), 44, quoted in Carruthers, *Esther Through the Centuries*, 241.

23. Paton, *Esther*, 264.

24. Livermore, *Scriptural Evidence*, 52.

25. Cushing, *Esther*, 95.

26. Kairos Theologians, *The Kairos Document: Challenge to the Church: A Theological Comment on the Political Crisis in South Africa* (Braamfontein: Skotaville Publishers, 1986), 8–9.

Haman's Defeat and God's Victory

Esther rightly names Haman as an adversary and enemy and calls him, "This vile Haman!" Haman has always been seen as a personification of evil and, as such, reminds us of other enemies of God's people; Haman's defeat gives God's people hope that other enemies will also be defeated. Frances Caulkins reads Haman's fall in this way and, preaching with her pen, encourages all God's people to trust the living God who not only hears the cries of his children who are oppressed by Haman-like enemies, but also will in the end crown the faithful and bring punishment to the guilty:

> Prone falls the oppressor, and a sway more bland
> Spreads like bedewing grace o'er Persia's land.
> Be all thy foes like Haman, Most High,
>   Defeated in their aims
> Thy church victorious, and by faith descry
>   What Esther's life proclaims:
> "Fear not, the living God looks down,
>   And sways the world below;
> Fear not, he will the faithful crown,
>   The guilty head lay low.
> Thy cry, thy plaint, Oh mourning dove, he hears,
> And kindly bends to wipe away thy tears.[27]

Although Haman's defeat is not the last battle in the book, it underscores one of the book's central theological messages, namely that God is active in the affairs of humans. The hope Caulkins hears in this text is one that all God's people doing battle with evil empires and evil Hamans should embrace. The final war in heaven, she reminds us, is one in which the great Dragon, the deceiver of the whole world, is defeated:

> And there was war in heaven, Michael and his angels waging war with the dragon. The dragon and his angels waged war, and they were not strong enough, and there was no longer a place found for them in heaven. And the great dragon was thrown down, the serpent of old who is called the devil and Satan, who deceives the whole world; he was thrown down to the earth, and his angels were thrown down with him. (Rev 12:7–9 ESV)

27. Caulkins, *Eve and Her Daughters*, 124.

CHAPTER 12

Esther 8:1–17

LISTEN to the Story

1That same day King Xerxes gave Queen Esther the estate of Haman, the enemy of the Jews. And Mordecai came into the presence of the king, for Esther had told how he was related to her. 2The king took off his signet ring, which he had reclaimed from Haman, and presented it to Mordecai. And Esther appointed him over Haman's estate.

3Esther again pleaded with the king, falling at his feet and weeping. She begged him to put an end to the evil plan of Haman the Agagite, which he had devised against the Jews. 4Then the king extended the gold scepter to Esther and she arose and stood before him.

5"If it pleases the king," she said, "and if he regards me with favor and thinks it the right thing to do, and if he is pleased with me, let an order be written overruling the dispatches that Haman son of Hammedatha, the Agagite, devised and wrote to destroy the Jews in all the king's provinces. 6For how can I bear to see disaster fall on my people? How can I bear to see the destruction of my family?"

7King Xerxes replied to Queen Esther and to Mordecai the Jew, "Because Haman attacked the Jews, I have given his estate to Esther, and they have impaled him on the pole he set up. 8Now write another decree in the king's name in behalf of the Jews as seems best to you, and seal it with the king's signet ring—for no document written in the king's name and sealed with his ring can be revoked."

9At once the royal secretaries were summoned—on the twenty-third day of the third month, the month of Sivan. They wrote out all Mordecai's orders to the Jews, and to the satraps, governors and nobles of the 127 provinces stretching from India to Cush. These orders were written in the script of each province and the language of each people and also to the Jews in their own script and language. 10Mordecai wrote in the name of King Xerxes, sealed the dispatches with the king's signet ring, and sent them by mounted couriers, who rode fast horses especially bred for the king.

[11]The king's edict granted the Jews in every city the right to assemble and protect themselves; to destroy, kill and annihilate the armed men of any nationality or province who might attack them and their women and children, and to plunder the property of their enemies. [12]The day appointed for the Jews to do this in all the provinces of King Xerxes was the thirteenth day of the twelfth month, the month of Adar. [13]A copy of the text of the edict was to be issued as law in every province and made known to the people of every nationality so that the Jews would be ready on that day to avenge themselves on their enemies.

[14]The couriers, riding the royal horses, went out, spurred on by the king's command, and the edict was issued in the citadel of Susa.

[15]When Mordecai left the king's presence, he was wearing royal garments of blue and white, a large crown of gold and a purple robe of fine linen. And the city of Susa held a joyous celebration. [16]For the Jews it was a time of happiness and joy, gladness and honor. [17]In every province and in every city to which the edict of the king came, there was joy and gladness among the Jews, with feasting and celebrating. And many people of other nationalities became Jews because fear of the Jews had seized them.

Listen to the Text in the Story: Biblical Texts: Deuteronomy 7:1–6; 20; 1 Kings 21:15–16; Isaiah 2:4; Amos 1:3–2:3; Ancient Near Eastern Texts: Herodotus, *Histories* 3.128–9.

Confiscation of Property: Xerxes Gave Esther Haman's Estate

In the ancient world, the estates of executed traitors or criminals became the property of the state to dispense with at will, as Xerxes did with Haman's estate. Jezebel used this policy to surreptitiously acquire Naboth's vineyard for her pouting husband:

> As soon as Jezebel heard that Naboth had been stoned to death, she said to Ahab, "Get up and take possession of the vineyard of Naboth the Jezreelite that he refused to sell you. He is no longer alive, but dead." When Ahab heard that Naboth was dead, he got up and went down to take possession of Naboth's vineyard. (1 Kgs 21:15–16)

Similarly, Herodotus recounts the dramatic story of King Darius's confiscation of the slaves and possessions of a traitor:

> King Darius instructs the Persians in Sardis to kill Oroetes . . . the spearmen drew their scimitars and killed him at once. . . . Oroetes' slaves and other possessions were brought to Susa.[1]

The Ethics of War: Destroy, Kill, Annihilate, and Avenge

Violence and war are themes featured in many ancient texts. Deuteronomy 20 sets out rules of warfare that include the promise of the LORD's support in battles against enemies (20:4), permission to kill males and take plunder from those who reject an offer of peace (20:10–11, 14) and in the case of certain enemies, such as the Amalekites, the command to wage holy war against them (20:4, 10–11, 14, 16–18; see also 7:1–6). Very few ancient texts address concerns about the ethics of war. Amos 1:3–2:3 stands out for its condemnation of war atrocities including genocide, the violation of women, and the desecration of bodies. Violators include the following: Gaza who "took captive whole communities and sold them to Edom," Ammon who "ripped open the pregnant women of Gilead in order to extend his borders," and Moab who "burned to ashes the bones of Edom's king" (Amos 1:6, 13; 2:1; see also Isa 10:7). Criticism of war is also implied in texts that present a vision of the future without war: "He will judge between the nations and will settle disputes for many peoples. They will beat their swords into plowshares and their spears into pruning hooks. Nation will not take up sword against nation, nor will they train for war anymore" (Isa 2:4). The book of Esther obliquely addresses issues related to genocidal warfare, but readers are not of one mind as to its message. As will be discussed further below, some read Esther as an argument for the rights of those threatened with genocide to counterattack, while others argue that the vengeful Jews are no better than the anti-Semites whose hatred and avarice motivated them to plan to annihilate an entire people.

Symbolic Clothes and Accessories: Mordecai's Royal Garments and Crown

As discussed earlier (see Esther 5:1–14: Listen to the Story), clothing such as Mordecai's blue, white, and purple garments and accessories such as his crown carried symbolic weight. The royals, those they desired to honor, and sometimes even royal animals wore crowns (Esth 1:11; 2:17; 6:8; 8:15). Herodotus recounts the story of how Xerxes used a gold crown to honor a man who had saved his life during a storm at sea. Unexpectedly, the tyrannical Xerxes then ordered his savior beheaded for his idea to lighten the ship's load by forfeiting human life:

1. Herodotus, *Hist.* 3.128–29.

> This storm bearing the harder upon him by reason of the heavy load of the ship (for the Persians of his company who were on the deck were so many), the king grew afraid and cried to the ship's pilot asking him if there were any way of deliverance. To this the man said, "Sire, there is none, if we do not rid ourselves of these many who are on board." Hearing that, it is said, Xerxes said to the Persians, "Now it is for you to prove your concern for your king, for it seems that my deliverance rests with you." At this they bowed and leapt into the sea. The ship, now much lighter, came by these means safe to Asia. No sooner had Xerxes disembarked on land, than he made the pilot a gift of a golden crown for saving the king's life but cut off his head for being the death of many Persians.[2]

EXPLAIN the Story

The Transfer of Property and Power (Esther 8:1–8)

This chapter begins "that same day"—the day of Esther's defeat of her "adversary and enemy! This vile Haman!" (7:6)—with a series of three ironic reversals precipitated by Haman's death (8:1). First, the extensive estate that Haman loved to brag about (5:11) becomes state property before being gifted to Esther, the very person who had exposed him and now negotiates a plan to counter his edict of death (7:4, 8; see Listen to the Story, above). Whether Xerxes gifts Esther out of a sense of guilt for his own role in the debacle (3:11) or out of compassion for his distraught wife is unclear. His lavish gift, however, is not unusual (see Esther 5:1–14 and 6:1–14: Listen to the Story).

Second, Esther reverses Mordecai's mandate that she hide both her nationality and family relations (2:10, 20; 8:1b). Accordingly, Esther introduces Xerxes, who needs a new second-in-command, to her uncle Mordecai. Xerxes had previously known Mordecai as the person he had forgotten to reward for saving his life and the man Haman had planned to impale (6:10). Recognizing Mordecai's qualifications for Haman's job and trusting Esther's endorsement, Xerxes invites Mordecai to enter the court and thus initiates the third reversal.

The Haman-Mordecai reversal that began in Esther chapter 6 when Mordecai received the honors Haman thought were his continues in chapter 7 when Haman is impaled on the pole erected for Mordecai's impalement. Now Xerxes gives Mordecai Haman's position and the very signet ring that Haman had used to seal the Jew's death edict (3:10). Continuing the Haman-Mordecai reversal, Esther adds wealth and power to Mordecai's position by setting him

2. Ibid., 8.118.

over his nemesis' vast estate (8:2). Zeresh's prediction that Haman would fall before the Jew Mordecai is almost fully realized—the death and impalement of Haman's sons will complete the prophecy (6:13; 9:10, 13).

At this point in the story, Esther's call to negotiate the deliverance of the Jews remains incomplete. The genocidal edict is still in place, and the Jews are still in peril. Not surprisingly, Esther initiates the next step in her strategic plan to fulfill Mordecai's charge that she "beg [Xerxes] for mercy and plead with him for her people" (4:8). Her final approach (8:3) unleashes a flood of emotion that could be either genuine or staged (5:1–2, 7–9; 7:2–6).

With dramatic flair, Esther falls at Xerxes's feet and pleads with intensity and tears (8:3). Scottish cleric George Lawson is typical of readers who judge Esther's approach as genuine but also stereotypically feminine: "Her beauty, her tears, the strong emotions of her heart apparent in her gestures, the amiable virtues which shone forth in her generous concern for her poor friends, were sufficient to have melted the most marble-hearted prince in the world."[3] While Lawson may be correct, Esther's wise use of tactics played into the king's need to feel in control, his desire to please, and his love for beautiful deferential women, and may also have been contrived. She pleads that Xerxes remove (the same verb used in 8:2 for taking off Haman's ring) the evil plan Haman the Agagite had devised against the Jews. While the significance of Esther's identification of Haman as an Agagite would have been lost on Xerxes, the narrator is purposely reminding readers that the historic and epic conflict between Haman and the Jews remained unresolved.

After Xerxes extends the gold scepter (8:4; see also 4:11; 5:2), Esther begins her formal plea. Commenting on this highly significant moment of favor that leads to the deliverance of the Jews, Harriet Livermore likens Esther to the Virgin Mary: "Happy Esther, highly favoured among women, the Lord is with thee, and the God of hosts is thy reward!"[4] Esther's petition echoes her previous requests, the language found in Memucan's deferential dealings with the king, and the account of the original conspiracy to kill the Jews. She prefaces her plea with four courteous and ingratiating conditional clauses (8:5) that alternate the importance of the king's valuing Esther's proposal ("if it pleases the king" and if he "thinks it the right thing to do") with the value of what Esther brings to the relationship ("if he regards me with favor" and "if he is pleased with me" or literally "if I am good in his eyes" as in 1:19, 21; 3:11).

Esther's carefully-scripted request that Haman's order be overruled by another edict places the responsibility for writing and implementing the initial

3. George Lawson, *Discourses on the Whole Book of Esther* (Edinburgh: J. Pillans & Sons, 1804), 178, quoted in Carruthers, *Esther Through the Centuries*, 244.

4. Livermore, *Scriptural Evidence*, 61.

edict of death squarely on Haman's shoulders. Esther wisely does not implicate Xerxes in the matter (8:5). Knowing that an argument based on the injustice of killing the Jews would be futile, Esther cleverly appeals to Xerxes's empathy and feelings for her situation (8:6). Her final double emotive rhetorical question, "For how can I bear to see disaster fall on my people? How can I bear to see the destruction of my family?" (8:6), echoes Judah's final plea to his brother Joseph: "No! Do not let me see the misery that would come on my father" (Gen 44:34).

Though Esther's appeal seems reasonable, the idea mentioned several times earlier in the book that Persia's laws were unchangeable meant that even the king could not formally rescind Haman's edict (Esth 1:19; 4:3; 8:8; Dan 6:8, 12; see Esther 1:1–22: Listen to the Story). Xerxes's initial response (8:7) is defensive. In his mind he had effectively dealt with Haman's sedition against the Jews by having him killed and by gifting his estate to Esther. Remarkably, Xerxes sets aside the crime of attempted rape that Haman was actually impaled for (7:8). Xerxes's comeback suggests that he knew all along that Haman was innocent of the charge of rape, but the charge had provided him with a convenient pretext to kill the man who had manipulated him into agreeing to an edict to kill the Jews.

In any case, realizing that Esther was not satisfied by what he had allegedly done for her, Xerxes offers a solution that is similar to the one he had offered Haman following his impassioned request to destroy a certain people group who followed distinctive laws (3:8–12). The "king"—a designation that is repeated four times in the Hebrew, three times in the NIV—authorizes both Esther and Mordecai (lit., "you" plural) to write "what seems good in your (plural) eyes" and seal an irrevocable decree concerning the Jews, that is meant to counter an ostensibly unalterable law (8:8).

At this point, even Xerxes seems to recognize the seriously flawed nature of the Persian legal system; as David Firth observes: "there is something intrinsically doubtful about a legal system that establishes irrevocable laws that are capable of being overturned by another decree which simply declares the opposite to apply! Once again, there is more than a hint of satire in dealing with the Persian legal system."[5]

Mordecai's Counteredict: Vengeance Belongs to Whom? (Esther 8:9–17)

Even before the content of the edict is revealed, the impressive royal administrative machinery is set in motion (8:9; see Esther 1:1–22: Listen to the Story).

5. Firth, *The Message of Esther*, 115.

Although Xerxes had tasked both Esther and Mordecai with writing a counter decree, Mordecai takes the lead at this point, as the orders are now associated with him ("They wrote out all Mordecai's orders"; 8:9). Mordecai writes in the name of the king and seals the dispatches with the king's signet ring (8:9–10).

The striking parallels between Haman's initial edict (3:12–15) and Mordecai's counter decree (8:9–14) continue to underscore the theme of reversals. Just as the king's scribes were summoned to inscribe Haman's royally authorized decree that was then sealed and widely distributed to officials throughout the empire (3:12), the king's scribes are called to write Mordecai's royally-authorized counter decree that is sealed and widely distributed. This time, the distribution begins with the condemned Jews who receive a copy of the counter decree "in their own script and language" (8:9–10).

The NIV translation of 8:11 indicates that the mirroring in the decrees is incomplete; the people to be destroyed, killed, annihilated, and plundered are no longer "all the Jews—young and old, women and children" as in 3:13, but only those attacking the Jews, namely "the armed men of any nationality or province who might attack them and their women and children." This translation effectively sidesteps the morally offensive issue of Jews slaying innocent women and children. Most translations—the NRSV, NASB, NKJV, and NAB, for example—reflect the fuller parallelism between Haman's decree and Mordecai's decree found in the Hebrew, which allows the Jews to stand up against their attackers, including women and children and to plunder their goods. Some who find this part of Esther's story morally problematic are quick to point out that just because the Jews are allowed to kill the innocent women and children, they may not have actually done so, just as they did not take the plunder (9:10, 15–16).[6] Others suggest that the Jews' proposed reciprocal vengeance supports the view that the "Jews in their actions, are not essentially different from the heathen."[7] Swiss pastor Wilhelm Vischer builds on this idea of the moral equivalence of the Jews and the Persians and argues that this counteredict points to the cross, where Jesus, through his death for sin once for all, solved the problem of retributive justice: "While God permits the sin both of Jew and Gentile to work itself out in the crucifixion of His Son by both parties, and judges it, He fulfils and reveals at the same time the unique and complete victory of His grace and truth over the world's iniquity."[8]

Perhaps the most faithful way to interpret the unmistakable parallelism between the decrees is to read this account of the conflict between the Jews and their enemies in light of the earlier holy war between the Amalekites and God's

6. See Jobes, *Esther*, 178–82.
7. Stan Goldman, "Narrative and Ethical Ironies in Esther," *JSOT* 47 (1990): 24–25.
8. Wilhelm Vischer, "The Book of Esther," *EvQ* 11 (1939): 15.

people (Exod 17:8, 14–16; 1 Sam 15:2–3; 30:1–20). Esther's request for a second day of killing and the hanging of Haman's ten sons (Esth 9:13) presents similar interpretive challenges. The moral offence to those who threatened to destroy God's people must be considered in these particular time-specific responses as part of a larger discussion of holy war.

The mirroring between the decrees continues as notice is given about the day appointed for the Jewish defense, the issuing of the edict as law throughout the empire, and the speedy dispersal of linguistically accessible copies of the decree by couriers mounted on the king's fastest horses (3:14–15; 8:13–14; see Esther 1:1–22: Listen to the Story). The timely distribution of the edict empowered the Jews to protect themselves and "avenge themselves on their enemies" (8:13).

The arresting parallels between the edicts come to an end as the reactions to the counteredict come to light (8:15–17). Haman's earlier edict of death had spawned a variety of responses, including Xerxes's and Haman's celebratory drinking, the city of Susa's dismay, Mordecai's public and symbolic mourning and protest, and the Jews' mourning, fasting, weeping, and lamenting throughout the empire (3:15–4:3). By contrast, Mordecai's counter decree generates celebration, joy, and gladness. The exalted Mordecai leaves the throne room dressed in a crown and regal blue, white, and purple clothing that signals his close association with the king (see Listen to the Story, above). His new position promises the traumatized Jews a more stable and secure future (10:1–3). All of Susa celebrates the good news. Jews throughout the empire experience gladness and joy, and host commemorative feasts—like those hosted by Xerxes, Vashti, and Esther (1–2; 5–7)—and (literally) "a good day," likely a celebratory holiday (NIV: "celebrating"; 8:16–17).

Chapter eight closes with a notice that many Persians "became Jews"—a verb that occurs here alone and is derived from the noun for Judahite (8:17). What is meant by converting out of fear of the Jews is not clear.[9] The extent of public knowledge about the Jews' God, who is so hidden in the book of Esther, is difficult to gauge. Haman's wife Zeresh certainly had a foreboding sense of fear about the Jews (6:13). But such a sense would not be likely to lead to the kind of knowledge that Rahab had when she testified: "our hearts melted in fear . . . for the Lord your God is God in heaven above and on the earth below" (Josh 2:11).

It is more likely that the conversions of many Persians were convenient rather than legitimate. The rabbis compared Persian "converts" to the "lion proselytes" of Samaria, who feared the Lord after he sent killing lions among

9. The LXX goes further to suggest the Persians "were circumcised!" (LXX 8:17).

them (2 Kgs 17:24–28).[10] We might also liken these opportunistic Persians to "rice Christians," a pejorative term used as early as 1699 by non-Christians in India and Macao to describe impoverished people, such as the casteless *pariahs,* who professed Christian faith in order to get rice to eat. The expression continues to be used to depict those who convert for material gain.[11] Harbona, the eunuch who took it upon himself to inform the king of Haman's plan to impale the man who had saved the king's life, was one of the first to align himself with the Jews whose fortunes had been so completely reversed (Esth 7:9).

LIVE the Story

Lifting the Needy from the Ash Heap and Seating Them with Princes

Missing from this chapter of great reversals is the theological framework found in other stories of great reversals in Scripture, which attribute the turnabouts to Israel's God. Hannah's prayer of thanksgiving following the birth of her long-awaited son (1 Sam 2) provides a helpful theological commentary on Esther chapter 8. Hannah's prayer attributes to the LORD the kind of striking reversals that we see in Mordecai's life:

> The LORD sends poverty and wealth [Mordecai is given Haman's estate];
> he humbles and he exalts [Mordecai is made second-in-command] . . .
> and lifts the needy from the ash heap [Mordecai casts off his mourning clothes];
> he seats them with princes [or kings such as Xerxes]
> and has them inherit a throne of honor. (1 Sam 2:7–8)

Hannah's prayer also recognizes that reversals silence the wicked who oppose the LORD. In Esther 8:17, the reversals push many to switch allegiance and "become Jews." Hannah's prayer also identifies the creator God as the one who protects his servants (from genocide) and who judges their enemies (such as Haman and other Persian anti-Semites):

> For the foundations of the earth are the LORD's;
> on them he has set the world.

---

10. Gary N. Knoppers, *Jews and Samaritans: The Origins and History of Their Early Relations* (New York: Oxford University Press, 2013), 4.

11. William Dampier, "As to the converts these People have made, I have been credibly informed that they are chiefly of the very poor People, and that in the scarce times, the Alms of Rice have converted more than their preaching," in *Voyages and Descriptions*, Vol. II (London: printed for James Knapton, 1699), 96.

He will guard the feet of his faithful servants,
but the wicked will be silenced in the place of darkness
[Haman and others are killed].

It is not by strength that one prevails;
those who oppose the LORD will be broken.
The Most High will thunder from heaven;
the LORD will judge the ends of the earth. (1 Sam 2:8–10)

According to Sarah Trimmer, the theological truths standing behind the great reversals in Esther "are powerful motives to induce us to trust in God and to live good lives that we may share in his protection."[12] Trimmer is not talking about a simplistic prosperity gospel nor is she talking about superficial "lion" or "rice" conversions. Instead she sees the story of Esther as a compelling admonition to believers to keep trusting in God even when God seems hidden or distant. This is how the story of Esther has been heard by countless generations of God's people who, even in the direst conditions, continue to trust in the sovereignty of God over their lives. They trust that if the silencing of the wicked and the blessing of God's faithful are not seen in this life, all things will be put right in the new heaven and earth. So too today, Christians who find themselves crushed by godless empires and vile Hamans are encouraged to trust the sovereign living God who delivered the Jews and who promises in Christ the ultimate victory of the righteous in the day of trouble (Ps 41).

"Hail, You That Are Highly Favored, the Lord Is with You: Blessed Are You among Women" (AKJV)

Esther's dramatic and effective appeal to the king has inspired much reflection and comment. Those living in cultures whose structures and values are similar to those of ancient Persia continue to regard Esther as a model showing how to use knowledge, position, privilege, and even allure to get what is needed from a person in power. Late medieval Jewish exegetes, for example, regarded Esther as an example of how subjects approaching their ruler should "emphasize the ruler's benefit, cite any favour the petitioner can draw on, assert the appropriateness of the request and the worth of the person as king."[13] More recently, eighteen wives of Haredi members of Israel's Knesset used the example of Esther's approach to Xerxes to persuade Sara Netanyahu to influence her husband, Benjamin Netanyahu, whom they likened to Xerxes in terms of his emperor-like control and power: "Please, we are crying out to

12. Trimmer, *A Help to the Unlearned*, 264.

13. Barry Dov Walfish, *Esther in Medieval Garb: Jewish Interpretation of the Book of Esther in the Middle Ages* (New York: SUNY Press, 1993), 53, quoted in Carruthers, *Esther Through the Centuries*, 244.

you," they wrote. Their cry in opposition to recent legislation to conscript Orthodox Jews for military service continued: "Fulfill your responsibility to the nation, and use your great influence with your husband the Prime Minister to prevent this mortal blow to such a large segment of Israel's population."[14]

In contrast, Filipina scholar Melba Padilla Maggay warns that Esther's "oblique and roundabout" method of gaining power "looks like feminine wiles to those who come from aggressively straightforward cultures . . . [and] a political tradition with a highly developed language for rights."[15] Maggay's point is well taken, but those who find Esther's approach offensive need to be reminded that when we read Esther's story within its ancient context, we can more fully appreciate the enormous challenges Esther faced as she negotiated with her narcissistic, impulsive, passion-driven, and tyrannical husband.

Esther as a War Hero and Savior: "So May All Your Enemies Perish, LORD!"

Although Esther's way to power should not be strictly emulated in most postmodern contexts, we can laud her wisdom and courageous actions. As Harriet Livermore recognized, Esther was "an honored instrument in averting ruin from thousands of [her] fellow mortals, yes a whole nation might call [her] a female Saviour!"[16] Recalling Esther's ancestry as "a descendant from Benjamin, the twelfth patriarchal character, whom good old Jacob blessed," Livermore reads Esther's story in light of the grand narrative of the story of God and connects her with her forefather Benjamin, whom Jacob described as being "a ravenous wolf; in the morning he devours the prey, in the evening he divides the plunder" (Gen 49:27). Esther, like her tribal ancestors, was a war hero who "devoured the prey, and at evening divided the spoil" to bring deliverance to God's people.[17] Livermore suggests that like Deborah and Esther, we too should pray: "So may all your enemies perish, LORD! But may all who love you be like the sun when it rises in its strength" (Judg 5:31).[18]

What about Destroying, Killing, and Annihilating Enemies Today?

The reversal of the genocidal decree brought great joy and happiness and was celebrated by both Jews and non-Jews in Susa. We too should celebrate

14. Frimet Goldberger, "Haredi Wives to Sara Netanyahu: 'Be Our Esther,'" *Forward.com: The Sisterhood Blog*, 28 February 2014, http://forward.com/sisterhood/193612/haredi-wives-to-sara-netanyahu-be-our-esther/.

15. Melba Padilla Maggay, "The Power & Potential of Women," in *The IVP Women's Bible Commentary*. Catherine Clark Kroeger and Mary J. Evans, ed. (Downers Grove, IL: InterVarsity Press, 2002), 269.

16. Livermore, *Scriptural Evidence*, 53.

17. Ibid., 65.

18. Ibid., 63.

the overturning of Haman's vindictive decree that was meant to annihilate God's people. The edict itself, however, raises an important ethical question: Is Mordecai's counter decree meant to give God's people today license to destroy, kill, and annihilate their enemies? Reinhard Achenbach believes that Esther's story does give Jews living as "an ethnic entity under foreign domination" sanction "to defend their fundamental right as an ethnic, cultural and religious integrity."[19] Achenbach argues further that the book of Esther more generally defends "the right to resist the violation of human rights especially under the threat of genocide."[20] This second, more general, argument aligns itself with the modern consensus regarding the immorality of genocide that the UN declaration of 1948 addresses and the legal tradition that permits the use of violence in defense of self, family members, and neighbors.[21]

Before using Esther's story to justify vengeful or even defensive combat, it must be noted that the Jews are not given permission to attack other ethnic groups, but only those determined to massacre them. In this respect, Goldingay suggests that Mordecai's counter decree is similar to what we see elsewhere in the Old Testament where, except for

> one or two spectacular occasions when God commissions them to take action against peoples just because of their wickedness, . . . God is not in the habit of commissioning them to take action against people just because they are their enemies. More often God is telling them to knuckle down under the authority of the empire of the day until the time comes when God decides to do something about it. . . . Haman and his edict are a different question.[22]

Moreover, as the post-conflict celebrations of Purim described in the next chapter strongly suggest, the events in Esther were not meant to provide an ongoing model for handling human conflict. Rather they were to celebrate the outcome that brought peace, truth, and rest to Jewish life, family, and community.

---

19. Reinhard Achenbach, "'Genocide' in the Book of Esther: Cultural Integration and the Right of Resistance against Pogroms" in Rainer Albertz and Jakob Wöhrle, *Between Cooperation and Hostility: Multiple Identities in Ancient Judaism and the Interaction with Foreign Powers* (Göttingen: Vandenhoeck & Ruprecht, 2013), 91.

20. Ibid.

21. See the United Nations Office on Genocide Prevention and the Responsibility to Protect at www.un.org/en/genocideprevention/genocide.html.

22. Goldingay, *Ezra, Nehemiah, and Esther for Everyone*, 185.

CHAPTER 13

Esther 9:1–32

LISTEN to the Story

1On the thirteenth day of the twelfth month, the month of Adar,
the edict commanded by the king was to be carried out. On this day the
enemies of the Jews had hoped to overpower them, but now the tables were
turned and the Jews got the upper hand over those who hated them. 2The
Jews assembled in their cities in all the provinces of King Xerxes to attack
those determined to destroy them. No one could stand against them,
because the people of all the other nationalities were afraid of them. 3And
all the nobles of the provinces, the satraps, the governors and the king's
administrators helped the Jews, because fear of Mordecai had seized them.
4Mordecai was prominent in the palace; his reputation spread throughout
the provinces, and he became more and more powerful.

5The Jews struck down all their enemies with the sword, killing and
destroying them, and they did what they pleased to those who hated
them. 6In the citadel of Susa, the Jews killed and destroyed five hundred
men. 7They also killed Parshandatha, Dalphon, Aspatha, 8Poratha, Adalia,
Aridatha, 9Parmashta, Arisai, Aridai and Vaizatha, 10the ten sons of Haman
son of Hammedatha, the enemy of the Jews. But they did not lay their
hands on the plunder.

11The number of those killed in the citadel of Susa was reported to
the king that same day. 12The king said to Queen Esther, "The Jews have
killed and destroyed five hundred men and the ten sons of Haman in the
citadel of Susa. What have they done in the rest of the king's provinces?
Now what is your petition? It will be given you. What is your request?
It will also be granted."

13"If it pleases the king," Esther answered, "give the Jews in Susa
permission to carry out this day's edict tomorrow also, and let Haman's
ten sons be impaled on poles."

14So the king commanded that this be done. An edict was issued in
Susa, and they impaled the ten sons of Haman. 15The Jews in Susa came

together on the fourteenth day of the month of Adar, and they put to
death in Susa three hundred men, but they did not lay their hands on
the plunder.

16Meanwhile, the remainder of the Jews who were in the king's prov-
inces also assembled to protect themselves and get relief from their enemies.
They killed seventy-five thousand of them but did not lay their hands on
the plunder. 17This happened on the thirteenth day of the month of Adar,
and on the fourteenth they rested and made it a day of feasting and joy.

18The Jews in Susa, however, had assembled on the thirteenth and
fourteenth, and then on the fifteenth they rested and made it a day of
feasting and joy.

19That is why rural Jews—those living in villages—observe the four-
teenth of the month of Adar as a day of joy and feasting, a day for giving
presents to each other.

20Mordecai recorded these events, and he sent letters to all the Jews
throughout the provinces of King Xerxes, near and far, 21to have them
celebrate annually the fourteenth and fifteenth days of the month of Adar
22as the time when the Jews got relief from their enemies, and as the month
when their sorrow was turned into joy and their mourning into a day of
celebration. He wrote them to observe the days as days of feasting and joy
and giving presents of food to one another and gifts to the poor.

23So the Jews agreed to continue the celebration they had begun, doing
what Mordecai had written to them. 24For Haman son of Hammedatha,
the Agagite, the enemy of all the Jews, had plotted against the Jews to
destroy them and had cast the *pur* (that is, the lot) for their ruin and
destruction. 25But when the plot came to the king's attention, he issued
written orders that the evil scheme Haman had devised against the Jews
should come back onto his own head, and that he and his sons should
be impaled on poles. 26(Therefore these days were called Purim, from the
word *pur*.) Because of everything written in this letter and because of
what they had seen and what had happened to them, 27the Jews took it on
themselves to establish the custom that they and their descendants and
all who join them should without fail observe these two days every year,
in the way prescribed and at the time appointed. 28These days should be
remembered and observed in every generation by every family, and in every
province and in every city. And these days of Purim should never fail to
be celebrated by the Jews—nor should the memory of these days die out
among their descendants.

[29]So Queen Esther, daughter of Abihail, along with Mordecai the Jew,
wrote with full authority to confirm this second letter concerning Purim.
[30]And Mordecai sent letters to all the Jews in the 127 provinces of Xerxes's
kingdom—words of goodwill and assurance—[31]to establish these days of
Purim at their designated times, as Mordecai the Jew and Queen Esther
had decreed for them, and as they had established for themselves and their
descendants in regard to their times of fasting and lamentation. [32]Esther's
decree confirmed these regulations about Purim, and it was written down
in the records.

Listen to the Text in the Story: Biblical and Apocryphal Texts: Exodus 15:14–16; Deuteronomy 7:1–6; 21:22–23; 1 Kings 2:25, 46; Nehemiah 8:1–22; Zechariah 8:19; 1 Maccabees 7:43–50 (see 2 Macc 15); Ancient Near Eastern Texts: Karnak, Campaign against the Hittites 2.4E.ii; The Gebel Barkal Stela of Thutmose 111 (2.2B); Herodotus, *Histories* 1.105; 3.79.

"Sins of the Fathers" and Post-Battle Celebrations

Ancients often killed people who were linked to conspirators, as they were judged guilty by association.[1] Herodotus tells the story of an attempted coup orchestrated by two magi that led to the massacre of many magi. Like the victory of the Jews over their enemies (Esth 9), the successful overthrow of the magi was celebrated and memorialized as a holiday:

> The Persians, when they learned . . . how the Magi had tricked them, resolved to follow the example set, and drew their daggers and killed all the Magi they could find; and if nightfall had not stopped them they would have left one Magus alive. This day is the greatest holy day that all Persians alike keep; they celebrate a great festival . . . the Massacre of the Magi; while the festival lasts no Magus may go outdoors, but during this day the Magi remain in their houses.[2]

Ancients also perceived family members to be security threats and killed them. Solomon, for example, had his older brother Adonijah murdered (1 Kgs 2:25). The notion that descendants were punished "for the sin of the

1. The notion that the family or tribe is the basic unit of society—not the individual—influenced their thinking in this area.

2. Herodotus, *Hist.* 3.73.

parents to the third and fourth generation" (Num 14:18) was also a common idea in the ancient world. Herodotus tells of the punishment of the descendants of the Scythians who plundered the sacred temple of Aphrodite—an act judged as morally wrong:

> But the Scythians who pillaged the temple, and all their descendants after them, were afflicted by the goddess with the "female" sickness: and so the Scythians say that they are afflicted as a consequence of this and also that those who visit Scythian territory see among them the condition of those whom the Scythians call "Hermaphrodites."[3]

The accounts of the Jewish triumph over the forces of the Syrian-Greek governor of Judea on the thirteenth day of the month of Adar in 161 BC in Maccabees reveal striking thematic parallels to the story of Jewish success in battle in Esther; these include plunder, the exposure of desecrated bodies and body parts, post-battle rejoicing, celebration, and the memorializing of the day of battle, and even the actual date of the conflict:

> When his army saw that Nicanor had fallen, they threw down their arms and fled. The Jews pursued them a day's journey. . . . People came out of all the surrounding villages of Judea, and they outflanked the enemy and drove them back to their pursuers, so that they all fell by the sword; not even one of them was left. Then the Jews seized the spoils and the plunder; they cut off Nicanor's head and the right hand that he had so arrogantly stretched out, and brought them and displayed them just outside Jerusalem. The people rejoiced greatly and celebrated that day as a day of great gladness. They decreed that this day should be celebrated each year on the thirteenth day of Adar. So the land of Judah had rest for a few days. (1 Macc 7:43–50: see also 2 Macc 15)

Fear-Inducing Hyperbole in Ancient Battle Reports

Battle reports were used as propaganda to garner support and strike fear into the hearts of adversaries. The triumphal account of the Egyptian pharaoh Seti I's military campaign against the Hittites is a case in point:

> Victorious King, mighty in power, whose battle-cry is like the Son of Nut's; he has returned triumphant, he has hacked up the foreign lands, he has trampled down Hatti-land. He puts an end to the rebels, and every foreign land languishes, becoming peaceable as dread of his Majesty has entered into them. His scourge (?) has broken their will ("heart"), and the

3. Ibid., 1.105.

> foreign lands are bound before him; he cares nothing for even hundreds of thousands gathered (together).[4]

Reports of Israel's victories in battle similarly depict enemies immobilized with fear:

> The nations will hear and tremble;
> anguish will grip the people of Philistia.
> The chiefs of Edom will be terrified,
> the leaders of Moab will be seized with trembling,
> the people of Canaan will melt away;
> terror and dread will fall on them.
> By the power of your arm
> they will be as still as a stone—
> until your people pass by, LORD,
> until the people you bought pass by. (Exod 15:14–16)[5]

In addition to exaggerating the extent of their victories, the ancients often embellished the numbers of the dead. The Gebel Barkal Stela of Thutmose III is an example of such hyperbole:

> Now let me report to you, pay attention folks! On the first campaign, [Amun-Re] ordained for me the lands of Retenu when they came in order to engage (in battle) with my majesty with a myriad of men, hundreds of thousands with the headmen of all foreign lands, standing on their chariots, comprising 330 chieftains, each one with their armies.[6]

The numbers of Persians killed by the Jews—500, 300, and 75,000—may also have been rounded up (Esth 9:6, 15–16).

EXPLAIN the Story

The Tables Turned: Killing, Rest, Feasting, Joy, and Gifts (Esther 9:1–16)

In this chapter that resolves the story's crisis, dates are important. The date of the reversal of outcomes, the thirteenth day of the twelfth month of Adar, begins the chapter, and dates continue to be stressed as the details about differences in when and how Jews in the empire celebrate their deliverance

4. K. A. Kitchen, "Karnak, Campaign against the Hittites (Undated) (West Side, Lower Register)," *COS* 2.4E:29.

5. See also Josh 2:11; 21:44; 23:9; Ps 105:38 and Esther 8:1–17: Listen to the Story.

6. James K. Hoffmeier, "The Gebel Barkal Stela of Thutmose III," *COS* 2.2B:16.

from their enemies are explained at length and repeatedly (9:1, 16–32). The book's theme of reversals is explicitly named as an overturning, "the tables were turned" (NIV) as the Jews "got the upper hand over those who hated them." The use of the passive verb, "were turned/overturned" is, as Firth suggests, "not random" but "as close as the narrator comes to mentioning God directly as the author of deliverance."[7]

The Jews were active participants in the overturning of the genocidal edict (9:2). The rules of engagement set out in Mordecai's counteredict (8:11–12) allowed Jews throughout the empire to organize themselves "to extend the hand" (NIV: "attack" 9:2) against those intent on annihilating them. The Hebrew expression, "to extend the hand," which was used earlier to describe both the murderous intentions of Xerxes's would-be assassins (2:21), and Haman's intent regarding Mordecai (3:6), now describes the Jews' military strategy.

The narrator's commentary, "No one could stand against them, because the people of all the other nationalities were afraid of them" (9:2), echoes the closing remarks in chapter 8 that fear of the Jews prompted many to become Jews (8:17). It also recalls earlier expressions among Israel's enemies of their fear of Israel and her God, whom they recognized was supporting Israel (see Esther 6:1–14: Listen to the Story). The narrator's intentional recasting of this battle in light of previous battles that the Lord had fought on Israel's behalf provides an important theological lens for reading the Jews' attacks on the thirteenth and fourteenth days of Adar as Holy War. It brings the hidden God into the story and suggests that the Persians' fears of the Jews, and of Mordecai in particular, had something to do with their numinous sense that God was with the Jews. Jacob articulated this same sense of mystery when he awoke from his dream and testified: "Surely the Lord is in this place, and I was not aware of it" (Gen 28:16).

Mordecai's greatness is doubly declared in verse 4 and frames the notice of the spread of his reputation throughout the empire. Mordecai's rise far exceeds the notice of Haman's rise to greatness and honor in 3:1. Mordecai is called "the man, Mordecai" in the last clause of verse 4 in the Hebrew, but these words are missing from the NIV, which collapses the notice to the simple pronoun "he." This full identification of "the man, Mordecai" is important, however, as it purposefully echoes the Hebrew of his introduction in 2:5 as "a man, Jewish," calling attention, as Jon Levenson suggests, "to the contrast between his status as a mere exile there and his elevation to great power here."[8] Mordecai's title also echoes the title given to "the man, Moses,"

7. Firth, *The Message of Esther*, 122.
8. Levenson, *Esther*, 121.

whose greatness among the people and officials in the story of the plague on the firstborn is explicitly attributed to the LORD (Exod 11:3; Num 12:3). This embedded allusion to Moses elevates Mordecai and anticipates the memorial to his greatness in Esther chapter 10.

Verses 5 to 14 focus on the killing of the enemies of the Jews on the day and month that had been chosen by lot to annihilate the Jews, and on an additional, second day of killing in Susa (3:7; 9:13). Verse 5 in particular accentuates the Jews' forceful assault as they struck their enemies with "the stroke of the sword, (KJV)" killing and destroying them—a word pair used in both edicts: 3:13, 8:11, and again in 9:6. The morally problematic comment, "they did what they pleased (lit., "according to their desire") to those who hated them" (9:5), recalls the first banquet scene where wine was supplied according to the desire or pleasure of each man (1:8). Just exactly how the Jews brandished their power is not clear: some suggest they exceeded the decree, but the kind of atrocities normally associated with vindictive attacks in the ancient world—rape, torture, and mutilation of bodies—are not mentioned (see Esther 8:1–17: Listen to the Story).

The narrator's triple mention of the Jews' refusal to take plunder is exceptional (9:10, 15, 16). In the ancient world, taking plunder was expected. It included taking valuables, portable livestock, and women and children, who became victims of rape. The question of why the Jews refused booty seems important, although it is left unanswered in this text. Is the narrator suggesting that the Jews were not interested in material gain? Did they recognize that plundering would only increase the anti-Semitic sentiments in Persia? Or is the narrator providing another clue that we are to understand the killing of the Persians who supported Haman as part of the completion of the unfinished conflict between Saul and the Amalekites (1 Sam 15; see Introduction to Esther)? Berlin speaks to this when she suggests that the Jews "correct" King Saul's error of taking plunder from the Amalekites when he had been specifically instructed not to, and that "this reversal in reference to booty wipes away the sin of the house of Saul."[9]

The numbers of Persians killed by the Jews are significant and troubling: 500 in the area of the citadel of Susa, as well as Haman's ten sons; 75,000 throughout the empire; and 300 on the second day of killing in the city of Susa (9:5–10, 15–16). Ancient accounts of war often exaggerated death tolls and omitted mentioning their own casualties for political and ideological purposes. At the very least, the numbers of Persians intent on massacring the Jews indicate the extent of the continuing hostility toward the Jews throughout

9. Berlin, *Esther*, 85.

the empire, given the change of heart experienced by so many who now feared the Jews (8:17). Reading this triumphal account within the context of the story of God suggests that the victory was not the Jews' alone. God was involved in delivering his chosen people from those who, like the enemies of old with hardened hearts, refused to make peace with God's people and were put under the ban (Josh 11:18–20).

Verses 7 to 9 list ten names, and only in verse 10 are they identified as the dead sons of Haman who had joined in the attack against the Jews. The list of names, like other lists of minor named figures in Esther, adds historical credence and pathos to the story; the death of these named sons who fueled Haman's excessive pride symbolizes their father's definitive demise (1:10, 14; 5:11). In Hebrew manuscripts, the list of Haman's sons' names are set out in columns, as is the long list of Canaanite kings defeated by Joshua and the Israelites (Josh 12:9–24). This unique tradition encourages readers to pause and consider the names of these particular enemies. It also contrasts with the later Jewish practice of reading the ten sons' names in one breath during the chanting of the book of Esther during the feast of Purim, a tradition which suggests that the names of vile Haman's sons are not worth pausing over.[10]

After passing on the report about the killing and destroying of five hundred men and the ten sons of Haman in Susa, Xerxes presents Esther another offer of whatever she wants (9:11–12). His unsolicited offer presents a different face of the man who previously displayed his need and desire to use and control women (1:11, 22). Like others who now esteem and fear the Jews, Xerxes has new regard for his Jewish queen and reaches out to support her. Commenting on this shift in the king's relationship with Esther, Hazony writes: "It is Esther who now embodies power in the king's eyes, and it is he who offers his favors—his service—in an effort to gain favor with her. Their relationship is finally and completely reversed."[11]

Esther's vindictive response is polite, brief, and exacting as she requests a second day of killing in the lower city of Susa, where most Jews lived, and the ultimate shaming of the dead bodies of Haman's sons (9:13). Her request was not unusual, as impalement of bodies or body parts was commonly used to desecrate the dead and to warn others against attempting to oppose those responsible. The impalement of the sons of Haman, the Agagite, provides another allusion to the story of Saul, as both Saul and his sons were impaled (1 Sam 31:10–13; 2 Sam 21:1–14). At the same time, Esther is silent about whether Haman's sons were dismembered before impalement as Saul was. Xerxes accedes to Esther's double petition, as he has to all other suggestions

10. Levenson, *Esther*, 122, citing b. Meg. 16b.
11. Hazony, *God and Politics in Esther*, 144.

and requests (1:21; 2:4; 3:11; 5:5; 7:1, 9; 8:8; 9:14). A factual report follows, documenting that Haman's sons were impaled, an additional 300 enemies in Susa were killed, and no plunder was taken (9:14–15).

Esther's last spoken words demonstrate her queenly self-confidence, initiative, and loyalty to the Jews. Indeed, her vengeful request can be read as a final strategic move to safeguard the future security of the Jews. It can also be interpreted as the final act in the ancestral Israelite-Amalekite conflict, as Esther does what Saul did not do in insisting that every enemy of God's people be annihilated. In this way, Esther puts her signature on the final battle in the holy war against the Amalekites and effectively shames Saul (see Introduction to Esther). Like Jael's killing of Sisera (Judg 4:21) and the unnamed woman's mortal wounding of Abimelek, who commands his armor-bearer to kill him lest people say that a woman killed him (Judg 9:53–54), Esther's initiative is an act of symbolic emasculation of Saul through death or defeat by a woman. The association of Esther with Ishtar, the Babylonian goddess of war and love, seems highly appropriate (see Esther 2:1–23: Explain the Story).

Not all readers view Esther's initiative in this vengeful killing and shaming as heroic. Cultural assumptions about gender and war shape the strong views of critics like the early twentieth-century pseudonymous author Wilhelmina Stitch, who judges Esther's story to be "an ugly narrative." She declares: "I like her not! Intrigue, deceitfulness, revengefulness, unforgiveness. . . . Haman was a bully; but, oh! How deceitful to hear Esther . . . actually asking for a free licence [sic] for a second day's slaughter."[12] To be sure, Esther is not the same young woman we met at the beginning of the book; she has developed "from a young woman, beautiful, charming, and silent, to a woman who speaks up and risks her life; from a morally quasi-innocent being to someone who becomes a moral person, who dares to take decisions, who takes on responsibility, and who is involved and entangled in violence and runs the risk of becoming guilty."[13] But does Esther's entanglement with violence really imply that she has gone too far by initiating further bloodshed? Has Esther, as a victim-survivor of trauma, become herself a victimizer? Does this episode in Esther's story—like David's sordid affair with Bathsheba—stand as an implicit warning about the seduction of power? Perhaps Esther should be seen as a hero with shortcomings, who fails to challenge the values of empire and becomes entangled in its messy values and morals.

---

12. Stitch, *Women of the Bible*, 248, 253, quoted in Carruthers, *Esther Through the Centuries*, 262.

13. Marie-Theres Wacker, "The Violence of Power and the Power of Violence: Hybrid, Contextual Perspectives on the Book of Esther," in *Feminist Frameworks and the Bible; Power, Ambiguity, and Intersectionality*, ed. L. Juliana Claassens and Carolyn J. Sharp (Oxford: Bloomsbury T&T Clark, 2017), 110.

Celebrating Life (Esther 9:17–19)

Following the final report of the Jewish killing of 75,000 enemies outside of Susa (9:16), the focus of the chapter shifts dramatically from the glorification of death to a celebration of life. Vengeance, destruction, killing, annihilation, and shaming are set aside as Jews throughout the empire spontaneously celebrate life and community. This shift is highly significant as it provides an implicit critique of traditional post-war celebrations, which specifically glorify gruesome and bloody events in the conflict, including the post-war rape of women (Judg 5:30). Also missing from the celebrations are songs of thanksgiving that attribute the victory to the Lord who "shattered the enemy" and did "not let us be torn by their teeth" (Exod 15:6; Ps 124:6).

At the same time, the post-conflict Jewish feasts that celebrate relief from battle and the end of the genocidal threat are not self-serving but rather community-building (9:17, 18, 19, 22). The root of the Hebrew word "relief" or "rest" (*noah*) that describes the Jews' post-battle experience recalls the rest/holiday that celebrated Esther's marriage (2:18) and Haman's instruction to the king that he should not tolerate (lit., "let rest") this certain people (3:8). It also echoes the motif of rest found in the conquest stories (Deut 3:20; 12:9–10; 25:19; Josh 1:13, 15; 21:44; 22:4; 23:1; 2 Sam 7:11).

The Jews in the provinces marked this rest from fighting with feasting and joy on the fourteenth of Adar. Their spontaneous celebration initiated what later became known as the feast of Purim (9:16–17). Their commemorative acts included the giving of presents or portions (for a similar practice, see Neh 8:10–12). The Jews in Susa also put violence behind them after the second day of killing and celebrated with feasting and joy on the fifteenth of Adar (9:18). The double celebratory traditions are part of the book's larger theme of banquets or feasts. They correspond to Xerxes's opening double banquets (1:2–4, 5–8), the banquets of Vashti and Esther (1:9; 2:18), Esther's double banquets with Xerxes and Haman (5:1–8; 7:1–9), and even the contrasting celebratory responses to the first and second edicts by Haman and Xerxes on the one hand and the Jews on the other (3:15; 8:17).

The Inauguration of Purim (Esther 9:20–32)

The final section of the chapter presents additional accounts of the origins of Purim. Although Purim became a very important Jewish feast, it was not divinely sanctioned, as were the feasts of Passover and Unleavened Bread (9:20–32; Exod 12). The variations in these accounts of the origins of Purim suggest that it took time for the feast to be formally established (note the addition of food for the poor in Mordecai's letter in verse 22, and the inclusion of fasting and lamentation in Esther's letter in verse 31). What may seem tedious and untidy in this chapter, however, has the effect of underscoring the importance of Purim and of the letters that Mordecai and Esther wrote that sanctioned Purim. Ironically, the messy repetitions call attention to the importance of repeating and remembering this story of deliverance that celebrates joy, life, and rest.

This section highlights Mordecai as he records the Jews' escape from Haman's evil genocidal edict and then, using the efficient Persian postal service, sends letters "near and far" (9:20) throughout the empire to institutionalize the spontaneous celebrations of the great turning of the tables on the fourteenth and fifteenth of Adar as days of feasting, joy, sharing food with neighbors, and gifts with the poor. Purim was clearly meant to celebrate relief from enemies, not a military triumph (9:20–22). Mordecai's letter establishes Purim's religious significance and introduces its obligatory nature as the repeated form of the Hebrew verb *qwm* ("to establish" or "to confirm") indicates (vv. 21, 27, 29, 31, 32). This emphasis is well reflected in the language of the NIV in 9:27–32 but less clear in verse 21. Mordecai's letter also normalizes the dates of the celebrations as the fourteenth and fifteenth of Adar. Esther's letter similarly speaks of establishing "these days of Purim at their designated times" (v. 31).

Verses 20 to 32 also feature a cluster of suggestive allusions to the larger story of God that add weight to the many other hints throughout the book of Esther that God is hidden rather than absent from this story of the deliverance of the Jews from annihilation. The comprehensive expression, "near and far" (20), suggests reading the deliverance of the Jews in the book of Esther as a partial prophetic fulfillment of the salvation oracle: "'Peace, peace, to those far and near,' says the LORD. 'And I will heal them.' . . .'There is no peace,' says my God, 'for the wicked'" (Isa 57:19, 21).[14]

The addition of gift-giving (9:22) to the expressions of celebration in verses 17 to 19 is consistent with the idea of sharing one's bounty with the poor, as mandated in the gleaning laws and exemplified by Boaz's treatment of Naomi and Ruth (Lev 19:9–10; Ruth 2:16; 3:17). As well, the language used to describe the overturning from sorrow and mourning into gladness (9:22) echoes Jeremiah's oracle of hope that promises redemption and return to Zion: "I will turn their mourning into gladness; I will give them comfort and joy instead of sorrow" (Jer 31:13; see also the promised reversals in Isa 61:3). This striking resonance, as Timothy Laniak notes, frames the saving reversal in Persia "in terms of God's covenant of faithfulness to the postexilic community."[15]

---

14. Levenson, *Esther*, 126.

15. Timothy S. Laniak, "Esther," in *Ezra, Nehemiah, Esther*, NIBCOT 9 (Peabody, MA: Hendrickson, 2003), 263.

Another account of the institution of Purim begins with the notice that Mordecai's letter was well received (Esth 9:23). This abridged summary of origins contains a number of unique features (9:24–25): the focus on Haman, the descendant of Israel's enemies and archetypal enemy of *all* the Jews (compare 3:10; 7:6); the mention of the casting of the *pur* (lot) (see 3:7 and Esther 3:1–15: Listen to the Story); the positive and politically correct recasting of Xerxes as taking considerable responsibility for countering Haman's evil scheme; the absence of Mordecai and, most likely, Esther from the story (see below); and the merging of the accounts of the deaths of Haman and his sons. The scholarly debate about whether or not Esther is the subject of verse 25, as she is in a number of translations (e.g., KJV, NRSV, CEB), arises from the absence of the feminine subject in the Hebrew. The NIV's choice of "plot" as the subject is to be preferred to "Esther," as it fits with this summary's exclusive focus on Haman and Xerxes.

Verse 26a links the origins of Purim to the singular word *pur* (lot) and the casting of the lot that determined the date for the genocide, which became instead the date of the first day of the Jews' deliverance. The reason why the feast is called Purim, the plural of *pur*, is not obvious; it may simply reflect the two days of celebration, or it may have been adjusted to fit with the names of other Jewish feasts that are plural nouns, namely, tabernacles, weeks, and trumpets.

The Jews responded positively to Mordecai's letter, as it corresponded with their own experience of the conflict (26b–27). They committed themselves to establishing and observing Purim "irrevocably" (NIV: "without fail"), an expression that calls to mind the notion of the unchangeable nature of Persian laws that was first mentioned in connection with Vashti's banishment (1:19) and was both parodied and challenged throughout the book. Verse 28 begins and ends with words related to memory ("remembered" and "memory") and repeats the notion of the irrevocability of Purim (NIV: "these days of Purim should never fail"). It stresses yet again the importance of recalling the story and message of Purim in every generation, everywhere.

The chapter concludes by focusing once again on Queen Esther as she writes with full authority to confirm, decree, and officially establish Purim (9:29–32). Since the verb "to write" is a feminine singular verb in verse 29, the question of Mordecai's role in writing this second letter is often raised. A number of scholars suggest that Mordecai's role in the writing of this second letter is secondary, and some emend the Hebrew text and omit Mordecai from this verse. In any case, Queen Esther's written support for Purim adds royal weight to Mordecai's written documents and reflects the book's repeated concern with recording events and writing and publishing edicts and letters (1:19–22; 2:23; 3:12–14; 8:8–13; 9:20–22). Such records carried authority and were meant to ensure that events, such as Mordecai's uncovering of the conspiracy to kill the king, were remembered and duly rewarded (2:21–23; 6:1–3). In addition, Esther's final authoritative letter provides an ironic commentary on the book's first letter, which was intended to limit women's power.[16]

Esther's letters were sent to Jews throughout the empire (9:30). Although the NIV assumes Mordecai is the subject of the masculine singular verb; some translations (ESV, NET) treat the verb as impersonal, rendering the clause "the letters were sent." More important than the identification of the person who sent the letters is the use of the theologically pregnant words "peace/shalom" and "truth/faithfulness" (NIV: "goodwill and assurance") to describe the intended effect and content of the letters. This word pair is also found in three other biblical passages (2 Kgs 20:19, Isa 39:8, and Jer 33:6) and is reversed in Zechariah's oracle that promises that fasts will be transformed into times of joyful and happy festivals associated with loving "truth and peace" (Zech 8:19). Since this transformation sounds very like the reversals celebrated by Purim, Jon Levenson suggests "the author of Esth 9:29–32 may have seen a fulfillment of ancient prophecy in the events narrated in the book to which he appended this passage."[17] The association of Purim with peace, "*shalom*," and its disassociation from war, violence, and vengeance provides an important clue as to how the Persian Jews interpreted the traumatic events they experienced, and how they wanted these events to be memorialized. Indeed, from its inception, Purim celebrations were distanced from the disturbing violence and vengeance of the thirteenth and fourteenth days of Adar, which, as Brevard Childs suggests, remain "forever in past history as unrepeatable."[18] Instead, Purim celebrates life and is meant to promote truth, peace, and goodwill in the community.

Esther's addition of fasting and lamentation to the celebrations of Purim suggests that it was important to remember the difficult backstory to the festival (9:31). Her addendum implicitly acknowledges what the early Greek editions of the story make explicit, namely, God's role in this epic story of deliverance. Esther's spiritual sensitivities are made explicit in the LXX as Esther prays fervently to God for deliverance: "My Lord, You alone are our king. Help me who am alone and have no help but You. . . . Be mindful, O Lord. Reveal Yourself in the moment of our affliction, and give me courage, king of the gods and ruler over every power! . . . Rescue us by Your power, and help me, who am alone and have no one but You, O Lord."[19]

---

16. Linda Day, *Esther*, AOTC (Nashville: Abingdon, 2005), 162.

17. Levenson, *Esther*, 130.

18. Brevard S. Childs, *Introduction to the Old Testament as Scripture* (Philadelphia: Fortress, 1979), 606.

19. Esther's Prayer, LXX C:14, 23, quoted in Levenson, *Esther*, 84–85.

The final verse of chapter 9 reinforces Esther's authority as it records the writing down of Esther's decree (*ma'amar*). This word was also used to describe Xerxes's command to Vashti (1:15) and Mordecai's instructions to Esther (2:20). This repetition, as Jobes suggests, "invites the reader to consider Queen Esther's word to be on par with that of Xerxes and Mordecai."[20] Moreover, as Fox suggests, Esther's final word "validates all the previous layers of confirmation and her statement is inscribed in a document as a witness to the future."[21] While the ongoing tradition in synagogues of reading the entire book of Esther during Purim may reflect the importance of the writing down of Esther's decree, the early association of "the letter of Purim" (9:26, 29) with the whole book of Esther was also an important influence in terms of reinforcing Esther's authority.[22]

Throughout history, Esther's act of writing the imperial edict has given a sense of agency to women who live in cultures where their access to education and positions of power have been restricted, and has authorized them to take up their pens. One example of such authorization is found in the pamphlet titled, *Esther Hath Hang'd Haman: or an Ansvvere to a lewd Pamphlet, entitled, the Arraignment of Women. With the Arraignment of Lewd, Idle, Froward, and Vnconstant Men and Hvsbands*, that was authored by the clever and learned pseudonymous author, Ester Sowernam (fl. 1615–1617). Sowernam self-identifies with Esther in her vitriolic attack on the misogynist pamphleteer, Joseph Swetnam, whom she effectively impales through her argumentation.[23]

LIVE the Story

"Purim Should Never Fail to Be Celebrated by the Jews—Nor Should the Memory of These Days Die Out among Their Descendants"

The popular carnival-like festival Purim that celebrates the reversal of the fortunes of the Jews in Persia continues to be celebrated by Jews throughout the world. Purim is popularly named "topsy-turvy" and the Jewish Mardi Gras, as it features partying with food and drink and transgressions of authority and sexual identity, including cross-dressing, betting, and deception.[24] Edith Pearlman captures the spirit of such Purim revels well when she describes the

20. Jobes, *Esther*, 223.

21. Fox, *Character and Ideology*, 204.

22. See Levenson's discussion of Colophon F:11 (Esth 11:1 in the Vulgate), which mentions "the foregoing letter of Purim," in *Esther*, 136.

23. Betsy Delmonico, "Sowernam, Ester (fl. 1615–17)" in *The Handbook of Women Interpreters*, ed. Marion Ann Taylor, 463–65.

24. Carruthers, *Esther Through the Centuries*, 267.

occasion as one "where you must drink until you cannot distinguish the king from the villain, the queen from the village tart."[25] The spirit of revelry is even found inside the synagogue, where noise makers called graggers are used to drown out the mention of the name of the evil enemy Haman during the reading of the book of Esther.

The Purim liturgy provides a clear framework for reading Esther within the larger story of God, and includes the reading of Deuteronomy 25:17–19, which fills in the backstory of Haman and Mordecai's antagonism as it describes Amalek's attack on Israel and contains the mandates to "blot out the memory of Amalek" and to "not forget." The early rabbinic blessing that follows the reading of Esther explicitly attributes the reversals in the fortunes of the Jews to God, and underscores God's character as Avenger and Savior of his people:

> Blessed are You, Hashem, our God, King of the Universe, Who takes up our grievance, judges our claim and avenges our wrong. And Who exacts vengeance for us from our foes. And Who brings just retribution upon all enemies of our soul. Blessed are You, Hashem, Who exacts vengeance for Yisrael from all their foes, and the God Who brings salvation.[26]

This blessing reflects the teaching of Scripture that vengeance is the Lord's. With this teaching in mind, the vengeful acts initiated by Mordecai and Esther are understood by some as carrying out the Lord's vengeance on those set on annihilating God's people. However, many argue that Esther's request for further revenge indicates a wrongful act. Paul speaks to the issue of our natural desire for personal revenge in Romans 12:19, citing Old Testament law as a precedent: "Do not take revenge, my dear friends, but leave room for God's wrath, for it is written: "'It is mine to avenge; I will repay,' says the Lord." Instead, Paul mandates overcoming evil with good (Rom 12:21). Arguably, personal revenge is different than communal retaliation in times of war.

Esther among the Persians and God's People Today

> The mill wheel turns, it turns forever,
> Though what is uppermost remains not so.
>
> —Bertolt Brecht[27]

25. Edith Pearlman, "Purim Night," in *How to Fall: Stories by Edith Pearlman* (Louisville: Sarabande, 2005), 183, quoted in Carruthers, *Esther Through the Centuries*, 271.

26. The prayer is cited in the Gemara, quoted in Yitzchak Sender, *The Commentators' Al Hanissim: Purim: Insights of the Sages on Purim and Chanukah* (Jerusalem: Feldheim, 2000), 128, 129.

27. Bertolt Brecht, *Roundheads and Peakheads,* trans. N. Goold-Verschoyle in *Jungle of Cities and Other Plays* (New York: Grove, 1994), 252.

> "Most Blessed of women be Jael. . . .
> She struck Sisera, she crushed his head. . . .
> At her feet he sank, he fell;
> where he sank, there he fell—dead." (Judg 5:24–27)

When we read Esther 9 within its ancient context, Queen Esther's request for a second day to finish the task of eradicating and shaming the enemies of the Jews is not only reasonable but arguably mild compared with other brutal practices of mutilation in war. Like Jael, another great woman of war, Esther can be lauded as "most blessed of women" for her courage and initiative in saving the Jews (Judg 5:24). But should Esther's deeds of heroism as a vengeful war hero be imitated? Baruch Goldstein's massacre of twenty-nine Muslims in Hebron on Purim in 1994 was inspired at least in part by the violent and vengeful actions of Esther and the Jews against their enemies.[28] South African scholar Gerrie Snyman tells about one of his students from a town on the edge of the gold mining industry who found encouragement in the Jews' response to their oppressors. Indeed, Esther 9 justified his community's goal "to seize power in terms of wealth and authority, if not dominance over both nature and the so-called (previous) oppressors, the white minority."[29] However, such a grassroots interpretation of Esther's "malignant spirit of revenge"[30] is countered by the institution of Purim itself, which reflects the actions of the Persian Jews in putting vengeance and violence behind them to celebrate life, rest, peace, and joy.

Instead of understanding Esther's actions as a model of bloodthirsty revenge, we should pick up on the self-critical ambiguities in the story at this point and follow the lead of those who interpret this chapter as a warning about the seduction of power or "the abused becoming the abuser."[31] Amos Gitai's powerful 1986 film, *Esther*, which was shot near the ruins of the old Arab neighborhood of Haifa that the Palestinians had abandoned after the 1948 war, shows what happens when the oppressed come to power and become oppressors themselves. It is a powerful critique of the ongoing violence between Jews and Palestinians.

Esther's actions also push us to reflect critically on what it means for God's people to live in an alien culture. It reminds us of how easy it is to adopt the moral values of our culture and become enmeshed in it. Elsie Stern argues

---

28. Chris Hedges with Joel Greenberg, "WEST BANK MASSACRE; Before Killing, Final Prayer and Final Taunt," February 18, 1994, https://www.nytimes.com/1994/02/28/world/west-bank-massacre-before-killing-final-prayer-and-final-taunt.html.

29. Gerrie F. Synman, "'Ilahle Elinothuthu'? The Lay Reader and/or the Critical Reader—Some Remarks on Africanisation," *RT* 6.2 (1999): 147–48.

30. Paton, *Esther*, 287.

31. Firth, *The Message of Esther*, 127.

that Esther's vindictive actions fit with other examples of Jews behaving like Persians—sending out decrees and banqueting—found throughout the book of Esther. These examples, she suggests, "are the stuff of assimilationist nightmares: Jewish residents of diaspora who follow no particularist Jewish practices and are, subsequently, unidentifiable as Jews."[32] God's people today, like the Jews living in Persia, face assimilationist nightmares daily. Jesus calls his followers to live distinctive lives as light and salt in the world (Matt 5:13–16; John 17:16–17). The apostle Paul also warns Jesus' followers about the dangers of accommodation. Eugene Peterson's paraphrase of Romans 12:2 speaks to the problem of assimilation and points to the issue of prevention:

> Don't become so well-adjusted to your culture that you fit into it without even thinking. Instead, fix your attention on God. You'll be changed from the inside out. Readily recognize what he wants from you, and quickly respond to it. Unlike the culture around you, always dragging you down to its level of immaturity, God brings the best out of you, develops well-formed maturity in you. (The Message)

The Anglican service of compline, said at the end of the day, includes prayers and scriptural texts that address the issue of our need for God's protection as we live in a world that wants to squeeze us into its mold.[33] The repeated prayer "Guide us waking, O Lord, and guard us sleeping; that awake we may watch with Christ, and asleep we may rest in peace" reminds us of our need for divine shelter.[34] First Peter 5:8–9a, one of the suggested readings in the Compline service reminds us how to deal with the spiritual battles we engage in daily: "Be sober, be watchful. Your adversary the devil prowls around like a roaring lion, seeking someone to devour. Resist him, firm in your faith."[35] The service includes the helpful reminder of our redemption in Christ and God's eternal promise of love and shelter:

> V. Into your hands, O Lord, I commend my spirit;
> R. For you have redeemed me, O Lord, O God of truth.
> V. Keep us, O Lord, as the apple of your eye;
> R. Hide us under the shadow of your wings.[36]

---

32. Elsie Stern, "Esther and the Politics of Diaspora," *JQR* 100 (2010): 25–53.

33. "With eyes wide open to the mercies of God, I beg you, my brothers, as an act of intelligent worship, to give him your bodies, as a living sacrifice, consecrated to him and acceptable by him. Don't let the world around you squeeze you into its own mould, but let God re-mould your minds from within, so that you may prove in practice that the plan of God for you is good, meets all his demands and moves towards the goal of true maturity" (Romans 12:1–2 Phillips).

34. See "An Order for Compline," *The (Online) Book of Common Prayer*, www.bcponline.org.

35. Ibid.

36. Ibid.

A Classic Theological Appropriation of Purim

Although Christians do not traditionally celebrate Purim, we do celebrate God's deliverance of the Jews. As early as the fourth century, Athanasius, Bishop of Alexandria, used the feast of Purim as a type of the great heavenly feast that celebrates Christ's victory over the devil. In the fourth of his Easter Letters, Athanasius reflects on the Feast of Purim as one example among many that celebrates the deliverance of God's people from bondage. Basing his meditation on the LXX, which makes explicit the fact that Esther both fasted and prayed to God for deliverance, Athanasius highlights Esther's role in this deliverance: "By faith she changed the ruin of her people into safety."[37] Christians also, he argues, celebrate their great deliverance from the greater Haman, "the devil, that tyrant against the whole world [who] is slain" through Christ.[38] He also compares the deliverance celebrated at Purim with that of Easter, arguing, "our feast does not relate only to time but to eternity. It is a heavenly feast! We do not announce it as a shadow or a picture or a type but as the real thing."[39]

Athanasius rightly calls our attention to the importance of remembering and celebrating Christ's ultimate victory that brings deliverance from sin and death. And, as David Firth writes, "There is for the people of God . . . always a significant theological content to our remembrance, for without this we cannot grasp the richness of what God has done."[40] Remembering and celebrating the great events in the story of God as the Jews did by institutionalizing Purim and other feasts such as Passover, is an important part of our Christian lives.

Psalm 107 speaks to the issue of the importance of giving thanks to the Lord for what he has done and calls for "the redeemed of the Lord [to] tell their story" as they "ponder the loving deeds of the Lord" (107:2, 43). Those of us who were not raised in Christian traditions that celebrate the great events in the story of God can learn much from Christians who use a liturgical calendar to order their lives around the momentous events of Christmas, Good Friday, Easter, Pentecost, Epiphany, and the Ascension. We should not be surprised that the truths ensconced in Scripture about the importance of remembering and celebrating, both as individuals and as communities, are now embraced by researchers who write and blog about the benefits of gratitude for our mental and spiritual health (see Esther 5:1–14: Live the Story).

---

37. Athanasius, *The Resurrection Letters*. Jack N. Sparks, ed. (Nashville: Thomas Nelson, 1979), 82, quoted in Conti and Pilara, *1–2 Kings, 1–2 Chronicles, Ezra, Nehemiah, Esther*, 397.

38. Ibid.

39. Ibid.

40. Firth, *The Message of Esther*, 133.

CHAPTER 14

Esther 10:1–3

LISTEN to the Story

[1]King Xerxes imposed tribute throughout the empire, to its distant
shores. [2]And all his acts of power and might, together with a full account
of the greatness of Mordecai, whom the king had promoted, are they
not written in the book of the annals of the kings of Media and Persia?
[3]Mordecai the Jew was second in rank to King Xerxes, preeminent among
the Jews, and held in high esteem by his many fellow Jews, because he
worked for the good of his people and spoke up for the welfare of all
the Jews.

Listen to the Text in the Story: Biblical Texts: 1 Kings 14:29; 15:23; 16:14; 2 Chronicles 25:26; Nehemiah 9:36–37; Zechariah 9:36–37; Ancient Near Eastern Texts: The Mesha Stela; Herodotus, *Histories*, 3.95–6.

Taxing Even the Distant Shores

Tens of thousands of ancient records now housed in museum collections around the world reveal that taxes (called "tribute" in the NIV) kept the wheels of empires turning. Expanded borders meant increased tax revenue. Xerxes, like his father Darius, valued such increases:

> Darius the son of Hystaspes collected a yearly tribute of fourteen thousand five hundred and sixty talents . . . This was Darius' revenue from Asia and a few parts of Libya. But as time went on he drew tribute also from the islands and the dwellers in Europe, as far as Thessaly.[1]

While increased revenue lined the king's coffers, conquered peoples who paid tribute often experienced oppression. The Jews in Jerusalem living under Persian rule likened the tyranny of taxes to slavery:

1. Herodotus, *Hist.* 3.95–96.

> But see, we are slaves today, slaves in the land you gave our ancestors so they could eat its fruit and the other good things it produces. Because of our sins, its abundant harvest goes to the kings you have placed over us. They rule over our bodies and our cattle as they please. We are in great distress. (Neh 9:36–37)

Speaking Peace

Mordecai spoke peace (*shalom*) to all his people, but the promised messianic king depicted in Zechariah would speak peace to the nations:

> Rejoice greatly, Daughter Zion!
> Shout, Daughter Jerusalem!
> See, your king comes to you,
> righteous and victorious,
> lowly and riding on a donkey,
> on a colt, the foal of a donkey. . . .
> He will proclaim peace to the nations.
> His rule will extend from sea to sea
> and from the River to the ends of the earth. (Zech 9:9–10)

Idealized Portraits of Kings and Their Legacies

When kings, dignitaries, and those writing up their histories recorded the past for posterity, they often idealized their legacies for political, ideological, and theological reasons. Esther 10 is one such record. In the famous Mesha Stela (ca. 840 BC), Mesha pridefully recounts his military victories—including those over Israel—and describes his extensive building projects:

> I am Mesha, the son of Kemosh, king of Moab. . . . Omri was the king of Israel, and he oppressed Moab for many days. . . . And his son succeeded him, and he said—he too—"I will oppress Moab!" . . . but I looked down on him and his house, and Israel has gone to ruin, yes, it has gone to ruin forever! . . . And Kemosh said to me, "Go, take Nebo from Israel!" And I went in the night, and I fought against it from the break of dawn until noon, and I took it, and I killed [its] whole population, seven thousand male citizens and aliens, and female citizens and aliens, and servant girls. . . . I have built Karchoh, the wall of the woods and the wall of the citadel, and I have built its gates, and I have built its towers, and I have built the house of the king, and I have made the double reser[voir for the spr]ing in the innermost part of the city. . . . And I am the kin[g over the] hundreds in the towns which I have added to the land. And I have built [the House of Mede]ba and the House of

Diblathaim and the House of Baal Meon, and I brought there [. . .] flocks of the land.[2]

EXPLAIN the Story

Esther 10:1–3: The Glorification of Xerxes and Mordecai

The short coda to the book of Esther takes us to a time after the events of the story. It begins with a notice of the king's imposition of a *mas*, a word that typically signifies "forced labor." Here it likely refers to a "tax" on "the land and the isles of the sea" (KJV)—an unusual expression that may be read as a figure of speech (a merismus) signifying the whole known world (see Isa 42:4, 10). This brief but intentional mention of the extent of Xerxes's kingdom forms a closing bookend to the opening chapter that emphasized the vastness of the Persian Empire.[3]

The notice of increased revenues through taxation picks up on the theme of wealth that runs through the book: Xerxes flaunted his wealth (1:2–8); Haman offered an enormous bribe and boasted about his wealth (3:9; 5:11); the taking of wealth-enhancing plunder was allowed but refused (8:1–2; 9:10, 15–16); Haman's wealth was transferred to Esther and Mordecai (8:1–2, 7). The reasons for the tax are not specified. Some suggest it was meant to reverse the holiday from taxes given when the king married Esther, as the ESV translation "remission of taxes" makes explicit (2:18 ESV). Others tie this tax to the need to make up for the revenues Haman promised the genocide would create (3:10). In either case, the idea of increasing taxes was likely Mordecai's. The parallel with Joseph's imposition of taxes when he was second-in-command (Gen 47:24–26) and Xerxes's tendency to rely on others to make decisions support this idea (1:13–21; 6:6).

Xerxes's taxation initiative is presented as worthy of inclusion in the king's records (10:2). However, given the book's underlying critique of Xerxes and all things Persian and the common association of taxes with injustice, oppression, and slavery in the story of God, a more negative reading of this tax is also possible (Neh 9:36–37; see Listen to the Story, above).

A full account of the "greatness" of Xerxes is not what the narrator of the book of Esther has presented to us (10:2). Instead we have seen a self-centered, pleasure-seeking, impulsive, irresponsible, indecisive, and callous king. Xerxes's

2. Smelik, "The Inscription of King Mesha," *COS* 2.23:137–38.

3. Sandra Berg is one of many scholars who see evidence of the book's chiastic structure in this narrative link to the book's initial description of Xerxes's vast kingdom; see Sandra Berg, *The Book of Esther: Motifs, Themes, and Structure* (Missoula: Scholars Press, 1979), 106–13.

elevation of Mordecai is arguably his most impressive act of greatness. The account of Mordecai's greatness, which is paired with the notice of Xerxes's significant acts, is more impressive. It recalls the "greatness" earlier associated with Haman (3:1–2). The rhetorical question, "are [the great acts of Xerxes and greatness of Mordecai] not written in the Book of the Chronicles of the kings of Media and Persia?" echoes the formulaic language found thirty-four times in similar questions in Kings and Chronicles (see also 2:23; 6:1; 9:32 and Esther 6:1–14: Listen to the Story on the importance of written records). This intentional allusion to the history of the kings of Judah and Israel elevates Mordecai's status as a leader in the diaspora and links Xerxes with the kings of Judah and Israel. More importantly, it insists that Esther's story of the Jews in Persia be read as historical, and an integral part of the larger story of God.

The praise of Mordecai continues, as do the implicit contrasts between Haman and Mordecai. Mordecai's greatness is defined in five ways in verse 3: he was second in rank to the king, a role previously held by Haman; he was "great among the Jews" (lit., in the Hebrew) in contrast to Haman, who was made great by Xerxes but was also the "enemy of the Jews" (3:1, 10; 5:11; 8:1; 9:10, 24); Mordecai was esteemed by the "*multitude* of his brothers" (NIV: "by his many fellow Jews") who were delivered from death, unlike the "*multitude*" of Haman's condemned sons (5:11); Mordecai sought good for his people in an ongoing fashion, unlike Haman whose narcissism drove his self-aggrandizing actions; Mordecai spoke "*shalom* to all his seed," (lit., in the Hebrew) unlike the self-centered initiatives of Haman. *Shalom*, as Joyce Baldwin suggests, connotes "prosperity of all kinds,—health, security, material plenty and good relationships."[4]

Mordecai's legacy of speaking *shalom* recalls Zechariah's oracle about the messianic ruler who will "speak *shalom*" (NIV: "proclaim peace") to the nations as he rules "from sea to sea" (Zech 9:10). While this allusion elevates Mordecai's actions, it also reminds readers that Mordecai's leadership was a temporary solution to a larger problem. The deliverance of the Jews was incomplete, and their future remained precarious. What happened to the Israelites in Egypt when a new king came to power who did not remember Joseph could happen again (Exod 1:8). The problem would be solved only with the coming of the Messiah, the deliverer, who would rule with peace and justice.

This final encomium to Mordecai fits with the view of many that Mordecai is really the dominant character in the book. An early witness to Mordecai's importance is ensconced in 2 Maccabees where the feast of Purim is called Mordecai's day (2 Macc 15:36). After all, as Fox notes, Mordecai is "introduced first (2:5) and praised last (10:2–3), and his glorification lies at the book's

---

4. Joyce Baldwin, *Esther: An Introduction and Commentary* (Downers Grove, IL: InterVarsity Press, 1984), 115.

turning point and presages the Jews' victory. His initiative begins the rescue effort, his edict is the mechanism of deliverance, and his epistle guides the people in the establishment of the new holiday. His unalloyed personal and public success for himself and his people shows that his behavior is to be taken as exemplary."[5] With good reason, readers have lauded Mordecai as a hero "for such a time as this" who was used by God as an agent of *shalom* for God's people. Carey Moore is not alone in his view that Mordecai was the greater hero because he "supplied the brains, while Esther simply followed his directions."[6]

Mordecai's devotees, however, generally fail to mention his role in precipitating the traumatic crisis, his repeated offending of Haman, and his crafting of the vindictive counteredict. Mordecai's darker side remains, as does the issue of his complicity with an irresponsible, self-indulgent tyrant in ruling an unjust empire renowned for injustice. Like Esther, Mordecai is a hero with shortcomings. As Timothy Laniak suggests,

> An honest interpretation of the protagonists in our story is one that takes into account the possibility of ethnic pride in Mordecai and overzealous vengeance in Esther. They are not heroes because they were perfect. Rather, they fit into the larger scheme of salvation history . . . often *in spite of* their shortcomings. Biblical history celebrates the deliverance of God (named or not), generally accomplished with the most unlikely partners.[7]

Esther's absence from the short ending of *her* book has bothered many readers. The Greek versions give even more attention to Mordecai, though Esther is included in Mordecai's prophetic dream and its explanation which shift the focus away from human heroes to God, who remembers and vindicates his people (F:8 LXX; F:8–10 A-text). A simple answer to this problem that lines up with what we know about women's roles in the ancient world is that Esther had completed her mission to save the Jews and had returned to her cloistered role in the palace where she continued to be Xerxes's wife and queen. Still, her absence in this closing chapter does add weight to the classic argument that the book should be called the book of Mordecai.

In his third century deliberations about the book's name, Hippolytus of Rome presents a compelling case for why the book is named Esther. He argues that while Mordecai did more than Esther in the book, she rescued her people: she "offered her life . . . [and] was held worthy to be honored as the principal accomplisher of the deed."[8] So even though Esther's greatness was

5. Fox, *Character and Ideology*, 185.
6. C. Moore, *Esther*, liii.
7. Laniak, "Esther," 183; emphasis original.
8. Hippolytus, *On the Apostolic Tradition*, 178.

not celebrated in the book of the annals of the kings of Media and Persia, the book's name and its inclusion in the biblical canon celebrates her importance. Esther was a traumatized, doubly orphaned Jew who found herself in a unique position of influence as queen of Persia. She risked her life for the good of her people and, like Mordecai, spoke up for their welfare. Both Esther and Mordecai model ways of surviving in a foreign culture.

LIVE the Story

Faith and the Public Place: Mordecai as an Ideal Political Leader

The idealized summary of Xerxes's and Mordecai's accomplishments communicates that the Persian Empire in general and God's people in particular flourished under the leadership of Xerxes and his second-in-command, Mordecai *the Jew*. Mordecai's success as a political leader stands behind the long tradition that views him as an exemplary figure or type. Fifteenth-century Spanish Rabbi Isaac ben Moses Arama highlighted three aspects of Mordecai's leadership: he ruled "through respect and not force," led "the people to their absolute good," not his own, and "spoke peace to his people."[9] John Stockwood (1584) similarly encouraged Christians in positions of power to "use their places to countenance the godly, against the pestilent policies of all proud and ambitious Amans" and to "aduenture to speake for the wealth of the church, and welfare of Israel."[10] This traditional reading of Esther 10 reflects what David Clines and others recognize as one of the story's original purposes, namely to affirm "the mutually beneficial roles of the Persian administration and of the Jewish people" and to reassure Jews living outside the land "that collaboration with the authorities is no sin against Jewish identity."[11] This strategy, of course, is temporary and needs to be set alongside the Old Testament hope of the coming Davidic Messiah who will rule nations with justice in contrast to the unjust, unpredictable, and inequitable King Xerxes. As the great creeds of the church affirm, Jesus is the long-expected Messiah who conquered all dominion and powers through the cross, and now reigns supreme at God's right hand and will, as the fourth-century Nicene Creed affirms, "come again in glory to judge the living and the dead, and his kingdom will have no end."[12]

---

9. Walfish, *Esther in Medieval Garb*, 48, quoted in Carruthers, *Esther Through the Centuries*, 277.

10. John Stockwood's 1584 preface to the English translation of John Brentius's Latin commentary on Esther, quoted in Carruthers, *Esther Through the Centuries*, 278.

11. Clines, *Ezra, Nehemiah, Esther*, 262.

12. See https://www.anglican.ca/about/beliefs/nicene-creed/.

In our postmodern context that is increasingly hostile to Christians, Mordecai's model of leadership and political engagement—and arguably Esther's model—has appeal. The need for thoughtful Christians to have seats at the tables where such culture-transforming issues as religious freedom, climate change, immigration, racial reconciliation, and human rights are being debated is acute. Although Jesus' call to be salt and light in this dark world (Matt 5:13–16) may seem daunting, we are not alone. The Holy Spirit, as Oliver O'Donovan reminds us, "surprises us, and leads us in ways we had not worked out beforehand . . . if we will follow, if we will be attentive, we shall be led to ways of being faithful witnesses."[13] To be ready to do this work, O'Donovan suggests we must "give our minds and attention to the deposit of faith and to the Scriptures. We must constantly renew our study, and make use of the resources we have been given, not abashed or discouraged by the fact that as Christians we never think exactly the same as everybody else around us."[14] Such constant reliance on the Spirit, together with the hard work of study and self-critical reflection, will protect us from absorbing the values of the empires we are living in as we work for the good of our world and of God's people.

An Ironic and Cautionary Reading That Looks to Something More

We also need to hear these closing verses of Esther as a warning to God's people. The men who are eulogized in the closing verses of Esther are presented as flawed characters in the story. Xerxes, narcissistic and indifferent, was hardly the kind of king the ancients would believe was the gods' representative and guarantor of the social and natural orders. Xerxes thoughtlessly used and abused individuals and groups he was meant to protect. The notice of taxation from the man who was "still in charge, still exercising his power and might in his own interests" is hardly good news.[15] "To laud the power and might of [Xerxes]," Wells suggests, "is really to poke fun at him because it hints that at the end of the story he will think it has been a story about him, whereas Esther and Mordecai [and I would add, we as readers] know better."[16] It is divine kingship, not human kingship, that Scripture presents as ideal. What the Jews experienced under Xerxes was temporary blessing and peace; what the larger context of Scripture suggests they need is divine kingship like that depicted in Psalm 72:

13. Oliver O'Donovan, "A Conversation with Oliver O'Donovan," *Vestigia Dei*, 28 November 2017, www.wycliffecollege.ca/blog/conversationodonovan.

14. Ibid.

15. Wells, "Esther," 91.

16. Ibid.

For he will deliver the needy who cry out,
  the afflicted who have no one to help.
He will take pity on the weak and the needy
  and save the needy from death.
He will rescue them from oppression and violence,
  for precious is their blood in his sight. (Ps 72:12–14)

This messianic Psalm, and arguably the ending of the book of Esther, look forward to the kingdom inaugurated by Jesus and, ultimately, to our hope of a new heaven and earth.

As noted above, Mordecai is also a flawed figure. While he worked together with Esther for the good of the Jews to secure their deliverance from genocide, he participated in the various structures of the hierarchy of power that we now recognize perpetrated numerous injustices.

In speaking "*shalom* to all his seed" Mordecai prefigures the messianic ruler who would "speak *shalom*" to the nations as he rules "from sea to sea" (Zech 9:9–10). Jesus is that Prince of peace (Isa 9:6). At his birth the angels sang peace to God's people on earth (Luke 2:13–14). The peace Jesus gives to his own is not like that the world gives—it is a peace that placates our troubled hearts and dissipates our fear (John 14:27). This gift of peace is to be shared, and those who do so are themselves blessed and called children of God (Matt 5:9).

"Can a Mother Forget the Baby at Her Breast? . . . I Will Not Forget You!"

When the veil that hides God in the book of Esther is lifted, we see that God did not abandon his people who had chosen to remain outside the land. Indeed, we see God working through imperfect people to save all the Jews from destruction. Through this remarkable story of the deliverance of the Jews, we are reminded that God does not forget his own. The theme of God's love for his people reverberates through the Scriptures. God's love is likened to the care of a viticulturist for his vineyard:

"Sing about a fruitful vineyard:
  I, the LORD, watch over it;
  I water it continually.
I guard it day and night." (Isa 27:2–3)

God's love for us is also compared to that of a nursing mother: "Can a mother forget the baby at her breast and have no compassion on the child she has borne? Though she may forget, I will not forget you!" (Isa 49:15). The book of Esther is about a loving God who rescued the Jews from genocidal destruction and who continues to watch over us even when it seems that we have been left behind or forgotten by God. And it is before this same Lord God Almighty, who was, and is, and is to come, that we are invited to worship with the living creatures and elders in the divine throne room depicted in the book of Revelation:

> "You are worthy, our Lord and God,
> to receive glory and honor and power,
> for you created all things,
> and by your will they were created
> and have their being." (Rev 4:11)

Scripture and Deuterocanonical Works Index

Genesis

Exodus

Leviticus

Numbers

Deuteronomy

Joshua

1 Samuel

2 Samuel

1 Kings

Job

Psalms

Proverbs

Ecclesiastes

Song of Songs

Isaiah

Jeremiah

Lamentations

Ezekiel

Daniel

Hosea

Joel

Amos

Jonah

Micah

Habakkuk

Zechariah

Revelation

Additions to Esther

Judith

1 Maccabees

2 Maccabees

Subject Index

Author Index

Ecclesiastes, Song of Songs

George Athas

A new commentary for today's world, The Story of God Bible Commentary explains and illuminates each passage of Scripture in light of the Bible's grand story. Its story-centric approach is ideal for pastors, students, Sunday school teachers, and laypeople alike.

Three easy-to-use sections designed to help readers live out God's story:

- LISTEN to the Story: Includes complete NIV text with references to other texts at work in each passage, encouraging the reader to hear it within the Bible's grand story
- EXPLAIN the Story: Explores and illuminates each text as embedded in its canonical and historical setting
- LIVE the Story: Reflects on how each text can be lived today and includes contemporary stories and illustrations to aid preachers, teachers, and students

Available in stores and online!

ZONDERVAN®
.com

The Story of God Bible Commentary

Daniel

Wendy L. Widder

A new commentary for today's world, The Story of God Bible Commentary explains and illuminates each passage of Scripture in light of the Bible's grand story. Its story-centric approach is ideal for pastors, students, Sunday school teachers, and laypeople alike.

Three easy-to-use sections designed to help readers live out God's story:

- LISTEN to the Story: Includes complete NIV text with references to other texts at work in each passage, encouraging the reader to hear it within the Bible's grand story
- EXPLAIN the Story: Explores and illuminates each text as embedded in its canonical and historical setting
- LIVE the Story: Reflects on how each text can be lived today and includes contemporary stories and illustrations to aid preachers, teachers, and students

Available in stores and online!

ZONDERVAN®
.com